LIKE A WAKING DREAM

Publisher's Acknowledgment

THE PUBLISHER gratefully acknowledges the ongoing generous support of the Hershey Family Foundation and in particular the contribution toward the printing of this book.

Like a Waking Dream

THE AUTOBIOGRAPHY OF
Geshé Lhundub Sopa

GESHÉ LHUNDUB SOPA
WITH PAUL DONNELLY

BOSTON • WISDOM PUBLICATIONS

Wisdom Publications, Inc.
199 Elm Street
Somerville, MA 02144 USA
www.wisdompubs.org

Library of Congress Cataloging-in-Publication Data
Lhundup Sopa, Geshé, 1925–
Like a waking dream : the autobiography of Geshé Lhundub Sopa / Geshé Lhundub Sopa
with Paul Donnelly.
pages cm
Includes bibliographical references and index.
ISBN 0-86171-313-3 (pbk. : alk. paper)
1. Lhundup Sopa, Geshe, 1925– 2. Lamas—China—Tibet Autonomous Region—
Biography. I. Donnelly, Paul (Paul B.) II. Title.
BQ970.H68A3 2012
294.3'923092—dc23
[B]
2012013287

ISBN 978-0-86171-313-4
eBook ISBN 978-1-61429-036-0

16 15 14 13 12
5 4 3 2 1

Cover design by Phil Pascuzzo. Interior design by Gopa&Ted2.
Set in Diacritical Garamond Pro 11.35/15.3.

Printed in the United States of America.

Table of Contents

Foreword

TODAY, INTEREST IN BUDDHISM is spreading throughout the Western world, encountering new cultures and new languages. In such circumstances it is very important that the Dharma be transmitted by scholars and practitioners who possess a deep and vast understanding of the Buddha's teachings, because that is the only way to protect their purity and authenticity. One such teacher is the monk and scholar Geshé Lhundub Sopa, whom I have known for over fifty years. Through his contribution as a scholar and a teacher of scholars, as a Buddhist mentor and guide to hundreds of Western students, and as a pure holder of the monastic tradition, Geshé Sopa has been an exemplary representative of Tibetan Buddhist culture. During my final geshé examination in Lhasa, he was one of several very able students chosen to challenge me in debate.

With my encouragement he left for America in 1962. In due course, he was invited to the University of Wisconsin, where he became one of the first Tibetan language instructors at an American university. His subsequent career as a professor spanned more than thirty years, during which time he taught many of the current scholars of Buddhist studies in America. It is a cause for celebration that Geshé Sopa, a man from faraway Tibet, could rise to the highest levels of Western academic attainment largely on the basis of his Tibetan monastic education and his own personal qualities.

It is my hope that this engaging account of Geshé Lhundub Sopa's exemplary life will allow interested readers to deepen their understanding and appreciation of what he has achieved, as well as of the value of Tibetan monastic education.

Tenzin Gyatso, the Fourteenth Dalai Lama
September 20, 2012

Editor's Preface

BEFORE THE ANNEXATION of Tibet by the People's Republic of China in the 1950s, Tibet was a nation where a significant portion of the male population entered the monastic life. In the area of the capital, Lhasa, there were well over twenty thousand monks just at the three great monasteries of Sera, Drepung, and Ganden. These monasteries were cities unto themselves, with their own way of life, scholastic traditions, complex economies, and a not insignificant amount of political power. They were the seats of Buddhist scholarship for the Geluk sect, and through rigorous training, superior scholars rose through their ranks and were awarded the geshé degree.

In the years leading up to the mass exodus of Tibetans from Tibet in 1959, Geshé Lhundub Sopa was one of the *virtuosi* scholars of Sera Monastery. In 1950, when he was only twenty-seven years old, he was chosen to be one of the examiners of His Holiness the Dalai Lama when the latter sat for his geshé examination. When the People's Liberation Army began their crackdown after the Tibetan uprising of March 10, 1959, Geshé Sopa, along with other members of the household he was a tutor in, left his monastery for a nearby retreat center a short distance from Lhasa, thinking that he would return after a few days. It soon became clear that there was to be no return to normal. After an arduous, month-long journey across the Himalayas, Geshé Sopa arrived in India and settled in a refugee camp along with many other fleeing Tibetans.

In 1962, the Dalai Lama chose Geshé Sopa to go to the Lamaist Buddhist Monastery of America in Freewood Acres, New Jersey, which had been established by the Mongolian monk Geshé Wangyal some years earlier. He was sent there as tutor and guardian to three young incarnate lamas who were being sent to America to learn English. In 1967, Geshé Sopa was invited by Professor Richard Robinson to come to the University of Wisconsin–Madison to teach in the Buddhist Studies program, which had been established in 1961 as the first such program in the United States. In 1975, Geshé Sopa founded the Deer Park Buddhist Center, and in 1981, Deer Park hosted the first of many Kālacakra initiations that the Dalai Lama would go on to perform in the West. Geshé Sopa eventually became full professor at the University of Wisconsin–Madison, where he trained numerous scholars of Buddhism. In 1990, he was made one of the directors of the Tibetan Resettlement Project, which helped Tibetans in exile to establish themselves in the U.S. Geshé Sopa is now professor emeritus, having retired in 1997.

Many Tibetans living today in exile never lived in Tibet. Many traditions have been carried on in exile, but the fact remains that an increasingly large percentage of Tibetans have little firsthand information about what life in their country was like before the occupation. This kind of information will be irretrievably lost when the last generation of Tibetans who lived much of their lives in Tibet has passed. It is our hope that this book will contribute to the preservation of this oral history and will make part of that history available to the Tibetan exile community, to scholars and students of Tibetan culture, and to the general public.

There is an abundance of studies of the doctrinal aspects of Tibetan Buddhism, yet comparatively little work has been done on how Buddhism was lived by monks in the various monastic centers that once existed across Tibet. The details of, for example, the process of how one became a monk, what the young novice's life was like, and how one progressed through the monastic education system are not widely known. With only a few exceptions, no outsider was interested in this kind of thing when the institutions of Buddhism existed in Tibet—and now these institutions are gone or have been radically transformed by the fifty-year-old Chinese occupation. The life stories of those who were monastics and lamas in Tibet at this time are vital resources for preserving this knowledge.

There are now several wonderful biographies and autobiographies in English of lamas who spent much of their lives in Tibet prior to 1959, including those of Lobsang Gyatso, Dezhung Rinpoché, Geshé Rabten, Chögyam Trungpa, Dilgo Khyentse Rinpoché, Dudjom Rinpoché, Arjia Rinpoché, Chagdud Tulku, Drikung Chetsang Rinpoché, Palden Gyatso, and the Dalai Lama himself. Geshé Sopa's story covers some of the same ground as these other accounts, but it is also unique in that it includes an account of a young monk at Shang Ganden Chönkhor Monastery. This Geluk monastery was one of several that were converted to the Geluk sect from the Kagyü during the reign of the Fifth Dalai Lama. While much of the way of life and education system is similar to that of the three large monasteries of the Lhasa area, there is also much that is unique, and it is recounted here from the perspective of a child and young man taking his early steps on the path of the Geluk scholar monk. The emphasis on the education system of the monastery carries over to Geshé-la's discussion of his time at Sera Jé. We thus have in this story a thorough firsthand account of the monastic education system in Tibet prior to the Chinese takeover in 1959.

This is neither a disciple's account of his saintly teacher's life nor an example of the traditional Tibetan Buddhist genre of the *full-liberation story* (*namthar*), a Buddhist master's account of his realizations. This book takes the form of a collaborative or "as-told-to" autobiography. My basic strategy in the interviewing process was to ask only open, general questions, allowing Geshé Sopa to determine how his story was ultimately to be told. This turned out to be very successful. On the first day we spent together, I came prepared with a long list of questions. Geshé-la was more talkative than I had hoped and seemed to genuinely enjoy recounting stories about his childhood. By about the third day, I arrived to find that Geshé-la had written out a list of things he wanted to talk about. Each day after this, Geshé-la was always prepared with what he called his "homework."

The interviews took place over a number of summers, for a week or two each visit. All the sessions were recorded. After listening to each day's recording, I asked follow-up questions the next day. After completing the first draft of the narrative, I read the entire draft to Geshé-la, and he clarified what was unclear and corrected what was incorrect. It was immensely satisfying to watch Geshé-la sitting on the edge of his seat listening to his own story. The process of editing and re-reading portions of the text has now been repeated numerous times.

Geshé-la's spoken English can be a bit difficult to understand for those unaccustomed to it. This necessitated a rather significant amount of participation on my part in the formation of the final narrative, and I hope I have accurately recorded the story of Geshé Sopa's life. Having known Geshé Sopa for twenty years, during which time I have studied Tibetan culture, language, and Buddhism with him, I am likely as suited to my role in this project as nearly anyone could be.

We have utilized Wisdom Publications' system for most Tibetan names and terms. This system has the advantage of rendering Tibetan words pronounceable while allowing those who know Tibetan to infer the actual Tibetan spellings. There are, however, a number of exceptions, in deference to familiar usage and the names of published authors. A table at the back lists Wylie transliteration for many of the most important names and terms. A map identifying many of the key locations mentioned in the text is found in the photographic section.

Paul Donnelly

Introduction:
A Brief History of Tibet

ANY DISCUSSION of the history of Tibet, especially its modern history, is potentially contentious. Tibetan accounts and those asserted by the People's Republic of China (PRC) stand in stark opposition, and it can be difficult for the beginner to sort out the facts based on such radically differing accounts. Tibetans have understandably strong feelings about what happened to them and the sovereignty of their homeland. The People's Republic of China has long striven to put the best spin on an undeniably disastrous policy toward Tibet from the time of the invasion in the 1950s, through the Cultural Revolution in the 1960s and 70s, and continuing on through subsequent years. Despite the potential pitfalls, a measure of historical background will nevertheless be helpful to frame the life story of Geshé Sopa.

The history of Tibet is inextricably connected to the history of Tibetan Buddhism, especially for Tibetans. In the seventh century, King Songtsen Gampo is said to have married a Chinese princess and a Nepalese princess. These women brought Buddhism with them to Tibet. In the late eighth century, King Trisong Detsen oversaw the first organized importation of Buddhism into Tibet and the establishment of the first monastery, Samyé. Traditional history has it that the great scholar monk Śāntarakṣita came to Tibet and ordained the first Tibetan monks, but before he could do this, the Tibetan gods had to be tamed. He convinced the Tibetans to invite the tantric master Padmasambhava to force the Tibetan gods to cease their disruptions and pledge their support to

Buddhism. This is the origin of many of the Dharma protectors that play such an important part in traditional Tibetan Buddhism.

Whether or not we accept the literal truth of this tale, it cannot be denied that this is an ingenious strategy for integrating the old religion into the new, and is characteristic of the way that Buddhism interacted with the cultures it encountered in its spread across Asia. We also see in this story exemplars of the two basic threads of the Indian Buddhist tradition that took root and thrived in Tibetan soil: Śāntarakṣita epitomizes the monastic and scholastic elements of late Indian Buddhism, while Padmasambhava is the archetypal *siddha*, a tantric master and wonder worker. These two approaches—the scholar and the yogi—are each essential to Tibetan Buddhist identity, and the spectrum between a life devoted to scholarship and the time left for tantric practice is something that Geshé Sopa is keenly aware of and interested in, as made especially clear in his accounts of his most revered teachers.

By the late eighth century, Buddhism was solidly established in Tibet and was supported by the king and the royal court. The close relationship between the monastic institutions of Buddhism and the king and his court meant that Buddhism was connected with political power in Tibet from the very beginning. In the third generation after King Trisong Detsen, another Tibetan king instituted a tax on all Tibetan households to support the growing monastic base of Buddhism. This king, popularly known as Ralpachen, not only instituted public support of what had been primarily a court interest, but also raised the power and prestige of the monastics to an unprecedented level. Some in the court, including officials who supported the pre-Buddhist Tibetan religion now known as Bön, were not happy with this, and this unhappiness culminated in Ralpachen's assassination by his brother, Langdarma, in 838. Only a few years later, Langdarma was himself assassinated, purportedly by the Buddhist monk Lhalung Palgyi Dorjé.

Following Ralpachen's assassination, for over one hundred years Buddhism had no state support. Though the monastic institutions in central Tibet were decimated in this period, interest in Buddhism continued to live on among the fragments of the old royal dynasty, a few of the surviving dispersed monks, and ordinary Tibetans. The Nyingma sect that traces its origin back to Padmasambhava is the only one of the four major sects to originate in this early spread of Buddhism in Tibet.

Following Langdarma's persecutions some monks had fled to far eastern Tibet and preserved the monastic lineage there. One important figure in the revitalization of the monastic tradition was Gongpa Rapsal, who took ordination with three monks living in eastern Tibet and three other local Chinese monks. In 978, two Tibetan monks who had been living in eastern Tibet returned to the central part of the country and reestablished the monastic lineage there.

A better-known revitalization happened in western Tibet. In 988, the monk Rinchen Sangpo returned to Tibet after studying Buddhism and Sanskrit for thirteen years in Kashmir. With the support of a king in the Ngari region named Yeshé Ö, Rinchen Sangpo translated numerous Buddhist texts into Tibetan and oversaw the establishment of many monasteries in western Tibet. Yeshé Ö's nephew sent a request to one of the great monastic institutions in India for a teacher, and in 1042 Atiśa arrived in Tibet. These events signaled the beginning of the later spread of Buddhism in Tibet. Atiśa reintroduced the monastic component of late Indian Buddhism, and his Tibetan disciple Dromtön Gyalwai Jungné established a new sect on the basis of his master's teachings called Kadam. This sect emphasized monastic discipline, and though it included tantric ideas and practices, these were practiced within a thoroughly monastic context.

During this same period, some Tibetans took it upon themselves to travel to India to seek teachings on their own. These Tibetans typically sought the teachings of the siddhas. Of these travelers, one of the most famous, Marpa Chökyi Lodrö, received initiation and instruction from the siddha Nāropa. Back in Tibet, Marpa led the life of a well-to-do farmer but attracted numerous disciples, for he was secretly a tantric guru. His most famous disciple, Milarepa, continues to be one of the most beloved figures in Tibetan culture. As we see in Geshé Sopa's story, even uneducated people knew some of the songs of Milarepa. Neither Milarepa nor Marpa were monks, but Milarepa's most famous and influential disciple was the Kadam monk Gampopa Sönam Rinchen. Gampopa skillfully combined the essentially tantric teachings and practices of Milarepa with the monastic teachings of the Kadam, and from him arose the various sects of the Kagyü school, including Tibet's earliest incarnation lineage, that of the Karmapas.

One of the teachers Marpa is said to have studied under before going to India himself was the translator (*lotsāwa*) Drokmi Shākya Yeshé. Drokmi Lotsāwa, the transmitter of the teachings of the siddha Virūpa to Tibet, was also the guru of Khön Könchok Gyalpo, the first hierarch of the Sakya sect. Like the Kagyü lineage, the Sakya also evolved into a predominantly monastic sect. Both the Kagyü and Sakya sects established relations with the political and military powers outside the borders of Tibet, most importantly with the Mongol Khans and the Chinese emperors. In 1249, the famous Sakya polymath Sakya Paṇḍita Künga Gyaltsen was appointed Tibetan viceroy by the Mongol ruler Godan Khan. In the next generation, Chinese and Mongol bases of power became one and the same when Kublai Khan became emperor of the Yuan dynasty. Kublai then named Phakpa Lodrö Gyaltsen—the head of the Sakya sect and nephew of Sakya Paṇḍita—imperial preceptor and viceroy of Tibet. Phakpa's ascendancy marked the beginning of religious rule in Tibet and the priest-patron relationship with the Mongol and Chinese powers to the east. This practice sometimes benefitted one or another group in Tibet, but it would also ultimately be a factor in the destruction of the nation, for in it the PRC sees proof of Tibet's longstanding subordination to China. The Mongol Yuan dynasty ended in the middle of the fourteenth century, but in Tibet's ensuing Phakmodrupa, Rinpungpa, and Tsangpa regimes, each lasting roughly a century, Tibetans continued to seek relations with, and be courted by, the chieftains of the now-fragmented Mongol tribes, as well as by the emperors of the Ming and the Manchu Qing dynasties. Particularly favored in this period were lamas of the Kagyü sect.

The end of the fourteenth century saw the emergence of a new sect, later called the Geluk, that also became engaged in these political maneuverings. Tsongkhapa Losang Drakpa, the founder of this new sect, trained and studied with teachers of all of the sects, as was the custom at that time. He became quite well known for his great scholarship and gained the support of some of the most powerful figures in central Tibet, perhaps because of his avowed Kadam-style emphasis on monastic discipline as well as his charismatic personality. Tsongkhapa founded Ganden Monastery, and three of his disciples founded the monasteries of Tashi Lhünpo, Drepung, and Sera. With this, the teachings of the Kadam sect, already in decline, were effectively dispersed into the remaining traditions, particularly the Geluk.

The members of the Geluk sect had to compete with the earlier established sects for patronage. Mongol chieftains and Chinese emperors remained interested in the great figures of Tibetan Buddhism during this time, due to their reputation for great scholarship and sanctity, and their supposed magical powers. In the late sixteenth century, Altan Khan of the Tumed Mongols invited Sönam Gyatso, one of the leading figures of the Geluk sect, to Kokonor. The Khan was so impressed by Sönam Gyatso that he converted to Buddhism, and he granted his teacher the title of Dalai Lama, which means "ocean lama" in the Mongol language, in honor of the extent and depth of his master's sanctity and learning. This title was also retroactively given to two of Sönam Gyatso's predecessors, effectively making him the Third Dalai Lama. This renewed the Mongol presence in Tibetan affairs both temporal and spiritual. In the middle of the seventeenth century, in the time of the Fifth Dalai Lama, the Geluk sect came to rule all of central Tibet with the help of another Mongol tribe, ousting the Tsangpa rulers and ending the dominance of the Karma Kagyüpas.[1]

The Fifth Dalai Lama was by all accounts a keenly intelligent man and an astute ruler. He began the construction of the Potala on a hill that was reputed to be site of the palace of the great early kings of Tibet. The choice of the name Potala was significant, for this is the name of the mountain in India where Avalokiteśvara, the bodhisattva of compassion, was said to dwell. It is from this time that the Dalai Lama became regarded not only as the reincarnation of his predecessors but also as the human manifestation of the bodhisattva of compassion.

In addition to having the support of the Mongols, the Fifth Dalai Lama was invited to China by the emperor and was received as a head of state. After the death of the Fifth Dalai Lama, the Sixth, Seventh, and Eighth Dalai Lamas lived in a period of intense competition for power between two different Mongol tribes and the Chinese emperors. None of them, however, can be said to have held significant temporal power. In the lifetime of the Eighth Dalai Lama, the Chinese emperor sent a garrison of Chinese soldiers with two representatives to oversee it to Lhasa. These men were called the *ambans*, and though this post continued up until the twentieth century, its power and influence varied. The Ninth through Twelfth Dalai Lamas did not reach an age at which they could rule, so regents ruled Tibet in their place.

The Thirteenth Dalai Lama came to power in the late nineteenth century, when the power of the Manchu Qing dynasty in China was beginning to weaken. This was also a time when the British sought to establish trade connections with Tibet, thereby also creating a buffer zone between their colony, India, and China. To accomplish this, the British in India first wrote to the Thirteenth Dalai Lama to try to begin talks, but the Dalai Lama returned the letters unopened. In 1904, the British sent an expedition into Tibet and engaged in numerous battles with Tibetan troops, emerging victorious each time. The Dalai Lama fled Lhasa and went into exile in Mongolia. He also went to Beijing and met with the emperor, who was still a child. In Tibet, the remaining officials reluctantly signed a treaty with Britain. The Dalai Lama returned to Tibet in 1909, only to learn that Chinese troops had invaded and conquered several eastern Tibetan cities and were on the way to Lhasa. The Dalai Lama fled again, this time to British India. Then, calamitous events in China provided a fortunate turn of events for the Tibetans. In

1911, there was an uprising against Manchu rule, and the last Manchu emperor abdicated the throne.

Taking advantage of the power vacuum caused by internal problems in China that persisted until the time of Mao, the Dalai Lama returned to Tibet and declared it an independent nation in 1912. The ambans were expelled from Lhasa, as were all Chinese troops. But although China had no presence or influence in Tibet in the years between 1912 and 1950, Tibet's independence was never officially recognized by China, Britain, or the United States.

The Thirteenth Dalai Lama died in 1933, and power passed to the new regent, Radreng—usually spelled Reting—Rinpoché. Reting oversaw the discovery of the Fourteenth Dalai Lama, who was enthroned in Lhasa in 1939. In 1941, Reting stepped down as regent, in his mind for a three-year period, and was succeeded by Takdrak Rinpoché. After the three years had passed, Reting attempted to regain his regency but was rebuffed. This led to a series of events that pitted Reting's monastery, Sera Jé, against the central government and sowed dissent in many of the monks against the government. These events are described here in Geshé Sopa's story.

In 1949, the Communist Party won the civil war in China, and the People's Republic of China was formed. Almost immediately, the PRC turned its attention to Tibet. The People's Liberation Army (PLA) began their assault on eastern Tibet in 1950. The fifteen-year-old Dalai Lama and many of his advisors fled south to Dromo, near the Indian border. While the Dalai Lama was in Dromo, on May 23, 1951, the Seventeen-Point Agreement was signed in Beijing by one of the members of the Kashak, the highest ruling body in Tibet. This high government official, Ngapö Ngawang Jikmé, had been in eastern Tibet at the time of the invasion, and he was taken to Beijing and convinced—or coerced—to sign the agreement without input from the Dalai Lama or the rest of the government in Lhasa. Coerced or not, the government of the PRC now possessed a document signed by Ngapö, a member of the Kashak, stating that the Tibetan government recognized China's sovereignty over Tibet and that "the Tibetan people shall return to the motherland—the People's Republic of China." This document effectively ended Tibet's independence.

By the time the Dalai Lama returned to Lhasa, Chinese troops and officials were already there. For the next several years, Tibet underwent a gradual transformation, with more power passing from traditional Tibetan political bodies to various Communist Party committees, most importantly the Preparatory Committee for the Autonomous Region of Tibet, to which total power would pass in 1959.

Though the Lhasa area experienced a gradual transformation, the inhabitants of the eastern regions of Amdo and Kham were not so fortunate. In the mid-1950s, Khampas revolted against the much more aggressive changes being instituted there. In response, the PLA bombed several monasteries and killed many Tibetans, both monks and laypeople, who had taken refuge in the monasteries. Many Khampas fled to central Tibet, significantly swelling the population of the Lhasa area. By 1957, several Khampa military groups were in open revolt against the PRC, and they were dealt with severely. The Khampas, however, were surprisingly successful, and it is because of their control of the southern route out of Tibet that the Dalai Lama, Geshé Sopa, and thousands of other Tibetans were able to go into exile in 1959.

The uprising of March 10, 1959, was precipitated by a perceived threat to the Dalai Lama, who had been invited by the Chinese officials to a performance at the Chinese military headquarters. On the day that the performance was to take place, thousands of people surrounded the Norbu Lingkha, the Dalai Lama's summer palace, in order to prevent him from going to the performance. The crowd's anger was unleashed on two Tibetans who were officials in the new Chinese government. One was injured and the other was killed. On March 17th, two shells landed near the summer palace, and the Dalai Lama's advisors decided that it was no longer safe to stay. The Dalai Lama, his two tutors, his family, and other members of the Tibetan government left the summer palace under the cover of night. On March 20th, the PLA was ordered to retake the city of Lhasa, which had been in uprising for over a week. This was the day that Geshé Sopa left Sera Monastery. After two days of fierce fighting, the flag of the People's Republic of China was raised over the Potala.

From this time, a mass exodus of Tibetan people began. It signaled the beginning of a period of crisis for both the people who stayed in Tibet and the ones who left as they have attempted to carry on their traditional culture in Tibet and in exile. In 1966, the Cultural Revolution began in China as a reaction within the Communist Party against perceived counter-revolutionary ideas that threatened the correct ideology of Mao Zedong. Mao encouraged people to smash the Four Olds (old ideas, old culture, old customs, and old habits), and his call was heeded and enacted by the Red Guards. Between 1966 and 1969, families were made to destroy their religious objects, monks and other religious figures were subjected to public ridicule, and most of the monasteries in Tibet were sacked, if not completely destroyed.

After the death of Mao Zedong in 1976, the attitude of the PRC toward Tibet began to change. These new attitudes were reflected in the declarations of the Eleventh Party Plenum in 1978, and real change began to take place in the PRC's handling of Tibet when Deng Xiaoping came to power. The new policies coming from Beijing were designed to redress the damage that had taken place in Tibet, and throughout China, during the Cultural Revolution. In Tibet, these reforms included a more tolerant approach to Tibetan religion, culture, and Tibetan language, as well as efforts to raise the standard of living of Tibetans and pour huge amounts of money into the economic infrastructure. Though Tibetans were understandably suspicious at first, it soon became clear that China was genuinely willing to allow Tibetans to again practice their religion openly and to reclaim long-suppressed aspects of their culture. Despite the worst excesses of the Cultural Revolution, the commitment and strength of ordinary Tibetans to their religion did not waver. When there was no longer a fear of showing this commitment, people again circumambulated the Barkor with prayer wheels spinning. A resurgence of Buddhism began not only in the Tibetan Autonomous Region but also in the greater Tibetan regions of Kham and Amdo.

This new openness extended even to monasticism, and some monasteries that were destroyed, damaged, or emptied during the Cultural Revolution were rebuilt, repaired, and re-enrolled, including Ganden Chönkhor and Sera. Monks were again able to take up the monastic life, but Chinese officials kept the numbers of monks at the large monasteries much lower than pre-1959 levels. Prior to 1959, Drepung, the largest of the Three Seats of the Geluk sect, had as many as 10,000 monks living within its precincts. After the uprising of 1959, the number of monks plummeted, with only about 700 monks living there in 1965. As the Cultural Revolution was unleashed, the number dropped to about 300, and the residents now were forbidden to practice their religion at all, having to dress in lay clothes and work in various jobs, and some married. With the liberalizing that took place in the early 1980s, monks were allowed to return to traditional monastic roles. To use Drepung again as the example, 1982 saw the first permitted enrollment of new monks, and by the late 1980s there were several hundred.

In 1987 the Dalai Lama appealed to U.S. and world leaders to pressure China to recognize Tibetan independence. This was heard by Tibetans in Tibet and seen as a sign that the tables were about to turn. A series of protests followed that caused the PRC to again take a more heavy-handed approach in Tibet, declaring martial law in 1989. The next major wave of protest and crackdown was in the period leading up to and during the 2008 Olympic games in Beijing. As of this writing in 2012, a tragic wave of self-immolations of Tibetans in Tibet has captured the attention of the world and brought renewed interest and concern for the Tibetan cause.

Those who fled Tibet have been faced with economic hardship, loss of loved ones, and the difficult prospect of somehow maintaining their culture in exile. By the end of June 1959, nearly 20,000 Tibetans had followed the Dalai Lama out of Tibet, and current estimates approach

150,000. The Tibetans very quickly organized themselves and gained the generous support of the Indian government as well as international supporters. Tibetans who followed the Dalai Lama into exile were first temporarily housed in two large transit camps—Missamari in Assam and Buxaduar in West Bengal—and then many took jobs in roadwork crews in northern India. The scholar monks of the three seats were sent to Buxaduar to try to continue the tradition of monastic education. After just over a year in exile, the Dalai Lama, with the help of Prime Minister Nehru, established his exile government in the former British hill station of Dharamsala in Himachal Pradesh. In order to secure a more stable base for the fledgling exile community, and to begin to create means of support for the exiles other than the backbreaking roadwork crews, the Dalai Lama approached Nehru to find the community a better home. Karnataka State stepped up and offered the exiles several thousand acres of arable land north of Mysore. Three thousand Tibetan exiles initially settled here and took up farming, and within a few years the camp became self-sufficient. By the beginning of the 1970s Sera, Drepung, and Ganden monasteries were reestablished in southern India as well.

Many other Tibetans settled in cities in northern India that had been bases of trade with Tibet before 1959. Here, numerous handicraft enterprises were begun that had the dual function of providing exiles with a means of support and of helping preserve traditional Tibetan handicrafts. As the home of the Dalai Lama and the government in exile, Dharamsala also of course became a major population center of Tibetan exiles.

Since the time of the establishment of the Tibetan government in exile, the Dalai Lama has consistently moved toward democratic reform of the institution. The Kashak remained the highest ruling body beneath the Dalai Lama himself, but the Dalai Lama early on took steps to first reduce and eventually eliminate his own political power. The highest position within the Kashak—the Kalön Tripa, or prime minister—was originally appointed by the Dalai Lama, but the position was made a democratically elected one in 2001. In 2011, the Dalai Lama renounced political power altogether, leaving the prime minister, currently Dr. Lobsang Sangay, the highest official in the Tibetan government in exile. Dr. Sangay is the first prime minister to have been born in exile and has never been to Tibet.

As this is a Tibetan's story, it should come as no surprise that it assumes a Tibetan perspective. The PRC comes out badly, and with good reason. Many people in Tibet suffered horribly, and it is undeniable that the Cultural Revolution devastated Tibet's indigenous culture. Still, the reader will see that Geshé Sopa's story is not simplistic or idealized. In it we see Tibetan individuals and institutions fail to live up to the very Buddhist principles so cherished by Tibetans. But it is also a story in which many exemplary individuals do live up to these principles, even in the worst situations.

Paul Donnelly

1. Life in Tsang

UNTIL I WAS about ten years old, I had many misfortunes: accidents, illnesses, and brushes with death. But when I entered into religious life, my situation improved. Once I entered the monastery I became healthier and happier, and possibilities began to open up that were inconceivable for a layperson from my rural part of Tibet at that time. After that, there was slow but steady progress. I still had many hardships of course, but when I think back on where and when I started, it seems almost unbelievable that I ended up in America. How is it that I am where I am today? I came from a small village in Tsang, went to Lhasa, was forced to flee from Tibet to India, and then somehow found myself in America. Even when I consider only what has happened to me here in America it is amazing. All these things that happened to me seemed like big things at the time. Now they seem like a dream. It's like a waking dream. When I was young, the West was a place you only heard about in stories; no ordinary person like me knew about such things firsthand. People said that beyond Tibet was India, which had been taken over and ruined by the British. Beyond that, far beyond the ocean, they said that there was a place called America. Ordinary Tibetans would never imagine that they could go to America. But here I am.

I was born in the Shang region of the Tsang province of Tibet.[2] Shang is best known as the region where the Shangpa Kagyü sect was established by Khyungpo Naljor at the beginning of the second propagation of Buddhism in Tibet in the eleventh century. Shang has many smaller areas within it, and as is often the case with settled areas in Tibet, my village was in a valley between two mountains. The valley itself was called Shum, and my village was called Phordok.

The name Shum comes from the word for "cry." There is an area of white sand on one of the mountains that can be seen from farther down the valley in the east. When you look up at the mountain from the valley, this white patch looks like a human face. Some say that this has a connection to the time when Padmasambhava was in this area. I'm not sure of the exact story, but it may have been that the name Shum came from people crying when they saw this face, the face of Padmasambhava, and remembered the great things that Padmasambhava did for Tibet. In Tibet there are many places that are named after such features. Phordok means any kind of a mound or bump that sticks up above flat ground. The name of our village was derived from the hill, so Phordok was both the name of the hill and of the village that lay at the foot of the hill.

My family consisted of only my father, my mother, and me. I am their only son. It was the custom in our part of Tibet to use just one part of your full name in everyday use. My father's name was Losang, and my mother's name was Buti. The full name that my parents gave me was Dorjé Tsering. My parents married late in their lives. When I was born, my mother was around forty and my father was already fifty, or maybe even older than that. I don't know for certain.

It was not common in Tibet for one to record the exact date of one's birth. The year was noted, and when the New Year came around everyone was considered to be one year older. Some high lamas and other important people would know their exact birth month and day, but ordinary people would know just the year and that was enough. I did not have many relatives, so after my parents died there was no one who remembered the exact month and day of my birth. So like many Tibetans, I don't know my exact birthdate. The Tibetan calendar has a twelve-year cycle. Each year is associated with one of twelve animals as well as one of five elements.[3] Finally, there is also a two-year cycle: the first year is male, and the second year is female. So every twelve years is the same animal though the element changes. I was born in a pig year. His

Holiness the Dalai Lama was also born in a pig year; he is twelve years younger than I am. His Holiness was born in the wood-pig year, and I was born in the water-pig year. In the Western calendar, this was 1923.

Pordok was a farming community; people in the area grew many crops. They grew barley, wheat, and a kind of black pea that we ground and added to tsampa. *Tsampa* is a Tibetan staple made of coarsely ground roasted barley flour. Tibetans usually eat tsampa by mixing it with butter tea and making a ball of dough. The black peas we grew were larger than the peas here in America. When they were coarsely ground, we also used them for horse feed. Wealthier people especially would use these peas in this way. Ordinary people ground them into flour and mixed this with barley flour for our tsampa. This gave the tsampa a slightly sweet taste. We also grew mustard plants and extracted oil from the seeds. The mustard plants had long rigid stems with beautiful yellow flowers on top. The plants had pods, with many seeds inside. We planted mustard and peas in a field together. The peas had a thin, weak stem and a tendency to bend down when the pods developed. By planting them mixed in with the mustard plants, they were protected, and the pods wouldn't lie on the ground and rot. That is the way farming was done in that area of Tibet. In the summer when the mustard plants flowered, the peas couldn't be seen. From high on the mountainside one would see entire fields filled with huge, beautiful yellow flowers.

My family had a small piece of farm land. I'm not sure if we owned the land we farmed or if it belonged to someone else. Land was often owned by the local or central government, or by aristocratic families or a monastery or a *labrang*, which is the estate of a lama, but ordinary people would work the land like their own. There was a basic unit of land called a *kang*. I don't know if it was an acre or more or less, but in any case it was a sizeable area. Some families held one of these units or only a half, and some families had two, three, or more. My family held half a *kang*.

People had to pay a tax based on how much land they farmed, so those who held several *kang* would have to pay more than someone who just had one or one half. A local official, who was something like a governor, collected this tax and sent it to the administration. Tsang was part of the domain ruled by the Panchen Lama's government in Shikatsé, so our taxes went there, but most other parts of Tibet would pay tax to the central government in Lhasa. The Panchen Lama was widely considered to be the second-highest religious figure in Tibet, after the Dalai Lama. The lineage of the Panchen Lamas began when the Fifth Dalai Lama bestowed the title of Panchen Lama on his own teacher, Losang Chökyi Gyaltsen. *Panchen* is a shortened form of *pandita chenpo*, which means "great scholar." The Panchen Lamas had political power over the Tsang region for centuries, though by our time this power was not absolute.

In the fall, people who worked the land had to send grain to the central government, or a local representative of the government would collect money from the people who lived in the area under his jurisdiction. Similarly, if the government needed to raise an army, each family would be responsible for providing support for it based on how much land they held. I don't really know the system very well, but it worked something like that.

On the hilltop above our village there was a Nyingma lama's labrang. It was not a monastery—the head lama there was married. There were three lamas living at this labrang, a senior one and two younger ones. Unlike the lama lineages that most people are familiar with, these lamas were actually a father and his two sons. The estate had a big house where the whole family lived. In the summer, the lamas were hired by people in the area to protect their crops from hail. The lamas were paid a salary to stay in a small house in the middle of the fields, where they would perform rituals to drive away hailstorms so that the crops were protected from damage.

Every year an elaborate series of rituals was performed at the labrang to drive away all negative forces. This was an important event in our area, and it was an exciting time for people all over the area. People dressed in their finest clothes, and everyone gathered to watch the public events. We children would imitate these things when we played.

The main ritual was performed on the twenty-ninth day of the twelfth

Tibetan month, which usually falls sometime in February. Before the main ritual began, there were preparatory rituals. For a week we heard horns sounding from inside the labrang, inviting the gods in. Part of the public ritual took place in the labrang courtyard. The ceremony could be viewed from a balcony that overlooked the courtyard, and people came from all over Shum to see it. I don't recall very much of that part of the event, but I remember the playing of trumpets and long horns, and that there was some kind of a religious dance. The other part of the public ritual took place outside the labrang compound. One implement used was a yak horn with mantras written on the outside that was filled with some substance, though I don't remember what. Arrows were shot in the ten directions,[4] and a human figure was drawn on the ground with a ritual dagger called a *phurba*. The lama took a large metal container, which had mantras written inside it, and turned it upside down on top of the figure, stepping up on it and performing a dance. Then ritual cakes called *tormas* were thrown into a triangular fire. There were more dances, and finally another torma was thrown over the side of the hill, which represented the final banishing of evil forces. This was all done according to the ritual system of the Nyingmapas. It was said that if the ritual were successful, the enemies of the teachings and obstacles to religion would be destroyed.

Some people said that this ritual could also be employed as a type of black magic and could be used against an evil person or family. It was said that when the ritual was done for this purpose, fire would be seen coming from the sky, landing on the house of the person. Much misfortune, including sickness and even death, would befall them as a result of this ritual. People said these things, but the basic purpose of the ritual was to drive away hindrances prior to the new year.

In Tsang, Buddhism was so deeply ingrained in the culture that it was customary for each family to have at least one son go to the monastery. If a family had three or more sons, then two sons would become monks, one son would stay at the family home and continue to tend the farmland, and the last would engage in business outside of the home. The lay sons could, of course, marry. If a family had several children and none of the sons were sent to the monastery, people would think badly of that family. Ordinary people were very religious, even if they didn't really know very much about their religion. There were many monasteries and nunneries then, and also many small shrines. Even ordinary families had a hanging scroll painting, called a *thangka*, or an altar in their houses. Everyone knew the refuge formula to the Three Jewels,[5] and they knew the mantra of Avalokiteśvara, the bodhisattva of compassion: *Oṃ maṇi padme hūṃ*. No one had to be taught these things; we grew up with them all around.

For ordinary people there wasn't really a sense of belonging to one sect or another in any exclusive way. It depended on what was present in the area where one lived, rather than individual people or families choosing one sect based on their own inclinations or consideration of the different teachings. I went to Ganden Chönkhor basically because I had relatives there, so there was a family connection. Not far beyond Ganden Chönkhor there was another smaller monastery called Dechen Rapgyé where others in our area had relatives. There were perhaps one hundred and eighty monks there. Dechen Rapgyé Monastery was connected to Tashi Lhünpo monastery and followed its traditions.

Historically, much of the Tsang region had been under the control of the Panchen Lama's government in Tashi Lhünpo dating back to the time of the Fifth Dalai Lama and his teacher, the First Panchen Lama. The Fifth Dalai Lama had given his teacher authority over the area around Tashi Lhünpo. So while we had to follow the orders of and send taxes to the central government in Lhasa, we also had to obey orders from Tashi Lhünpo and send taxes there too. There was a fortress above Ganden Chönkhor that was the government center of our area. The government administrator there was sent by the central government in Lhasa. If there was an order to be delivered or a punishment to be dealt out, it was done by this administrator. Ganden Chönkhor, however, was connected to the Dalai Lama's government in Lhasa and to the three great monasteries there. For the most part these two systems were similar in that they were both of the Geluk sect, but there were differences. Because of my years at Ganden Chönkhor, my knowledge and experience is primarily of the system followed by the three great monasteries in the Lhasa area.

2. Early Memories

I STILL REMEMBER A story that my parents told me from when I was very young, around the time that I first began to talk and walk. I think it may have been an indication of a previous life. Far down in the eastern part of the valley, there was another town where an important noble family lived. My parents said that when I was very young I said, "My house is down there, and I have a horse that's bluish gray. I want to see my horse." They said, "Where is your horse?" I pointed my finger in the direction of the lower part of the valley, saying, "Way down there." I was pointing in the direction where the noble family lived. Perhaps one of the old grandfathers or some religious person had died there, and my family thought that I was the rebirth of this person. But my parents never said anything to anyone in the other family or took me there. They were a high noble family and we were just ordinary people, so nothing came of it.

When I was very young I encountered many illnesses and accidents. The first time I came close to death I was only two or three years old, but I remember it clearly. In front of our house there was a hill of piled-up dirt from which you could get up onto the roof. One day my mother laid me down at the bottom of the hill because she had to go up on the roof for some reason. Then she stumbled, which caused a large rock to roll down the hill and hit me where I was lying. I started crying of course, and my mother screamed, "I've killed my baby!" The rock hit me on the forehead and, curiously, on the foot. I still have the scars. If the rock had hit me more squarely, I think I would have been killed instantly. Instead it wasn't really that serious, but there was a lot of blood, so it looked pretty bad. We didn't have modern medicine then, but we had our own ancient methods. In old houses like ours there were many spiders' nests. My mother collected some of these and put them on the wounds. This was supposed to stop the bleeding and keep the wounds from getting infected. It must have worked. It's funny that I so clearly remember my mother crying out and running to me. That was my first brush with death.

In Tibet many natural locations such as mountains, lakes, and streams are considered to be sacred places where deities and *nāgas* live. One type of deity called a *sadak* was said to inhabit such places, and it was said that one must be careful not to bother or upset the sadaks or they would become angry. Often, when a child was born, the parents would go to one of these sacred places and make an offering to the deity. They offered prayer flags and incense, and the child would then always have a connection with that deity, who became known as his birth deity.

Because my family farmed a little piece of land, they needed a bull to pull the plow. We had some some cows and sheep as well. Our house had a courtyard where the animals were tied when they came home. There were many trees around our house, and a huge willow tree grew right next to our door. The tree was bent way over, parallel to the ground, with branches that reached all the way to the earth. A pillar supported the trunk of the tree to keep it from bending all the way to the ground or breaking. The branches of the tree formed a closed-in area, and when I was young, maybe five or six years old, I really enjoyed playing around that tree. I went there to sit or play, and I probably didn't bother to go somewhere else to go to the bathroom, so you can imagine what it was like. Old trees like this were also home to deities and nāgas. We believed that if someone harmed or cut one of these trees, then he would get sick because he had upset the deity. It was said that nāgas did not like dirtiness or impurity, so their places had to be kept clean and protected or they would cause problems. My constant playing under the tree probably made it dirty, and I became very sick.

I grew weak and was afflicted with a kind of rash or pimples. I was sick almost constantly. Though my parents were very poor, they called in an oracle healer. While people are more familiar with the famous major oracles such as Nechung, at that time there were numerous local oracles as well.[6] Many local deities had oracles whom people consulted on many matters, including sickness. Usually a person would begin a career as an oracle because he had been possessed by one of these deities. Though it began involuntarily, eventually these people came to be able to control and utilize these possession states. They were then trained by another older oracle, and they learned the rituals and methods of divination that were used to help people. The oracle called the deity and then went into a trance in which the deity would answer questions about the person's problems.

I must say, I am a little skeptical about some of these oracles. There were so many of them, and this was a way of earning a living. Horses had to be sent to bring the oracle, which most people would have to hire, and when he arrived he had to be offered good *chang*—Tibetan beer— and be well compensated. With so much to gain, I wonder about the legitimacy and intentions of at least some of these oracles.

In Tibet, it was generally believed that sickness was the result of some kind of unseen being. The oracle that my parents consulted said that my illness was due to a female, conch-colored nāga, who was angry at my behavior around the tree. Nāgas do not like people running around without their clothes, and they don't like bad smells or other kinds of dirtiness. The oracle said that my parents had to keep that place clean by keeping me out of there and that they shouldn't cut any of the branches. Whether one believes in this kind of thing or not, I had been very sick, and I did get better after my parents took the oracle's advice.

When I was seven or eight, another curious incident happened. In our village all the cattle were taken together to graze in an outlying area every morning. It was the children's job to take the cattle out to graze, and at least one child from each family was sent to do this. We were sort of like cowboys. We'd take the cattle out beyond the village, keeping them together until we reached an open place. Then we'd let them go freely wherever they wanted, and they would go in all directions. In the summer we had to make sure that the cattle did not get into anyone's cultivated fields, and we had to chase them out if they did.

There would usually be a group of about fifteen children. One of them would be an older boy who was in charge, but the rest would be young children, probably between the ages of seven and ten. Every morning we took the cattle out, and every evening we brought them back to our own houses. We took tsampa, or something else to eat, and something to drink, and we would stay out all day. Sometimes we would go far out where there weren't many fields, so we didn't need to worry about the cattle getting into them. There were many nice valleys and pastures from which to choose. This was very enjoyable for us.

One day we went farther than usual to a valley where all the fields were on one side of a little stream. On the other side of the stream there was a nice open area where there were no fields, so the animals could roam and just enjoy themselves. We children stayed in this valley for a long time and played. If an animal found its way across the stream to a field, we took turns going to chase it out. There was a nunnery there, and farther up the mountainside there was a small yellow house that was a hermitage (*ritrö*) where someone was living.

Next to this hermitage was a small cemetery. Cemeteries in Tibet were not like cemeteries in the West. There were no nicely maintained lawns, headstones, or flowers. Here they were solitary, frightful places where the bodies of the dead were taken. The bodies were chopped up, and vultures came and devoured them. Most people were afraid of such places because it was thought that there were spirits there. People avoided cemeteries, but we children weren't aware of these beliefs yet. We learned this kind of thing later in life.

While we were in that valley, one of the cows crossed through the cemetery toward a cultivated field, and it was my turn to chase the cow back to the rest of the herd. I walked up to the hermitage and around the cemetery and chased the cow back toward the others. When I came back, I cut through the cemetery. As I went through, I saw a strange figure between two rocks. It was small like a baby but it had a big head and hair hanging down to its huge eyes. I didn't know what it was. At first I thought it was a rock, but when I looked more closely, I saw that this strange creature was moving its head, looking around. When I saw this I was terrified; there was a real living thing there!

Later, people had some explanations of what I had seen. Some said that I saw a type of being called a *lord of the cemetery*. Others said that maybe I saw a being called a *theurang* that is associated with dragons and thunderstorms. When dragons take off there arises a great noise, and the theurang, who is a little man with a hammer, is said to be hitting the dragon on the head. When there is a lot of lightning and thunder, people say that there are many theurang around. It sounds strange to modern ears, but these were the beliefs people had. I don't know what it was that I saw. Maybe it was an appearance arisen through my karma, or maybe there was nothing there and it was just some type of negative vision. Whatever it was, this event was the beginning of a period of great suffering for me. But it also set in motion a chain of events that would lead to my entering the monastery, so who is to say whether it was positive or negative?

When I saw this thing, I ran away as fast as I could toward the others, running over stones and through bushes and thorns. I was barefoot, so I was hurting my toes and feet, though I didn't realize it at the time. I was running and jumping without looking where I was going, and eventually I jumped and landed right in a bush that had very thick, very strong white thorns. These thorns went deep into my legs and feet, especially in the heels, but I didn't feel them. I was scared so I just kept running. When I got down to where the other children were, I told them what had happened and what I saw. They didn't believe me. But some children picked up sticks and stones and went back to the cemetery looking for this "baby" I had seen. They did not find anything there, and when they came back down they said that I was lying. I was very bloody, and only then did I begin to feel the pain and realize that there were many thorns sticking into my flesh. We took most of them out, but there were three very strong thorns deep in the heel of my foot that we couldn't get out without digging into my flesh. They simply would not come out, so I had to walk all the way back home with the thorns in my foot. I was in a lot of pain, and the walk home was horrible. I couldn't stand on that foot at all. I made it home, but we still could not get the thorns out of my heel, and the wounds became infected.

Because my foot was infected and painful, I did not want to walk on it. When I sat down, I drew that leg against my body. From sitting like that all the time, and from limping for a long time to avoid walking on that foot, I developed a knotted-up lump high on my leg, and this became inflamed like a boil. If someone pulled my leg straight it was excruciating, and eventually this lump became infected and filled with pus. Between the injury on my heel and the bump on my leg, I stayed in bed for months. I was very sick. The longer I stayed with my leg curled up, the more difficult it became to straighten the leg at all. There was a monk-doctor who lived some distance away, and my mother carried me there. He gave me some treatments and some medicine, but I was still in great pain day and night. I became very weak and dehydrated, and again I came very close to death.

My parents were already quite old by this time. There were three other families in the area that were relatives, some of whom were a little wealthier than us, and they helped some. When my parents had to work, some of these relatives would come and take me out to sit with the other children who were playing, or sometimes they would sit me with the older people who were chanting and spinning prayer wheels. This helped me. Back then, people were not so busy like they are here in America. People had time to spend with each other and could more easily help others. That was a good thing about the situation then.

My parents tried all kinds of things to help me. They sent for doctors and for lamas and oracles who did divinations. One of the lamas said that the problem was not just the injuries; there was also a karmic obstacle. He said that I should not become a farmer but instead should be sent to a monastery to become a monk. Then, he said, everything would be all right. Otherwise I would die. It was then that my parents, or I should say my father, decided that after I recovered I should not stay at home and live a farmer's life. If I did not die, I would be sent to Ganden Chönkhor Monastery. This was not usually an option in a case like mine. At first, my father kept this plan to himself because the local government official would not have agreed to let the parents of an only child send him to the monastery. This is because if I went to the monastery, there would be no one left to take care of the land after my parents were gone. My father planned to take me to Ganden Chönkhor in secret. Once I was there, it would be difficult for the government official to argue with the monastery officials. So it was by my father's determination, and my own, as you will see, that I would become a monk. We had two relatives at the monastery, so that also made things more feasible. The younger one often came to our house to visit. I called the older one Ashang-la.[7] This uncle was a very important person in my life.

After my father resolved to send me to the monastery, my immediate condition still had to be treated. A doctor came every day and pulled on my leg to try to straighten it out. It was incredibly painful, and I dreaded these visits. I cried the whole time, and they had to hold me while they pulled on my leg. It was really terrible, like being in hell. I became very thin and weak because I wasn't eating very much. I think my parents must have given up hope many times and thought that I would die. This went on for a long time, probably six months or more. Eventually the doctor dug into the heel and was able to remove the three thorns. After that, it got better. Somehow, after a long time, through prayers, medical treatments, and determination, I didn't die. And my father did not forget what the lama had said about my entering the monastery.

3. The History of Ganden Chönkhor

PRIOR TO WHEN Ganden Chönkhor became a Geluk monastery during the time of the Fifth Dalai Lama, there was constant fighting between the region of Ü, which is central Tibet, and Tsang, to the south and west of it. The king of Tsang favored the Karma Kagyü sect and opposed the Geluk sect. The Fifth Dalai Lama held some power in central Tibet. The Mongols had great respect for him, and they came to his aid in the fight between central Tibet and the king of Tsang. With the help of the Mongol armies, the king of Tsang was defeated, and the Fifth Dalai Lama became the ruler of all of Tibet. He was the first of the Dalai Lamas to do this.[8]

Prior to this, the Geluk sect was not very strong in Tsang. Tashi Lhünpo was already there, and there was another monastery near Ganden Chönkhor which at that time belonged to the Karma Kagyü sect. About one mile west of the present Ganden Chönkhor was the small Geluk monastery called Laru Dratsang, which means "monastery of the rotten scraps of cloth." It was so called because that was all the monks there had for clothes. It was a very poor monastery, especially compared with the big Kagyü monastery. The old temple manager told me that in those days when the monks from Laru Dratsang went to visit the Kagyü monastery, they always wore their hats inside out. As Gelukpas, their hats were yellow, but they were lined with red wool inside. When the Laru Dratsang monks went to the Kagyü monastery, they would wear their hats with the red side facing out to appear to be Kagyüpas, for if they showed up in yellow hats they would be beaten up. That's how bad the situation was then.

After the Fifth Dalai Lama took power, nearly all of the Kagyü monasteries in the area were taken over and changed into Geluk monasteries. They say that the Fifth Dalai Lama established thirteen of these converted monasteries, including Shang Ganden Chönkhor, Nyuk Ganden Chönkhor, Phenpo Ganden Chönkhor, and others. The first part of these names refers to the region in which they were located. *Ganden* signifies the monastery and system of Tsongkhapa, and *chönkhor* means "wheel of Dharma." Thus the name given to these converted monasteries means these places were teaching the Dharma of the Ganden system of Tsongkhapa.

The assembly hall of Shang Ganden Chönkhor was the original assembly hall of the old Kagyü monastery. The monastery had massive thick walls—one could put a bed in the recess for the windows—and there were huge, elaborately carved beams and pillars like those in the Potala. The great shrine room (*lhakhang chenmo*) was located at the far end of the assembly hall and rose two or three stories. A beautiful two-story Buddha statue was housed there, and the story of this Buddha image, telling how it was made and so on, was written on the age-darkened wall of the entrance to the room. The inscription dated back to the Kagyü era. In front of the statue to the side, there was a door to the room where the temple manager (*kunyer*) lived. He was in charge of such duties as offerings, making tormas, and other ritual activities. I learned most of the history I've discussed here from the old temple manager who lived here in this room, who was eighty-five when I returned to visit in 1987. These days the monks there may not know about these things. Some of this history was written down in books at Ganden Chönkhor, but most of it only exists orally. And the old Ganden Chönkhor was entirely destroyed during the Cultural Revolution.

When I returned to Tibet and visited the rebuilt Ganden Chönkhor, I was shown some relics in the temple that they said dated back to the ancient period. In a glass case there was something wrapped up in a five-colored cloth, so I asked what it was. They took it out and showed me that it was Milarepa's walking stick. It was a wooden walking stick, crooked, shiny, and smooth from much use. I was skeptical that this was really Milarepa's stick, so I asked them how they came to have it. They told me that there was a family in the area who had gotten hold of it when the Chinese came in the 1960s and had kept it hidden during that time. They had acquired it right after the Chinese destroyed the monastery and everything in it, including the old Buddha image. The stick was one of the things that had been inside the statue. When the political situation improved in the 1980s, the family offered it back to the monastery. This seemed plausible, but I wasn't convinced right away.

At first I thought, Ganden Chönkhor is a Geluk monastery—how could it have Milarepa's stick? Even if the family had gotten hold of the relics from the Buddha image after the Chinese destroyed it, I still wondered how the stick of the great saint Milarepa got to be one of the things that was put inside this Buddha statue in the first place. But it was the Karmapa that had installed the statue, and he was probably the most powerful religious figure of his time. It was possible that he could have had such a rare relic. It was quite reasonable when I thought it out, so I believed it. There were two other objects there that were also said to have been found among the things from within the destroyed statue. Both, like the walking stick, were kept hidden by local people until the reestablishment of Ganden Chönkhor. One was a small stupa from Atiśa's time, and the other was a wooden bowl that was supposed to have belonged to the ancient King Gesar.[9]

Gelukpas say that in the Fifth Dalai Lama's time, after the Karmapa was defeated and driven out, he was sent to Tsurphu Monastery, which had long been a seat of the Karmapas. The landscape around Tsurphu Monastery is characterized by triangular ground and triangular sky because of the way the valley and surrounding mountains are arranged. In Tibetan magical practices, black iron triangles are used to trap spirits and other negative forces, so one can imagine the implications of the physical attributes of the site where Tsurphu is located. The place is very narrow and has a little river. There are some bushes, but the ground is black. Gelukpas say that the Karmapa was purposely put in a bad place by the Fifth Dalai Lama, but the Karma Kagyüpas probably do not see it this way.

At one time I wanted to go to Tsurphu, but somebody told me that I shouldn't. The person said that in the time of the Fifth Dalai Lama, the Kagyüpas had gotten some of his hair and put it under the front steps of the monastery. Walking on the steps would be like stepping on the Fifth Dalai Lama's head. It was probably true. After the Fifth Dalai Lama's rise to power there was strong animosity between the sects; the Kagyüpas probably thought of him as their enemy. They could have gotten some of his hair and done this. Every time I went by that valley and saw the golden roof and the beautiful buildings, I wanted to go, but I never did. I was afraid that it might be true about the Fifth Dalai Lama's hair under those steps.

There are many connections between the Fifth Dalai Lama and Ganden Chönkhor in addition to the circumstances of its founding. The main philosophical textbooks (*yikcha*) used at Ganden Chönkhor are those written by the Fifth Dalai Lama. And the Fifth Dalai Lama himself established Palden Lhamo as the principal protective deity of Ganden Chönkhor.[10] It is said that the Fifth Dalai Lama sent a special thangka painting of Palden Lhamo to Ganden Chönkhor. Part of this thangka was supposed to have been painted with blood from the nose of the Fifth Dalai Lama. It was on a pillar in the temple under many banners of yellow and red cloth on which were written the sacred mantra of Palden Lhamo, *Jho*. We never saw this thangka, because it was completely covered up with offering scarves (*khataks*) and banners. Every time there was a special ceremony, if someone were making a big offering to the monks, one of these banners would be brought in on a long pole and added to the others. There were so many banners that they looked almost like a tent around the pillar. There was also supposed to be a mask of Palden Lhamo on that pillar under all the cloth. We never saw that either.

In the 1980s, when the Chinese administration began to ease restrictions on religion, the rebuilding of Ganden Chönkhor began. First they rebuilt just a new assembly hall. Then, slowly, more buildings were erected. It was primarily wealthy families who sponsored the rebuilding so that their sons would have a place to live at Ganden Chönkhor. Now they have even rebuilt the Dalai Lama's palace, where he would stay if he were ever to visit there.

4. The Beginning of My Life as a Monk

AT GANDEN CHÖNKHOR the monks gathered in the great assembly hall at least twice each day, in the morning and around noontime. Sometimes this happened three times, and occasionally they would assemble for the whole day, in five separate sessions. In the morning, monks did not have to prepare food or cook. They came to the assembly hall with their bowls, and tsampa and tea were served. There was no luxurious dining room; everything was done together in the assembly hall.

Before I entered the monastery, I often visited there with my father. When I visited, I would go up to the balcony to watch when my two relatives went to the assembly. Below were rows and rows of monks. The prayer leader (*umzé*) was there, the disciplinarian (*gekö*) was there, and at the end of the rows were young monks who were children just like me. I watched these children very carefully. I observed that their conduct was very good. I admired how they looked sitting there in their robes, and I had a strong desire to do that too. I very much enjoyed listening to the chanting and watching the older monks go back and forth doing their duties, and I especially admired how the children were so disciplined and well behaved.

When I returned home from my visits to the monastery and played with the other children in my village, I played as if I were their leader. I'd make them line up in rows and walk back and forth like I was the disciplinarian, saying, "Don't do this! Do this!" I would make them behave like monks. I even went and found some red or yellow cloth to make a kind of robe. I think many of the children had never seen this kind of thing themselves, so they enjoyed it too. From the time that I was about ten, I knew I wanted to become a monk. I kept insisting to my parents that I wanted to go to the monastery. Other people from the village said that since my mother and father were old and I was their only son, I should stay at home and take care of the land. My mother didn't want me to go to the monastery either. She wanted me to stay at home.

My father, however, was a very religious and determined man, and he wanted me to go to the monastery as I wished. We had an altar in our house, and my father read the *Vajracchedikā Sūtra* every day.[11] He also knew some Nyingma texts. For instance, he could recite *The Liberation through Hearing in the Intermediate State*, which Westerners know as *The Tibetan Book of the Dead*.[12] He recited this when we traveled to distant places. (Remember, we walked everywhere we went.) Most people had a generally positive feeling for, and faith in, Buddhism, but my father was unusual. Though he did not have a formal education, he knew how to read, and he had a better understanding of these texts than most people. He wanted me to have an education at the monastery, even though most people were against the idea. I was very insistent that I should become a monk, even though I was still a child. I talked about it constantly at home and outside among others. Even when I played, I was a monk all the time.

But there was a problem. In order for me to become a monk, we had to get permission from the local government official. Since our land would not have a caretaker if I left, we had to ask special permission. The official said he would not grant this request and that I should be kept at home, just like the people of our town were saying. But my father had great courage and determination, so he defied the local official and popular opinion. He said that they could do what they liked to him, but he was going to take me to the monastery anyway, without permission. He knew that I would be cared for by our relatives there, so there was no need for anyone to worry about me. So early one morning he just took me to the monastery.

That was how I first got to Ganden Chönkhor. It was my idea and desire. I was determined to be a monk. My father supported me, especially after what the lama said after I hurt my foot at the cemetery, but in the end it was my decision. In most families, it was the parents who decided who would go to the monastery, who would stay home, who would go into business, and so on. The same was true with marriage in the old system. As in most places, in Tibet it was primarily the family, the parents, who made these decisions for their children. In my case, though, it was different.

I was almost ten when I entered the monastery. It was during the time called the Festival of the Buddha's Descent from Heaven, which commemorates the time when the Buddha came back down to earth from the Heaven of the Thirty Three, where he was visiting and teaching his mother who had been born there as a god. It falls on the twenty-second day of the ninth month of the Tibetan calendar. There were only three months left until the twelfth month and the New Year, when I would turn ten years old.

At the monastery I was entrusted to the care of my older uncle. My other younger relative also lived at Ganden Chönkhor when I entered, and I stayed with him a lot in the beginning since my elder uncle was often away. My younger relative had a very nice voice. He was not a great philosopher, though he was a scholar monk. Later he became a ritual specialist (*chogawa*) for the monastery. There were special rituals that had to be done at the time of death, and people contacted the monastery to get someone to perform them. The disciplinarian had a list of people who were qualified to do these rituals, and the monastery would send someone when a request was made. The ritual that is done is from a text of the *yoga* class of tantric texts.[13] The monastery trained a group of people who memorized the text and ritual actions. There were many mantras and symbolic hand gestures, called *mudrās*, that had to be mastered. Then, before these monks could be sent out to perform rituals, they had to complete a retreat on the practices. Once they finished, they were put on the disciplinarian's list and sent out by turns when people requested a ritual specialist from the monastery. My relative was one of these ritual specialists.

5. My Relative the Ritual Specialist

M Y ELDER UNCLE didn't come to visit my family often, so I didn't know him very well prior to entering the monastery. But my younger relative, whose name was Shākya, had come to visit our house ever since I was a baby, so I knew him well. He was from my mother's side of the family, as was my elder uncle. I'm not sure how to describe the family relationship in English, but Shākya and my mother were not brother and sister. He called my mother Tsomo-la, which is a term for an older female relative.

I once heard an interesting story about Shākya. There was a town about ten or twenty miles away called Katsé. It was similar to a monastery in some ways, but it was partly occupied by laypeople who were religious but were married and had children. Someone had died in Katsé, and they requested a monk from Ganden Chönkhor to come to do the necessary rituals. Katsé had a reputation for being a little rough, and it was infamous for strange occurrences involving the dead, such as corpses rising up like zombies or vampires. This was the first time my relative was sent out by the monastery to do the rituals for the dead. The disciplinarian sent Shākya to do the rituals, but afterward, remembering what kind of place Katsé was, he thought, "Why did I send a first-timer to this place? I shouldn't have done that."

The ritual specialist had to stay with the dead body for almost a week. The first three days the body was left in the home. They sat it upright in the corner of the room with a lamp and a full cup in front of it, and a curtain across it so that no one coming in would see the corpse unless they pulled the curtain back. The ritual specialist sat next to the curtain in front of a small altar where there were butter lamps and other offerings.

The first couple of nights in Katsé were uneventful for Shākya, but on the third night something strange happened. It was late, around midnight. The only light in the room was coming from two small lamps. As Shākya was doing the rituals, he thought he saw the curtain pull back a little bit. At first he thought that he might just be imagining things, so he resolved to have more confidence and keep doing what he was supposed to do. He had been taught not to be superstitious or to let this kind of thing bother him, to just have confidence in his training and in the power of the rituals. He knew he had seen something, but he decided to ignore it and continue.

A little while later it looked like the side of the curtain was being pulled back again, as if the dead person on the other side were trying to peek out. Shākya became a little bit afraid, but he continued on with the prayers and rituals. Finally, the curtain moved again, and this time Shākya was very uncomfortable and decided to get up to look behind the curtain. The dead man behind the curtain did not look like a normal corpse. His whole face had become completely red and swollen. His hair and beard were all standing straight up. He was about to rise.

Shākya had been taught what to do when something like this happened. He was supposed to do special mantras and rituals using a vajra and bell[14] and use special black sand that had been blessed by the entire assembly of the Ganden Chönkhor monks. First he threw some of the sand over the face and body of the dead person. He put the vajra and the bell on top of the corpse's head and then spoke the mantra loudly several times. Then he kicked the body in the stomach three times. A huge noise, like gas, came from behind, and the body started to change. The hair came down, and the face got thinner until it looked like a corpse again. After this success, Shākya was confident in the power of these methods and substances, and he never worried about this kind of occurrence again. This was his first experience as a ritual specialist.

The black sand that Shākya used had been blessed in the second month of the year when Ganden Chönkhor had a special period of intensive recitation of the *maṇi* mantra. During that month the mantra of Avalokiteśvara, *oṃ maṇi padme hūṃ*, was recited from morning to evening. After fifteen days there was a day of silence, and in the evening the prayer leader recited a special prayer. There were trays of protection cords that were blessed that would later be given out to the laypeople who came for a blessing. The black sand was also on trays in the assembly hall throughout the ritual. At the end of this period, the trays were passed around to all the monks, and each monk blew on the tray, his breath having been purified by the mantra recitation. The black sand was blessed in that way. This sand was very powerful, so the ritual specialists always carried some of it when they went out to perform death rituals. The sand was also used by farmers. In the summer, there were sometimes a lot of caterpillar-like insects that were very destructive to the black pea pods, endangering the entire crop. If a farmer scattered some of this black sand in the fields, the insects went away or died.

There were two types of ritual specialist at Ganden Chönkhor. The *kangsowa* were tantric ritual specialists who did rituals to drive away demons and hindrances, through rituals similar to the one that took place every year in my village at the labrang. They did this on the twenty-ninth day of the twelfth month of every year. At Ganden Chönkhor there was a group of twenty-five monks who performed these rituals. When the rest of the monks were gathered in the main temple, these twenty-five gathered in a small temple above and did their own tantric rituals for the monastic community.

The other ritual specialists, like my relative Shākya, were sent out to do rituals for laypeople. Many of the *kangsowa* were also sent out for death rituals, but the *chogawa* only did these death rituals. They had to memorize a large text that was a ritual compendium, learn the mudrās and the way of chanting, and do the retreat. After the retreat they were included in the society of ritual specialists. When a layperson showed up at the monastery needing these services, a message was sent in. The disciplinarian's assistant consulted the list of ritual specialists, chose one, and immediately went to get that person from the assembly. The layperson waited outside with horses and went together with the ritual specialist to get the ritual equipment, and then they left. That was the system. This happened almost every day. Sometimes people came from far away, other times from nearby. It didn't matter whether the person who had died was wealthy or poor, ordinary or noble; the monastery sent ritual specialists regardless. This was one of the things that the monastery provided to the laity.

Shākya came often to our house to visit. I remember shortly after he had completed his mastery of the text and its rituals, my mother asked him to recite it for us one night. It was wonderful to hear Shākya's beautiful voice and his melodious way of chanting, accompanied by the ringing of the bell and the graceful way he did the mudrās. This was never done in the assembly hall, so most monks had never heard it. The only time that laypeople would hear it was when someone had died, so we were very lucky to hear it in these happy circumstances.

6. Living the Religious Life
at Ganden Chönkhor

ENTRANCE INTO monastic life consists of several rituals that are done step by step. Though sometimes people nowadays call children in monasteries "monks," one cannot take full ordination as a monk (*gelong*) until adulthood. Prior to that time the child is a novice (*getsül*). Novice status is attained through two rituals that mark one's leaving lay life behind and entering religious life. Until the boy has gone through these rituals and taken on the signs and vows associated with them, he is not considered a genuine member of the monastic community.

The first ritual marks the stage of entering the status of renunciant (*rapjung*), and the second one marks the boy's entrance into being a novice. The first ritual and its vows are called the *rapjung parma*, or "supplementary renunciant vows." This consists of the adoption of three signs of the renunciant life that demonstrate outwardly that the boy is dedicated to living the spiritual life. The first of these is the ritual act of going before the abbot (*khenpo*) of the monastery and performing three prostrations to formally request entry. The second is the renunciation of the trappings of lay life by changing into monks' robes. The third is the ordaining monk cutting the boy's hair. The young renunciant's head is shaved except for a small tuft of hair, and this is cut in a later formal ceremony. In the course of these rituals, the boy also receives a new name, which signifies his entering a new life. At this point, the boy is a renunciant. Next comes the taking of the full ten precepts[15] that prohibit the boy from engaging in harmful activities. After this he is considered a novice. As a novice, the boy is able to participate in monastic life, go to the assembly, and other such things, but he isn't yet a fully ordained monk, or *gelong* (Skt. *bhikṣu*).

At Ganden Chönkhor, these two novice rituals were generally performed together, one after the other, in a group ceremony in a large room in the monastery palace (*phodrang*). They were presided over by the abbot and some senior monks. In my case, it was my teacher, Lhündrup Gönpo, who performed the hair-cutting ritual and from whom I received my ordination name. It was the monastic custom for a novice to take part of his ordaining teacher's name as his new name. My ordaining teacher had Lhündrup as part of his name, so each of the boys that he ordained was also given Lhündrup as one of his names.[16] All of the novices who were ordained together were called *Dharma friends*. For the rest of their lives they always referred to each other this way because they had all received ordination together. I took the novice vows very early, only about a month after getting to Ganden Chönkhor.

Once entering the monastery as a novice, one had to observe a strict set of monastic rules and precepts, though not the entire body of vows that are laid out in the Vinaya.[17] One began to learn to read, and from the very beginning, there were prayers to be memorized. The word *prayer* here does not mean exactly the same thing as I understand it to mean in Christianity, where prayer means praising God or making requests for blessings or confessing the bad things that one has done. In our tradition we have prayers to buddhas, bodhisattvas, lamas, and many other beings for many purposes. For instance, there are poetic praises of the Buddha and his followers such as the great Indian masters. While these are mostly recited out of a spirit of devotion and reverence, they are also done for the sake of inspiration in one's own practice. There are also short liturgical texts that describe the lives of the Buddha and other figures like Tsongkhapa, and a short text that accompanies prostrations to the Buddha as well.

There are also prayers of dedication, which have the function of dedicating all of one's merit toward the welfare of all sentient beings—their deliverance from suffering and attainment of awakening. When we make such requests, we are not asking some god to do these things for us; we are stating our aspiration to develop our own spiritual practice so that we can help other beings ourselves. We ask the awakened beings for support, guidance, and inspiration in these aims. In Buddhism we make requests to other realized beings for aid, but we know that ultimately, awakening is attained by oneself and is available to all. We do not believe that there is some being or beings out there who can do these things for us without our efforts.

As a young monk, there were many things to memorize, and in the beginning this took up most of our time. We started with a selection of three or four verses that were taught orally, and then we memorized them. My relatives taught me many such verses. Later, we had to memorize whole texts. The first thing was the refuge formula that was used at Ganden Chönkhor, which was recited every day at the assembly.

The ordinary tasks of everyday life were also difficult. The monks in Ganden Chönkhor had to get all food, matches, and other supplies from Namling, the biggest and most widely known city in that area of Tsang. Since there was no water available on the mountainside where Ganden Chönkhor was, water had to be brought from the river outside the monastery. Young monks would go down to the river and bring water back in large clay pots. It was nice in that the young monks would also have a chance to play outside a bit before bringing the water back. Wealthy monks[18] had large copper storage containers with an inner white coating to prevent the copper getting into the water. But most people had to bring their water in every day. In most kitchens there was a large clay pot in the corner that the water would be put in. Sometimes this had to be filled more than once a day. Getting water took maybe thirty minutes round-trip. Bathing also had to be done out in the river, since one could only wash his face and hands in the monastery. Laundry was done at the river as well. The young monks were responsible for washing the clothes for the household, so the students would do the washing for the teacher. This was the old way of doing things.

We had to sit still and quietly each day in the assembly, and we were fearful of the disciplinarian. My relatives at the monastery were also quite strict, so after several months I really missed home. Despite my early conviction to be a monk, I missed my mother, and I wanted to go home and stay with the cows. I remembered playing with the other children and tending the animals, spending the whole day out in the fields and valleys. Those cows weren't so strict; they were almost like friends. In the monastery I felt miserable thinking about those memories. I think most children would have had these feelings.

7. A Young Monk's First Two Teachers

MONASTIC LIFE in Tibet was completely different from anything most people are familiar with in the West. Every Geluk monastery had some of its own unique traditions, but they all followed the same basic tenets, practices, and way of life. My experience was of course specific to Ganden Chönkhor, but life in other Geluk monasteries was largely the same.

A young monk had two primary teachers, called the *fundamental teacher* (*tsawai gegen*) and the *text teacher* (*pechai gegen*). The fundamental teacher was the monk who sponsored the novice and took care of him, acting almost like the young monk's parents within the monastery. This teacher was typically a senior monk who was a relative or friend of the family, and he was responsible for teaching the boy the customs, rules, and regulations of the monastery. The young monk lived with this teacher, and regardless of where the boy went during the day, he left from this home and returned to it. When the boy was old enough, the fundamental teacher found a suitable text teacher for him, and the novice began his education. In my case, my elder uncle was my fundamental teacher.

The text teacher was responsible for the student's learning of prayers, chanting, and so forth. He was also the one who taught the student to read, starting with the alphabet, then how to read short passages, and eventually to read texts quickly. The student first had to memorize passages given to him orally by the teacher. Later, when the student was able to read, he was assigned sections of text to memorize on his own. The teacher would say that the student had to memorize from one point to another in a text for a given day. In later education at Ganden, Sera, or Drepung, it was assumed that one had already memorized numerous texts. Many of the texts were common to all Geluk monasteries, but some were unique to an individual monastery. The main objective at this stage of education was for the student to be able to read and recite from memory.

One's text teacher was also called his *Dharma recitation teacher* (*chöjökyi gegen*), because he was the one who taught the young monk the necessary prayers, recitations, and so on. The Dharma recitation teacher had two basic teaching responsibilities. First, he helped the young monk memorize a volume of many small prayer texts that were specific to the monastery. At Ganden Chönkhor, this volume included small sūtras such as the *Heart Sūtra* and other prayers that originated with the Buddha himself.[19] It also included other prayers by Tibetan authors and Indian masters such as Nāgārjuna.[20] These texts were mostly in verse form, so they were suitable for recitation. There were prayers for prostrations, offering prayers, dedication prayers, and aspirations prayers. There were also other liturgical texts by great teachers and lamas. Altogether, these made up a huge volume that was to be memorized by the young monk. The student had to read and recite the texts in this volume over and over until he had committed them to memory, which took several years. This was the young monk's first duty as a student, and it was his Dharma recitation teacher who helped him with this. While the young monk was memorizing these texts he also learned to read. All the emphasis was placed on reading; there was very little concern for learning to write.

8. Daily Assemblies and Classes

AFTER I JOINED the monastery, I was finally able to participate in all the activities that I had formerly watched from the balcony overlooking the assembly hall. All the monks came together at least twice every day in the great assembly hall, once in the early morning and again around 11:00 a.m. The monks had tea together in the first assembly and more tea with some kind of light meal in the later assembly. At certain times during the year there could be as many as five assemblies in a day for several days in a row, but there were always at least two. Because tea and a meal were served, these were called *wet assemblies* (*löntsok*); they were always held in the assembly hall. *Dry assemblies* (*kamtsok*) were what we called the gatherings in the Dharma courtyard (*chöra*), where we would do prayer and, later in our educations, debate. There wasn't any tea or food at the gatherings held outside.

The morning assembly began around 7:00 or 7:30 a.m., but we awoke much earlier for recitation, meditation, and other practices. Each year a monk was selected for the special job of calling all the monks of the monastery to the first assembly. This man was called the *charkepa*, and he was selected for this job because he had a good voice. Each morning he walked along the roof of the assembly hall from the eastern corner all the way to the western corner so that the monks all across the monastery could hear this call from their homes. By that time many monks would have already been meditating or doing other practices in their rooms. It wouldn't have been good to startle them with a loud voice, so the charkepa called out to them in a special way.

First the charkepa did three prostrations. Then he slapped his hat on the palm of his hand, the first time softly, then a little harder, and then as hard as he could. After that, he put on his hat. Then he coughed or cleared his throat three times, the first time quietly, then a little louder, and then very loudly. Gradually, the charkepa began to make a little more noise. Initially he recited a verse so quietly that no one could even hear the words, but after the final words of the verse, "we pray," he called out, "oooohhhhh," and then repeated this a second time more loudly. He remained silent for a little while and walked to the middle part of the roof, where he repeated the entire sequence. Then he did the same thing at the opposite corner of the assembly hall. Finally he began the whole process again back where he had started. This took maybe an hour or more. The monks who lived at the far corner of the monastery may have been called a little later, but they still had time to get ready and get to the assembly hall. This was how it was done at Ganden Chönkhor. I've heard that in Japanese monasteries and other such places they have a gong, but we did not have that.

When the charkepa was finished he came down, and two other monks blew conch shells on the roof. It was said that one of the shells was a male sound and the other was a female sound, because one had a lower tone and the other had a higher tone. The two monks stood next to each other but faced opposite directions. At the end they blew the conches with a wavering sound. By that time most of the monks were already in the assembly hall, but there was still time to get there if one hadn't gone yet. Once this was finished, however, it was too late, and one was in trouble if he came in late. He might as well have gone home unless he wanted to feel the disciplinarian's stick, which would have been waiting for him in the assembly hall.

After a day of going to assemblies, the young monk returned home to the fundamental teacher's home for a meal. Then after dark, the student went to the text teacher's home for tutoring. This teacher had five, ten, or maybe even twenty students, but certainly no more than that. The place one went was not a school but rather a private room, so it wouldn't fit any more students than that. The whole night was spent at the Dharma recitation teacher's house. The students spent the evening sessions memorizing the monastery's prayer texts. The Dharma recitation teacher helped the students with the texts and checked what they had memorized. Every night each student reviewed what he had memorized the previous night and recited it to make certain that he had learned it correctly. If he had, he would begin a new section. Lessons lasted until maybe 11:00 p.m. or midnight, and then the student slept there.

In the morning he woke up, got ready for the first assembly, and went directly there. He didn't return to his home until the afternoon, usually sometime between 2:00 and 5:00, when he went home for dinner. The whole day was spent at assemblies and at the Dharma recitation teacher's house memorizing and reciting. If there weren't many assemblies on a given day, then one would stay at the Dharma recitation teacher's house until it was time to go home for dinner. After dinner, at dark, it started all over again. It wasn't like it is here in the West, where students go to school during the day and return home for the evening. We stayed at school through the night and only went home for brief periods to eat.

9. Running Away from the Monastery

AT MONASTERIES such as Ganden Chönkhor, the year was separated into various educational and religious sessions or semesters. In between these sessions, there were short breaks, and during the fifth Tibetan month there was a vacation period, and we could go anywhere. During this time, young monks usually went to stay with their parents, which was very nice. Going home at any other time required permission from the disciplinarian, and that was very difficult to get. However, during the semesters, one's mother and father could come to visit. When I first entered the monastery, my parents often came to see me, but when they visited, I wanted to go back home with them, and I always cried when they had to leave. The monastery was built on a hillside and rose way up from the plain, like the Potala. On the days that I thought my parents would be coming, I watched for them. From the monastery I could see them coming from a long way off, and when they left I could watch them going for a long time. That was a very hard thing to watch.

There was a time early on when I was so unhappy at the monastery that I ran away. It was during the period when I had to memorize all the prayers and ritual recitations. Some Dharma recitation teachers were stern and fierce, and some were patient and gentle. My fundamental teacher, my uncle, chose a monk named Gelong Dompelpa, who was very well known and respected but was a very strict teacher. Everyone feared him, including me. He made me work very hard on my memorization and chanting. He insisted that I do my chanting loudly and very clearly. I had to memorize the passages very quickly too. The end result was good, but at the time I didn't see it that way.

Every day I had to go to Gelong Dompelpa's house in the evening and read a portion of text over and over. Then I had to recite that section to prove that I had learned it. In the beginning I had some difficulty with this, and my teacher became angry with me. One day I was unable to do the recitation, and he became very angry and scolded and beat me. He told me that I had to work harder. The next day I was still unable to do the recitation, and again I received a scolding and a beating. Then he showed me two whips that were hanging from a post in his house and told me that if I didn't do my recitation properly, the next day he would whip me with them. I was very frightened. I didn't think I would be able to do the recitation the next day and knew I would have to face a whipping. When I returned to my home the next afternoon, my uncle tried to be encouraging in his stern way, but that did very little to ease my mind. All I could do was worry about the whipping. I decided to run away that night.

When it was time for me to go back to Gelong Dompelpa's house, I went instead down to the main gate of the monastery and hid behind the open gate. I knew I couldn't make it all the way home that night, so I sat there for a long time, crouching behind the gate. I knew that the gatekeeper came around midnight to close and bolt the doors, so when midnight approached, I ran to the doorway of a nearby house. The doorway had a step down into the door, which made a small space where I could hide. I stayed there until the gatekeeper came and closed the gates. Then I returned and hid in the space of the gates, up against the doors. The gatekeeper would come out every so often on his watch, so I had to keep running back and forth between the gate of the monastery and the doorway of the house.

At one point when I was crouching in the doorway of the house it began to rain. I was protected from the rain by the doorway. However, just outside the doorway, there was an indentation that quickly filled with water. A small dog came by and began to drink from the little pool.

Sometimes children do strange things, and for some reason I decided to scare this dog, who could not see me. I jumped out and the dog ran off, terrified. Unfortunately, when I did this, my foot bumped the door of the house, and it got the attention of the monk who lived there. He called out, "What is going on there?" and I had to run back to my spot by the main gate. He came out with a lantern and looked around, but he did not see me. I spent the whole night going back and forth between the two spots. When morning approached I knew that the gatekeeper would reopen the gates and the monks would begin to come out and gather for the morning assembly. So I found another spot to hide and waited. Finally, when the gates were opened and all the monks were in the assembly hall, I ran from the monastery.

It took me almost all day to get back to my home, but when I got back to the village I was afraid to go home because of what my parents would say. For a while I hid in a hay barn. I stayed there until I was so hungry and thirsty that I could no longer bear it, and finally, I went home. My mother scolded me and said that it was foolish and dangerous for me to walk all that way by myself. She was worried about me. When my father came home he didn't scold me much. He said that it was too late in the day to take me back to the monastery, but he would take me back in the morning. My mother then said that since I had come all that way I could stay a day or two, and then I would have to go back. They sent a message to my uncle to let him know that I was safe.

After several days my father took me back to the monastery, even though I really didn't want to go. I was afraid of what my uncle would say and even more afraid of my text teacher. To my surprise, my uncle was not very angry. He asked me why I had run away and caused everyone so much worry. I told him that I was afraid of my teacher and that I had not been doing well and was afraid of being whipped. My uncle went to see my teacher and told him that there was no need for me to be hurried through my memorization; I could do it at a slower pace. This made matters much better. After that my text teacher became more patient with me.

10. Completing One's Basic Education

AFTER A YOUNG monk completed his memorization of prayers and texts, he had to demonstrate this by reciting the entire volume of texts in front of the whole assembly. That was how we were tested. In the Tibetan language, we say that a student "gives" an examination, unlike in the English language in which a student is said to "take" an examination. We said that we gave the examination to the teacher, but really we gave it to the entire group of monks in the assembly hall.

In the assembly hall the monks sat in long rows. The young monks who were being tested sat in the first one or two rows. After the tea or food had been distributed, the prayer leader recited an offering prayer. Then all the monks ate their meal in silence while one young monk changed his sitting position to face up toward the altar and gave a recitation of a portion of the text that he had memorized. He did this according to a special rhythm and very loudly. The young monk had to keep reciting until the disciplinarian gave the signal that he could stop.

The disciplinarian had a long staff, which was the symbol of his position. When he struck the staff down on the floor, with a *chak* sound, the boy could stop his recitation. It was the disciplinarian's decision as to whether the student had proven himself. If the boy was doing a good job, pronouncing everything correctly and using the right rhythm, volume, and speed, the disciplinarian would let the recitation continue on some time. If the boy had difficulty with any of these things, the disciplinarian slammed down the end of the staff—*chak*!—and stopped the boy in mid-sentence. When a young monk was giving the examination, he didn't want to hear this sound because it meant that he was doing a poor job. When his turn came he paid very careful attention to all the aspects of the recitation so that he didn't hear this sound. This was a very nerve-wracking experience. The whole assembly hall was quiet; there was only one voice in the hall, and it was his. All the monks were there, his teachers were there, and of course he knew that the disciplinarian was listening very carefully.

Each student had to recite the entire volume to the assembly. This process was controlled by the disciplinarian's signal and could take years to complete. The young monks who were being tested took turns reciting. Sometimes there were only five or six boys giving exams at a time, sometimes more. Recitations would only take place during the wet assemblies held in the assembly hall. During normal days when there were two wet assemblies per day, three boys would be tested in each session. During times when a patron sponsored multiple assembly sessions each day or when there were special occasions, there might be up to five sessions a day. These occasions included the month leading up to the full moon of Buddha Śākyamuni's birth, awakening, and passing into final nirvāṇa (*parinirvāṇa*); the celebration of Tsongkhapa's birth, awakening, and passing into final nirvana; and the one-month Avalokiteśvara retreat. At these times there were more opportunities for recitations.

During the special Avalokiteśvara retreat period, for instance, the chants and other practices associated with this period only took up one morning and evening session, but the monks spent all day in the assembly hall, in five sessions all together. That meant that the rest of the day's sessions were available for giving exams. In the early morning session the prayer leader chanted *oṃ maṇi padme hūṃ* in his deep voice, and then everyone sat in silence. During the subsequent three assemblies, the prayer leader would recite this mantra again, and everyone chanted the tea-offering verses, but after that there were no further rituals to be done, so this time could be used for the students' recitations.

The frequency of these occasions would determine how often a boy would get his turn to recite and thus how long it would take for him to finish. Regardless of the time of year, it was always better for the young monk if only a small number of boys were taking the examination. If there were only a few students, he might be able to give a recitation every day. If there were more students, his turn came every other day or only once a week. That resulted in an extension of the period of his testing. If the boy were very sharp, it could be finished quickly, but if not, it took much longer.

Thus a young monk's first three or four years at the monastery were spent memorizing and being tested on this large volume of texts. The entire process could take as long as six or seven years. It took two or three years just to do the memorization, and then the examination period could take years as well. Until this was finished, the Dharma recitation teacher was the student's guide and teacher. Every young monk did this. There were no exceptions to this requirement.

II. My Uncle and His Position in the Monastery

As I SAID, my fundamental teacher was my uncle. It was always the case that a young monk had some family or social connection to his teacher—people weren't turning their children over to strangers. It was the fundamental teacher who went to the abbot to obtain permission for the boy to become a monk. Then he was responsible for that boy. If the boy got in trouble, it reflected badly on his fundamental teacher. In addition to taking care of the boy's basic needs, the fundamental teacher also had to arrange for the boy's education. A good fundamental teacher was therefore very important for a young monk.

My uncle was not a scholar monk; he was a kind of monk called a *dopdop*.[21] Dopdops were usually monks who had not studied extensively but served as the workers in the monastery. They had to complete the recitation examination like everyone else, but after that they did not continue their education. It's like the stages of education in the U.S. After high school some students go on to university, but others do something else. Dopdops were like those who do not continue their education after high school. The big monasteries had many jobs that needed to be done and much business that needed to be conducted. The dopdops did all kinds of jobs—they were sent out to do business with nomads, they worked in the kitchen, and they served in the assembly hall. When soup was prepared, it was the dopdops who prepared the meat, chopped the bones, and so forth. Among the dopdops, some were big and strong. They were selected for security work at special ceremonies, such as the Great Prayer Festival, the Mönlam Chenmo, in Lhasa.

Dopdops who were wild and badly behaved sometimes fought among themselves. The monastery had to monitor their behavior diligently. Generally, however, dopdops were just monks who did not pursue higher studies. My uncle was one of these. At a young age he was very wild, but later in his life, he held one of the most important jobs in the monastery—he was the tea master. The tea master oversaw the preparation of the tea or whatever other food was offered during the assembly. The tea master was the boss of the kitchen and its workers.

Interestingly, the person who took the job of tea master was selected differently from most other positions in the monastery, which were appointed by the abbot or the disciplinarian. The tea master was elected by the monks of the monastery. At the end of each year there was a formal meeting of the monks to elect the next year's tea master. If the person had done an excellent job in his first year, then the monks called for him to continue in the job for another year. They each called out "*rang ja!*" to indicate that they wanted the same tea master again. The disciplinarian monitored the meeting. At the end, if all the monks loudly called out together, "*rang ja, rang ja!*" the tea master had no choice but to continue in the job for another year. My uncle was called back twice.

When my uncle accepted the responsibility for taking care of me, he had a few statues and thangkas in his room, but like most dopdops, he didn't have many books. One book that my uncle did have was a copy of Milarepa's *Hundred Thousand Songs* that included the yogi's biography.[22] My uncle had a special affinity with this text. He was familiar with many of the songs, and he could even recite some from memory. Sometimes he made me read from that book as an exercise in fast reading. It was typical for a fundamental teacher to do this, and of course Milarepa was a great role model for the dedicated spiritual life. Later, when I was considering whether or not to go to Sera to continue my studies, the book proved to be important in the decision. My uncle recited a verse from the *Hundred Thousand Songs* as his dedication to helping me continue my education. The verse goes:

Atop the valley is the great meditator.
Below, donors offer what he needs to live.
Both perform auspicious acts that lead to buddhahood.
The first and foremost auspicious activity is the dedication
of merit.

My uncle quoted this verse to show that even though he himself was not able to study and progress in practice, through his support and sponsorship of me, we would both accumulate merit. Even though my uncle was a dopdop, he had a practical understanding of, and serious dedication to, the Dharma.

12. Sustenance in the Monastery

IN ADDITION TO being responsible for the boy's education, the fundamental teacher also had to provide all a monk's material support. It was the custom in Tibet for laypeople, wealthy monks, and lamas to occasionally distribute money to all the monks of the monastery. The donor did this in order to generate merit. The money received by the fundamental teacher contributed to the support of the young monk. As a member of the Sangha, the young monk also received these disbursements of money. The fundamental teacher, like a parent, kept this money for the novice. The teacher also received support from the novice's family as well as from his own family. Of course, in the monastery, one didn't have to worry about a morning meal because every monk received tea and brought his own tsampa to both of the early assemblies. During special occasions, the monks didn't have to worry about any meal for that day. In general, however, it was not the case that the monastery fully supported the monks who lived there. Rather each monk relied upon his family home to provide support.

The monastery owned farmland and fields, which were worked by laypeople. When the crops were harvested, half of the grain usually went to the monastery, though in some cases farmers gave less. Either way, the monastery always had a store of grain. People also offered animals such as yaks and sheep to the monastery. Some richer monasteries had arrangements with people in the nomadic areas. A group of nomads raised and tended animals that belonged to the monastery, and the monastery received a portion of their milk, butter, and cheese.

During the semester, each monk received an allotment of barley, which he would have someone roast and grind to make tsampa. This grain came from the monastery's granary, which had originated from the fields owned by the monastery. The monastery oversaw this system of distribution. The amount of food was not great, but it was enough to keep one from starving. Some monks, based on their families' wealth, were comparatively rich, but most of us had just enough to survive. We brought our own tsampa to the early morning assembly. When we drank our tea, we would leave a small amount in the bottom of the bowl. From the bag of tsampa on our belts, we would take a small amount out and mix it with the remaining tea into a ball of dough. We did this underneath our outer robe and then quietly ate it. This was our breakfast. We also did this at the second assembly later in the morning.

At those times when there was a third assembly, such as when a wealthy patron sponsored a ceremony, we would have a very delicious soup. Such a soup could not be duplicated, even at home. It was made with a special kind of meat, lamb or something, and large bones that were roughly chopped and put into huge cooking pots in the monastery kitchen.

These pots were huge, as tall as a man. Just one of these pots would fill most of a normal-sized room. The monastery kitchen took up nearly an entire floor of the building and had three or four of these pots. One was the main teapot, one was filled with water, one contained the soup, and one was for the ingredients that were added to the soup. They all sat over wood fires. I heard that after the destruction of Ganden Chönkhor during the Cultural Revolution, the Chinese troops used these pots for toilets. They did many terrible things like that.

Along one wall of the kitchen were the teapots used for serving. They were wooden with three decorated bands of metal that wrapped all the way around them. Wooden poles were put through the handles to carry the teapots, which also had spouts from which to pour the tea. The opposite wall held similar pots for the soup, which didn't have spouts but instead had ladles for serving. The monks sat in rows in the assembly hall, and each row had one person who went into the kitchen and picked up the pot that was marked with his row number. This was always done the same way. The young monks had to take turns doing this, and so did the dopdops of all ages.

The tea masters were the overseers of the kitchen, and they maintained a very strict environment there. They were really quite intimidating, and they didn't allow the young monks and dopdops to talk or joke. The kitchen was part of the monastery after all, and the monastery was a place of discipline. This was true of every part of the monastery; there were no exceptions. At Ganden Chönkhor, the tea and soup were well known for being delicious. The tea, of course, was Tibetan butter tea. The tea leaves came in bricks, and as many as twelve of these bricks were crushed and boiled at a time to make tea for the entire monastery.

To make the tea, two dopdops stood on the top edge of the stoves and used huge, long-handled spoons to mix the tea as it boiled. They had to stir it for a long time, scooping down into the pots and pulling the spoons way up overhead and then down again in a circular motion, over and over. They did this hundreds of times for each pot. The men selected for this job had to train in the summer before beginning. For practice, they went out to the river and used an old heavy handle for exercise. It was hard work.

Before the tea could be served to the assembly, the tea leaves had to be taken out of the pots. The dopdops who worked in the kitchen had long-handled strainers made from a metal hoop with a piece of thin cloth stretched over them that they used to strain the tea. The job was also physically demanding, and it required a great deal of skill to get all the tea leaves out efficiently. When all the leaves had been removed, what was left was a delicious strong black tea. Then the butter was added. They used the same method to mix in the butter, though it didn't take as long as removing the leaves. At first the butter floated on the top, glistening yellow, but it only took about ten or fifteen strokes for the dopdops to mix it in. This tea was so delicious! It's difficult to accurately describe it, but hopefully this gives you some idea.

When I was very young I used to go through the upper level of the kitchen on my way to the assembly so I could watch the tea-making process from the balcony. While the dopdops stirred the tea, they had a special chant to count each stroke. As they brought the spoon down into the tea, they sang, "*chik cha chik*,"[23] ending as they scooped the leaves out. When they put the spoon in again they continued in the same manner chanting, "*nyi nya nyi*," then "*sum sa sum*," "*zhi zha zhi*," and so forth, eventually counting to well over one hundred.

I think this special method was unique to Ganden Chönkhor. It was not done the same way at Sera or the other great monasteries. They didn't mix the butter in this way. At Sera, what they called "tea" was really little more than hot water. Today in the monasteries in India, I think they mostly use churns. But Ganden Chönkhor had this wonderful tradition of making tea in this way, and it was delicious. When there was a special ceremony and a donor sponsored one of the offerings to the assembly, the tea would be even better—only the best tea and very good butter were used. At such times, everyone went to the morning assembly. No one wanted to sleep in and miss this tea!

13. The Structure and Schedule of Education at Ganden Chönkhor

IKE ALL the great Geluk monasteries (*densa*) in the Lhasa area, Ganden Chönkhor was divided into smaller units. There were eleven units altogether: three large ones, which were called *regional houses* (*khangtsen*), and eight smaller ones, which were called *personal residences* (*mitsen*). The difference between these two units was basically just size. It was traditionally said that Ganden Chönkhor had five hundred monks altogether, but actually there were many more than that. The regional houses were organized according to the areas from which the monks came. Each regional house had its own temple, gathering place, and dormitories. There were some private homes as well, where just a single monk or an elder monk and his student lived, but they were usually associated with one of the regional houses or personal residences.

I lived in Shum regional house with my elder uncle, who was my fundamental teacher, because we were both from Shum. This regional house was one of the three large ones. The other two were Sharkyu and Hralsum. Shum regional house was on the northwest side of the monastery, Sharkyu on the east; Hralsum was on the southwest side and was the biggest of the three. Many of the personal residences were also divided according to the monks' home regions. For instance, my younger uncle and his parents were from Gyantsé. The monastery there was called Serkhang, so anyone from around that area would live in Serkhang personal residence.

Semesters (*chöthok*) at Ganden Chönkhor were the periods of active study and varied in length. Each season had a longer semester and a shorter one. A shorter semester lasted maybe fifteen days, and a longer semester was twenty days or a month. The semester courses were referred to as *chöra*. *Chö* means "Dharma," and *ra* refers to the fence that enclosed the area where students practiced their debating and prayed. *Ra* can also refer to the circle that the students sat in, but originally it referred to the fenced-in area where debating took place. At Ganden Chönkhor this place was a courtyard in front of the main temple that was paved with large flat stones. The word *chöra* can thus either refer to the actual space where these activities took place, which I call the *Dharma courtyard*, or the period when a class was in session.

While the semester was in session the students went to the Dharma courtyard in between the first and second assemblies. As I've said, the monks had nicknames for the two different kinds of assemblies: "wet assembly" and "dry assembly." Since wet assemblies had food and tea, no monk wanted to miss these. Dry assemblies were long and difficult, partially because they were held outdoors. Nevertheless, during the semester monks had to go to both types of assemblies. They couldn't miss one without first getting the permission of the disciplinarian. If they missed an assembly without permission, there was trouble.

Between semesters we were free in that we didn't have to go to the assemblies or the Dharma courtyard sessions. We could go outside the monastery or stay home. The between-semester periods allowed us much more freedom. This time could be used for many different purposes, but mostly it was used for studying, especially when one was young. What one did depended on how much time there was between the sessions— which, like the length of the semester periods, varied. During the fifth month, many people left the monastery to visit family, but most of the between-session periods were too short for that.

When a monk wanted to study, he went to find a quiet place where there were no distractions, and he spent all day memorizing the texts that had to be learned. He read the text verse by verse in a loud voice so that he heard the material. At night he tried to recite it without looking at the text. This was not an easy thing to do. Though it was easier when one was young, it was never truly easy. We didn't focus on the meaning. We probably didn't even understand it at the beginning. We just learned the words and only later came to understand them. We young students were almost like parrots at that stage, first memorizing the recitations for the assemblies. In higher study, we memorized logic primers and philosophical textbooks. This was very intensive and required great self-discipline. Finding a solitary place to study was really the only way to memorize the huge amount of material that had to be learned. As you can see, young monks worked very hard both during the semesters and in between.

For the first year or so after I entered the monastery, I stayed at home with my uncle. Then he decided that I needed to begin going to a text teacher. My memorization of the volume of prayers and recitations took two or three years to complete, from the age of ten to the age of thirteen. I gave my examination when I was about thirteen; it took a little less than a year. As I've said, students took turns giving examinations bit by bit, and the amount of time that it took varied. In my case, the timing was good, so I finished fairly quickly. After finishing the memorization examination, I stayed at home for another two or three years. During that time I still attended assemblies and participated in other monastic ceremonies, but I didn't take any classes. It was like a vacation, similar to American students who take time off after finishing high school. After this time I was sent to a philosophy teacher.

14. The System of Philosophical Education

AFTER THE FIRST memorization examination, the monks at Ganden Chönkhor were divided into two groups: those who went on to more education and those who became dopdops. Those who were beginning the philosophical level of education were further divided into two different sections called the Eastern School (*chöra shar*) and the Western School (*chöra nup*). Each of these had its own buildings and teachers, and formed its own entity. A student came to identify himself by the school to which he belonged. Each school also had its own small temple, though the students didn't actually meet there every day.

Each of the two schools had several high-ranking scholars and teachers. The highest one was the dean (*chörai gegen*); he was the leader of the school. The dean was appointed by the abbot, and he was second only to the abbot. His status was even higher than the reincarnate lamas (*tulku*). When he came and went from the assembly, and when he went anywhere else in the monastery, the rest of the monks paid him special respect. This was an honor that very few ever received.

The dean lived in a house with the other high-ranking teachers, and students went there in the same way that they had gone to their Dharma recitation teacher's house in their earlier education. The students went to school in the evening and spent the night there. In the morning they went to the morning assemblies, returning to their school after each one. They stayed at school until sometimes as late as five o'clock and then went home to eat. After dinner, they returned to their school, and it started all over again. This level of the monk's education focused on memorizing introductory philosophical texts and on learning how to debate. For the first two or three years, the students concentrated on elementary logic primers (*düra*). The classes were large, with ten or twenty students. The dean's house had room for all these students to sleep, and during the day they spent most of their time together memorizing logic primers. Some of the time was spent learning the method of debate from the teacher as well.

The students of the two schools had an important function in the monastery's evening activities, because they were the ones who called the monks to the debating sessions at the Dharma courtyard. The two schools took turns doing this; one night the Eastern School went, and the next night the Western School went. The dopdops didn't come to these sessions. When the students called the other scholar monks to this debate, they made a lot of noise. They didn't have a gong or a horn. They called out the syllable *dhīḥ*, which is the seed syllable of the bodhisattva Mañjuśrī's mantra, *oṃ a ra pa tsa na dhīḥ*. Mañjuśrī, the bodhisattva who embodies the wisdom of all the buddhas, is something like the patron saint of scholar monks. The students moved around the monastery calling out *dhīḥ, dhīḥ, dhīḥ*, and all the debaters came.

The dean stayed throughout the session and monitored the debating in the light of his lantern. During the debate the disciplinarian came on his rounds to monitor what was going on, and to check up on who was there and who was not. He came with his stick, his lantern, and his two assistants, looking over everything. This went on for an hour or so, and then the disciplinarian left. No one was allowed to leave until the disciplinarian left. Once he left, other people slowly began to leave. The dean of whichever school was on that night left shortly after the disciplinarian, and when he left, his students followed him back to the school.

I studied at the Western School of Ganden Chönkhor, and my principal philosophical teacher was Lhündrup Mönlam, who was the dean of the school. He later became abbot and abbot emeritus of Ganden Chönkhor. He had first gone to Sera and then had come back to Ganden Chönkhor. He was part of the same extended monastic household (*shaktsang*) as my later teacher Khensur Thapkhé, who at that time was already at Sera.[24] A monastic household is the home of a monk or a group of monks. It is similar to a labrang, but here there is no lama. Like labrangs, ordinary monastic households can also have many monks: a manager,[25] cooks, and other workers. Some monastic households were small, and some were quite large. The one that I'm talking about here was rather large.

It was a monk called Kunyer Tsöndrü who started this monastic household. He was the senior member. It first consisted of him, his students, and the students of those students. The old temple manager that I met in 1987 was also part of this household unit. The other members of the monastic household were: Geshé Losang Chönden, who later became the tutor (*yongzin*) to Drupkhang Rinpoché at Sera, and who was also the teacher of Geshé Ngawang Gendün and Khensur Thapkhé; Palden, who was not a philosopher monk but was the brother of Geshé Thapkhé; and finally there was a young monk who was a relative of Palden and Khensur Thapkhé and who later came to Sera.

A student's philosophical teacher was chosen by the student and his fundamental teacher. The monastery and its administration played no part in this. In my case, my uncle asked around to find out who was a good teacher and was well respected and trusted. He eventually decided on the dean of the Western School, Lhundrüp Mönlam, whom we called Gen Mönlam. *Gen* is used as a respectful yet affectionate title for one's principal religious teachers. In some cases, the student and his fundamental teacher could decide on someone other than the dean, like a private scholar, if they thought it was more appropriate. Private teachers didn't have all the same responsibilities as the dean, but generally they taught according to the same schedule and in the same way as the dean.

Once the teacher had been chosen, there was a traditional method for the first meeting of the student with the teacher. The student had to prepare tea that would be offered to the prospective teacher, as would a fine silk khatak and a silver coin that had to be of the best quality without any blemishes or imperfections. The quality of the tea was particularly important. People watched the tea offering to see how the tea turned out, because it was believed that the result was significant in indicating the student's future success. Sometimes when one made tea and churned it with butter, it just came out black. Other times it came out a beautiful reddish color, which was considered more auspicious. So when the student was making the tea, he tried very hard to make it come out just right. This made the students a little uneasy, because so much was at stake.

This tradition was an ancient one. There is a story about Milarepa asking Marpa to be his teacher. Milarepa offered Marpa just an empty pot, I suppose because he didn't have anything to put in it. Marpa looked at the pot and said that this was symbolic. He said that though Milarepa was already famous and everyone knew the sound of his name, he didn't really have much inside, like the sound of striking an empty pot. At that point in his life, Milarepa was already a famous yogi, but Marpa was trying to say that Milarepa still needed to develop. This is an example of the importance of the first offering to one's teacher. Every monk goes through this the first time that he meets his teacher. From that time on, the person to whom he made this offering was considered his teacher and was revered almost like a guru. The student must then obey the teacher's every word.

15. The Status of Scholar Monks

THE FIRST TEXT that the students memorized and studied in their philosophical training was an elementary logic text called *types of evidence* (*takrik*). After the students had memorized, debated, and passed an examination on this material, they were called *those who studied types of evidence texts* (*takrikpa*). The Tibetan word for "evidence," *tak*, is pronounced the same way as the Tibetan word for "tiger," though they are spelled differently. In Tibetan the word for the great wild animals is *takzik*, literally "tiger-leopard." Tigers are the highest of the great animals, while leopards (*zik*) are second best. At Ganden Chönkhor, those who mastered this level of education were known as *tigers*, while the dopdops and the monks who did not pass the first exam on logical method were called *leopards*. At Ganden Chönkhor we had these nicknames for different kinds of people.

These different statuses had practical implications for the monks. At the end of each semester, grain was distributed to all the monks. There were two lists kept by the monastery, one for tigers and one for leopards. Within both of these lists, the names were ordered in terms of seniority, according to how long one had been a monk. When the grain was distributed, the tiger list was read first, and no leopard's name was called until after the very last of the tigers. Kunyer Tsöndrü, the eldest member of the monastic household that I described, was first in seniority among all the leopards, but he didn't get his measure of grain until the youngest of the tigers had received his. This demonstrates how important and respected scholarly knowledge was in the monastery; intellectual accomplishment brought a higher degree of privilege.

It should be noted that there were many reasons why a monk did not go on to philosophical training. Some simply did not want to, some were unable to, and there may be other reasons as well. This is similar to the situation in America: some people complete college, some finish high school, and some don't even make it that far. There are many different situations. In the monastery, it was clear in any case that those who pursued higher education were more respected and valued.

16. The Education of Scholar Monks

THE FIRST SEVERAL years of philosophical study were dedicated to learning basic epistemology, logic, and debate. Students memorized texts and began to debate on them. There were different levels or classes, each of which had different subject matter that had to be learned and mastered. There were three texts: a short one, a medium one, and a long one. It wasn't a matter of staying in each class some particular amount of time. A student worked on each text until his teacher determined that he was ready to move on to the next. Each monastery had its own philosophical textbooks. Since we at Ganden Chönkhor were connected with Sera, we used their textbooks, which were written by the Fifth Dalai Lama and by Sera Jetsünpa.[26] These were our main textbooks, but we also read logical primers that were written by Phurbuchok Jampa Rinpoché.[27]

Every year in a special semester in the summer, there was a period of debate in the assembly that pitted the students of the Eastern School against the students of the Western School. In one of the morning assemblies and then again in the afternoon, two monks stood up and debated in front of all the monks assembled. The monks debating had to dress up in their best robes and be impeccably groomed. One monk had to recite a thesis in the form of a chant, and then the other monk challenged him on this thesis. Monks of all ages and stages of education participated in this, but the students who were just in the beginning stages of their philosophical education had an important role during this period. Every year some junior students were chosen by the dean of the school to debate during this semester. The dean also assigned the subject that would be debated. The two contestants in these debates were from the two different schools.

Prior to the actual debate, these junior students had to memorize the materials connected to their thesis. The dean took the chosen students to practice every afternoon outside the monastery, some distance away. The Eastern School and the Western School each had their own territory outside the monastery that was used for these exercises. The debate opponents were not supposed to see or hear each other because one could not know what the other was doing.

There was a particular way that the thesis had to be chanted and a particular way that students debated, and all this needed to be learned precisely. The deans of the two schools went with their respective students to make sure that they learned to do this just right. The students were evaluated and ranked by the deans in this process based on who showed the best scholarship and skill in debating. This was similar to what happened at Sera, though at Sera this ranking was much more important because if a monk didn't get first or second ranking, he would not progress any further, as I'll discuss later. At Ganden Chönkhor it was not so serious. Because there were not so many monks, a student might end up having more than one chance to debate. At the end of the debate, no winner was declared officially, but everyone knew who won.

While the junior level was serious and strict, the senior level was much less so. Senior debaters were generally scholar monks from the more advanced classes, but there were also older monks from Ganden Chönkhor and some who had gone to Sera and then returned. In these latter cases, the monks would debate on more advanced topics such as Vinaya and Abhidharma.[28] The senior monk debates were enjoyable, and everyone was allowed to laugh and joke with one another. It was much more comfortable and pleasant than at the junior level, where the young monks were too nervous to enjoy themselves.

I still remember my debates as a junior monk. It was serious and a little frightening, though the practice sessions outside the monastery were rather enjoyable. There was a very pleasant and dry area near a riverbed that had a stone path, stone paving, and a raised stone seat on which the dean sat and taught us everything we needed to know. The dean called on each student in turn. It was difficult when one's turn came, but after the student was finished with his turn, he was free. He could go even farther out and just enjoy himself. It was really a very nice place.

The students of the two schools intermixed in the assembly most of the time, but there were times that the students from each school would gather with their dean at their own temple. One month before the debate assembly, the students who had been chosen to debate in the assembly and their teachers gathered for a three-day period of all-day sessions and were treated each day to a very nice meal. Local government officials and reincarnate lamas were also invited, even if they were not participating in the debate. The youngest students had to recite some short texts, but the rest of us didn't really have any particular tasks at these meetings. We just drank tea and enjoyed very good food. It was basically a ceremony to honor us. These events were sponsored by the schools themselves, not the monastery.

Interestingly, monks who did not finish their memorization of the philosophical texts, and even some dopdops, considered themselves to be associated with either the Eastern or the Western School, even though they didn't participate in events such as these. I suppose this is like people supporting a sports team. I don't know how such relationships were originally determined, but these affiliations got passed down from fundamental teacher to student. My uncle, for example, who had done no philosophical study, considered himself connected with the Western School, and he rooted for them when they competed with the Eastern School. This was so even before I started my philosophical education. Because of my uncle's preference, I was destined to be associated with the Western School.

17. My Teacher Gen Mönlam

M Y FIRST PHILOSOPHICAL teacher, Gen Mönlam, was dean of the Western School. The dean had many official duties and responsibilities. Almost every night he taught philosophy and other subjects, but sometimes he also gave practical advice. Gen Mönlam-la would give various kinds of teachings such as the stages of the path,[29] or teachings on morality, monastic conduct, karma, and so forth. Sometimes this advice was based on the life stories of the Buddha or great teachers, lamas, or yogis such as Nāropa, Milarepa, and Tsongkhapa, or even great teachers from our monastery or Lhasa. Gen Mönlam was very kind to me, and his advice helped me be a disciplined, serious student. My uncle was often gone on monastery business, and I was left alone, but I lived strictly and religiously because of what I had learned from these teachings and the personal advice Gen Mönlam gave me.

Gen Mönlam's spiritual advice was excellent. Some people took this advice to heart, and some didn't. Many young monks got themselves in trouble, and some were even kicked out. Living by the monastic code was not easy. There were four major offences that would get one kicked out: murder, theft, sex, and lying about spiritual attainments. For instance, if a monk killed a human or animal, he had to leave the monastery. If he stole something and was caught, he was automatically kicked out. He wasn't allowed to stay in the monastery because he had broken a fundamental rule of monastic life. This was strictly enforced. Being expelled from the monastery was very serious because it meant losing the respect of the other monks and the laypeople. If a monk got involved with a woman or broke another of the major rules, he lost a great deal. I saw this happen from time to time. In some cases the person would just leave if he knew that he had broken one of these rules, but in other cases he would try to stay, and the monastery would censure and expel him.

18. Taking the Kālacakra Empowerment the First Time

GANDEN CHÖNKHOR was not a tantric monastery; it was based exclusively on sūtra.[30] The same was true at Ganden, Sera, and Drepung. These monasteries had separate tantric colleges for such practices and rituals, but for the rest of us this was not allowed. Ringing bells and so forth was considered a distraction. Therefore, if someone wanted to do any tantric practices, he had to get permission first and keep the practice very low-key.

About five miles west of Ganden Chönkhor was a monastery called Dechen Rapgyé that was associated with Tashi Lhünpo. It was a tantric monastery. They had a regular schedule of tantric rituals that took place at New Year and other such times throughout the year. Dechen Rapgyé had about one hundred monks in residence. The monastery had a large courtyard in which the monks would perform the annual ritual dance (*cham*) on the last day of the year. The monks dressed in colorful costumes with black hats and several different kinds of masks. The masks represented Buddhist saints, deities, and Dharma protectors. The purpose of the ritual was to dispel all the inauspiciousness, negative karma, and bad omens that had accumulated that year so that the new year would begin positively. Many nearby townspeople and the monks of Ganden Chönkhor would come to watch the ceremony. I went many times to see it myself. During these times the crowd was so large that a chalk circle was drawn on the courtyard to keep people back, and the dance was performed within the circle. Often, however, the crowd was too large, and people would start to squeeze in and push into each other. A monk would come and crack a whip to push the crowd back.

Every year Dechen Rapgyé also had a special ritual period devoted to the Kālacakra tantra in which they created the mandala and performed all the rituals. One year, they invited a great lama from Tashi Lhünpo named Ngakchen Rinpoché. His name means "great master of the tantric ritual." I heard that during the Ninth Panchen Lama's time, Ngakchen Rinpoché had given many thousands of people the Kālacakra empowerment all over Tibet, even in Amdo and China. He had a long white beard and was very striking in appearance, and at the time, he was the highest lama at Tashi Lhünpo, since the Panchen Lama was not there.[31]

Everyone at Ganden Chönkhor was talking about this event. Many people wanted to go, and I wanted to go too. Of course, I didn't really know anything about it, but I wanted to go all the same. I was about fifteen at this time. I had never taken any kind of empowerment before, and all I knew was that during the empowerment the lama gave a mantra that had to be recited every day. In fact, I have recited this mantra faithfully ever since. But at that time I had no understanding of the practice. Still, I very much enjoyed going to Dechen Rapgyé for the empowerment. We stayed two or three days. The empowerment took place under a huge tent with a mandala in the middle.

This empowerment was attended only by monks. Dechen Rapgyé was a small monastery that could not accommodate very many people, though it did have a Kālacakra temple. Most of the monks who attended were senior monks, so I was fortunate even to have been able to go. Any monk from Ganden Chönkhor was allowed to come, but I was probably the youngest one from Ganden Chönkhor to attend. Some of the senior monks were planning to go, so I asked if I could go along with them, and they agreed.

We took some food and tea with us. I had a cousin from Shum living at Dechen Rapgyé, so I told the older monks that we could cook at his house. But when we got to his house, his door was closed and sealed, and there was a stupa-like marker outside it indicating that no one was going to come out and no one was to go in. It turned out that at that time my cousin was in the midst of a three-year retreat. Fortunately, the house had a nice quiet courtyard so we were able to use that space for our cooking. We never saw my cousin.

I don't know now if it's accurate to say that I received the empowerment at that time since I didn't really know anything about what was happening. In general, a person has to know what he is doing and be ready for such an empowerment in order to really receive it. I'm sure I at least received the blessings. In Tibet, great lamas like the Dalai Lama went all over the country and gave the Kālacakra to thousands of Tibetans. Most of those people didn't know much of anything about what they were doing, but they at least received the blessings. Similarly, today when His Holiness gives the Kālacakra in the West, people go even if they don't know anything about the significance of what will happen. But at the least they receive a blessing just from going.

At Ganden Chönkhor, tantra was not a part of most monks' lives. As I mentioned before, there were twenty-five monks there who did special rituals to protectors and other rituals in the room above the main temple. All the monks at Ganden Chönkhor recited some prayers to Palden Lhamo in the assembly, but beyond knowing these prayers and the fact that our protector was Palden Lhamo, we didn't know much about such things. Even at Sera and the other great monasteries in the Lhasa area, tantric practice was a matter of personal choice and a private matter. If someone wanted to get an empowerment from some great lama, then that was his business. The monastery did not offer such things. Afterward, if one wanted to go into retreat, he had to make all the arrangements himself. He had to arrange for space in the monastery or at some small hermitage outside the monastery.

19. Deciding to Go to Sera

AFTER SERVING as tea master, my uncle worked for the monastery in a job that often took him far away. For part of the summer and most of the fall, he went to villages to collect the grain that had been promised to the monastery. This meant that he was gone for long periods of time, sometimes for several weeks on end. During those times, when I was at my home I was alone. My uncle had to make preparations for me so that I had everything I might need during his absence. He would get the tsampa, meat, butter, and anything else I needed before he left. Some boys were not well behaved; when left alone, they would overeat or have many people over. But I lived simply. I was very strict with myself, and I studied diligently. I took care of the home as well, so when my uncle returned, he was always happy and satisfied with my behavior.

My uncle tested me during the times that he was gone, and I proved to be responsible and hardworking. This gave him confidence in me. Though I was still very young at the time, eighteen years old or so, my uncle felt that I could take care of myself. I'm sure this helped in the decision to send me to Sera. My teacher Gen Mönlam was the one who first pushed for me to go. He said to my uncle, "Tea master, this boy should not stay here, he should go to Sera." My uncle would have to sponsor my stay in Sera, paying for my food, clothing, and everything else. This would be a major commitment, but my uncle was convinced that I could succeed. He told me that he would send me to Sera because he himself had never had any such opportunity. Citing the verse from Milarepa's story, he said that he and I together would accomplish something meritorious through his sending me to Sera.

I could have continued my education at Ganden Chönkhor. However, it was not possible to earn the geshé degree there.[32] They did have a degree known as *kachen*, which was similar to the geshé degree. In ancient times, one could only attain the levels of *kachen* and *rapjampa*. Like the geshé degree, the kachen degree was granted through examinations and a ceremony, and it had a ranking system that could lead to one becoming the disciplinarian of Ganden Chönkhor. One could also eventually become the dean of the Eastern or Western School with this degree. Although this system at Ganden Chönkhor was similar to what they had at the great Geluk monasteries, many of us still wanted to go to a bigger and more prestigious place. Many of our best teachers had been educated at Sera and had come back to teach at Ganden Chönkhor. Those teachers had a different manner than those who had never left, so we had seen examples of how an education at Sera changed a person.

During my education at Ganden Chönkhor I had heard about the three great monasteries, the Three Seats (*densasum*) of the Geluk sect, and their system of education and way of life. I knew even then that I wanted to strive to become a geshé. I learned about the geshé degree, the various ranks of geshés, and how these geshés could attain high positions, all the way up to being Ganden Throne Holder (*ganden tripa*), the head of the Geluk sect. This position was open to anyone; it didn't matter what background one came from. It was like an open hand. I heard these things from teachers and lamas, and it brought about my motivation to strive for this goal. Some people wanted to go to the great Geluk monasteries for educational reasons, some wanted to be great practitioners or yogis. In either case, the emphasis was not on worldly comfort or gain but on a simple, strict life that had a religious motivation. One had to be aware of this fact in order to decide that this was the life that he wanted. Without knowing the purpose behind monastic life, one might have thought that such a life was all poverty and hardship. But once he realized the positive qualities of humility, a restrained and virtuous personality, and a simple life dedicated to spiritual education, he would understand that poverty and hardship are actually good things. Everyone respected those who lived like this.

Even at a young age, I was intrigued by the idea of being a high-ranking geshé and all that entailed. My teachers taught me about great religious figures from the past, the great Indian and Tibetan masters who were exemplars of the life of religion, devotion, and virtue. From these stories, I learned about the dedication and humility that constitute the essence of real religious life. As young monks we heard that the Three Seats were like an ocean of people who lived up to these high ideals. Of course we also had such models at Ganden Chönkhor, and our whole system of life and education was based on that of the Three Seats, which caused my mother to ask, "Why do you need to go to Lhasa? You are already at a great monastery."

Geshé Riksal, Geshé Gendün, and many other scholars from Ganden Chönkhor had gone to Sera and accomplished great things there. Gen Mönlam had also studied at Sera. There were already thirty or forty scholars from Ganden Chönkhor at Sera when I was considering going. They were all highly respected. Others who had been at Sera and returned to Ganden Chönkhor would talk about the city of Lhasa, and since we were all from small villages, it sounded strange and exciting. The same was true when they talked about Sera Monastery and its thousands of monks. They talked about the disciplinarian and the sergeants-at-arms (*shalngo*), who wore elaborate outfits and wielded great power. We heard stories of hundreds of monks debating at the same time. It all sounded amazing. I had never been to Lhasa, but hearing respected scholars talk about it in this way made me want to go. The monks who had returned were held in the highest esteem and received special treatment. Very few said much about the hardships and the sheer difficulties of being at Sera; they mostly talked about the vast size, the splendor, and so on. We were amazed by these descriptions.

Lhasa was a holy city to Tibetans, like Mecca is to Muslims. Lhasa was home to the Jokhang Temple, the largest temple in Lhasa and the most important pilgrimage site for Tibetans, and also the Potala, where His Holiness lived. Lhasa was also home to the three most famous and important centers of the Geluk sect: Sera, Drepung, and Ganden. Traditionally, it was said that Drepung had 7,700 monks, Sera had 5,500, and Ganden had 3,300, though there were in fact nearly 20,000 monks all together when I came to Lhasa.

These three monasteries were sometimes called the Three Seats or *densasum*. *Den* means "seat," which referred to the Dalai Lama's seat at each of these three monasteries. *Sa* means "place," and *sum* is the word for the number three. Another name was the abbreviated form *sendregasum*. This word is formed of the first syllables of Sera, Drepung, and Ganden and then the word for the number three. Tibetans often use this kind of abbreviation, forming a shorthand term by taking the first syllables of several distinct words and combining them into one word. Another such term is *trasasum*, which means the "three monastic centers." Sometimes Tashi Lhünpo was also included in the list of the great Geluk centers, in which case people said *densazhi*, or the Four Seats.

People sometimes swear on the name of something that they hold dear or sacred, such as their mother's name or their country. Gelukpas, especially people from Kham, swore on the *sendregasum*. If someone was asked, "Are you sure about that?" his response was, "Yes! *Sendregasum!*"

Of course I was also interested in excelling in my education. With a geshé degree the highest position that one could reach was that of Ganden Throne Holder. The person who held that position was a successor of Tsongkhapa himself. There was a saying that the throne of Ganden had no owner, which meant that anyone could have this honor if they worked hard enough. It was like being president in the United States or becoming the pope. It didn't matter what family you came from, what monastery, or anything. Anyone could attain this if he worked hard. Since I was a young boy I had been intrigued by this, and I thought that I wanted this position for myself. I wanted to go to Sera, I had my uncle's support, and the monastery put me forward as a boy who had potential.

If I had come from a wealthy family, it would have been easier, but that was not the case. The monastery itself did not ever provide support for its monks who were going to Sera, so my uncle accepted all the financial responsibility.

20. Getting My Parents' Permission

BEFORE I COULD go to Sera I had to get the permission of my parents. Because I had become a monk, there was no one left in Shum to take care of them. So by that time they had given up the land that they farmed and begun new lives that had been arranged by my uncle. They too were my uncle's responsibility.

My father was the older of my parents, and my uncle had arranged for him to be the temple custodian for a noble family he knew. Like a person who was entering the religious life, my father had taken lay vows. He wore a red *chuba* and had shaved his head.[33] The family he worked for had a temple with a copy of the complete Buddhist scriptures, the Kangyur and Tengyur, and various buddha statues.[34] His job was to arrange the offerings, fill the water bowls, and take care of the temple first thing every morning. Then in the afternoon he returned and cleaned the water bowls and did whatever else needed to be done. The rest of the day he spent turning a *mani* wheel in another temple.[35] He earned his keep this way, getting his meals and lodging from the noble family.

My father had no problem with my going to Sera. Like when I originally wanted to become a monk, my father was supportive of the idea. He knew that my uncle would take care of me and that I would have great opportunities if I became a monk. Later, two or three years after I had gone to Sera, I visited him. It was the first time I had returned to Shang. The people there were surprised that the old man that they knew as the temple custodian had a well-educated son in Lhasa.

My mother did not want me to go to Sera. She was living near Ganden

Chönkhor in another noble family's estate. We had a relative from Shum who had married into this family, and with my uncle's help, an arrangement was made for my mother to live there. The estate had a big central house and a number of smaller houses. My mother lived in one of the small houses. My parents were living separately at this time, but they saw each other sometimes. I saw them both occasionally, but especially my mother since she was close by. Even though my uncle was willing to send me to Sera, my mother opposed the idea.

She gave two reasons for wanting me to stay. First of all, I would be far away from my parents, who were very old. She said I shouldn't go until after they had died. Secondly, she said that Ganden Chönkhor was a great monastery with great scholars and great fame. There was no reason I should go off to Sera when everything I needed was right there at Ganden Chönkhor. She asked me not to go. I was faced with a very difficult dilemma. If I did not go, I would be going against the advice of my teacher, my uncle, and my father. And I wanted to go. But if I went, I would be going against the wishes of my mother. It was a difficult decision, but in the end I chose to go.

21. The Journey to Sera

O N   T H E   D A Y that I left for Lhasa, some special events were going on at Ganden Chönkhor. A sponsor was making major offerings to the Sangha at the late morning assembly. There would be rice served, money distributed, and other special things. However, my uncle was concerned about my going on this long trip because I was young and not very strong. He said we should take it easy the first day, and that we wouldn't have to hurry because he already had a place in mind to stop the first night. He decided that we would go early, spend some time at my mother's house, and then set off. Two other monks, dopdops, would be traveling with us, but they would meet us later so that they could go to the second morning assembly. Since my uncle and I were leaving before this, we had to miss all the events of the day.

We set out early, and as we approached the great gate of the monastery, we came upon someone carrying a basket that was full of the husks and remains of sesame seeds that had been pressed for oil. After sesame seeds are pressed there are some leftover parts that are useful for feeding animals and other purposes, and this person was carrying them to the monastery. When one sets out on a journey, khataks are offered if one encounters auspicious signs. We had a number of khataks with us for this reason. The first person we met was this person carrying the basket. My uncle said that this was very auspicious and that I should offer the man a khatak. This was a little before sunrise.

Right outside the walls of the monastery was the home of a noble family who often had important guests. That morning someone from the monastery was going there with an ornate teapot for offering. We all ended up at the start of the wall at the same time. Again, my uncle said that it was a great omen and that I should offer another khatak. This was an omen that even I recognized as auspicious, because I had seen such offerings made to teachers in the monastery.

A little farther on, at the limits of the monastery's property, was a small shrine to a protector deity. The small square building with a stone enclosure around it had many prayer flags fluttering above it. People put these up on certain days to propitiate the protector. We went into the enclosure, and my uncle recited some prayers. I didn't know anything about this practice. My uncle threw some grain into the air as an offering, and at that very moment, the sun struck the prayer flags in the first morning light. Again, I didn't know that this was significant, but my uncle was very happy, saying that this was a great omen for our trip. Consequently, we were optimistic about our journey.

We then went on to my mother's house. When we got there, she made tea and some *khapsé*, a deep-fried Tibetan pastry. She was crying a little, but she tried to hide it to avoid being scolded by my uncle. After we drank the tea together, we set off. From her house we had to walk a long way across a vast plain to a hill on the horizon. We would be staying at a place just over this hill, but we couldn't see the place from where we were. My mother came a short distance along with us, but then my uncle said that she shouldn't come any farther. When we parted, both my mother and I were close to crying. I was choked up and my eyes were filled with tears, but I couldn't let my uncle see this. I kept turning away and wiping my eyes so he wouldn't see me. My mother was doing the same. My uncle told us not to cry because crying when people were parting was considered inauspicious. It was said that this was a sign that we would not see each other again in the future. But in that moment my mother and I couldn't help it.

My uncle and I set off, and my mother stood there, watching after us. As we were about to go over the mountain pass I looked back, and my mother was still standing there. She looked so small. My uncle said something stern about her still standing there, and again I had to secretively wipe away my tears. Then we went over the hill, and I couldn't see her anymore and she couldn't see me. That was a very strange, emotional experience. I never saw her again after I left that day. In my second year at Sera, I received the news that my mother had died.

We stayed the night a short distance from my old home. The other two monks met us there, having left after the special assembly and traveled very fast. They each carried a big load, but it was mostly paper so it wasn't terribly heavy. My uncle carried all my provisions along with his own. All I was carrying were my new robes for Sera. It is very far from Ganden Chönkhor to Lhasa, and the trip had many hardships. Of course there were no cars, planes, or trains to get us there. The journey took thirteen days by foot. We had to cross four mountain passes, but even the valley parts of the journey were difficult. Sometimes it took all day to get across a valley, which left no time to get across the pass before dark, so we had to stay the night at the foot of the pass. We collected firewood to cook tea and tsampa and maybe some dried meat. We didn't have a tent; we just slept outside on the ground.

It was the twelfth month, about February in the Western calendar, so the weather was very bad, very cold. On the other hand, traveling in the cold was good in the sense that you would get warm, but not too hot, while walking. The passes were all covered in snow and ice. At the start of some passes that had been used by many people, a simple stone shelter had been built to block the wind. Even in these shelters it was very cold. My uncle and I slept together lying head to toe under one covering to keep warm. Sometimes my uncle's feet would be in my face, but I was shorter so he didn't have that problem. The other monks who had accompanied us on this journey slept the same way. It was very important to keep our legs covered, because otherwise they would get frostbitten. Sleeping like this kept us warm enough.

Every morning we began before sunrise and walked all day. Often there was no trail at all, but the two dopdops had taken this route many times before and served as our guides. They were special emissaries from

Ganden Chönkhor who delivered mail, money, and prayer or blessing requests to the Dalai Lama and other high lamas at Sera such as Reting Rinpoché and Phurbuchok Rinpoché. The reason we went in the twelfth month was that these two monks were taking prayer requests for the New Year. It was really very rare for people to go from our monastery all the way to Lhasa. Our guides, these dopdops, were very large and intimidating men. They wore laypeople's clothes and openly carried knives to dissuade anyone that we came across from bothering us. They each had a short knife for eating and another longer one for fighting. Some areas that we passed through were very wild, with no one around for miles. We had heard that some people had been robbed or even killed along this route, which is why we traveled with these two monks. They were rather fierce in appearance, so we didn't have any trouble. On this trip we passed by Tshurphu Monastery, and it looked very beautiful off in the distance. I wanted to go to see it but didn't because of the story about there being some hair of the Fifth Dalai Lama under the steps to the monastery, as I mentioned earlier.

After almost two weeks of walking, my first glimpse of Lhasa was the sight of the Potala far in the distance, rising high above the valley. The city itself was covered by haze and smoke, but the Potala rose above it. We could see it from maybe two days away. Sometimes we could see it, then we couldn't, and then we'd see it again. When we started to get closer to Lhasa, we saw Drepung Monastery, and as we went farther we saw Sera Monastery way up on the foot of the mountain. Finally we passed right in front of the Potala. Lhasa city was to the east. I had never been to any large city before, not even Shikatsé, which was not very far from Ganden Chönkhor. In fact the biggest city I had ever seen was Namling, and that was quite small. Lhasa was amazing to me.

22. History of Sera Monastery

TSONGKHAPA LOSANG DRAKPA (1357–1419) was the founder
of the Geluk sect of Tibetan Buddhism. He was a great Buddhist
scholar and practitioner who tried to clarify and spread the pure teachings and practices of the Kadam school of the great master Atiśa, who
was one of the central figures of the second propagation of Buddhism
in Tibet in the eleventh century. In 1409 Tsongkhapa established Ganden Monastery, which Tibetans call the *mother monastery*. This is so
because Sera, Drepung, and all other Geluk monasteries follow the system laid out by Tsongkhapa at Ganden. The Geluk sect was originally
called *Galuk*. *Ga* is the first syllable of *Ganden*, and *luk* means "system"
or "method," so *Galuk* means the "Ganden system." This later became
Geluk, which means "system of virtue," but it still referred to the system
of Tsongkhapa. Some people say that it comes from the word *Ger-luk*,
which means "private system" or "exclusive system," but that is completely false. Drepung and Sera were both established by disciples of
Tsongkhapa, Jamyang Chöjé and Jamchen Chöjé. These men were not
quite of the stature of Gyaltsap Jé Darma Rinchen and Khedrup Jé Gelek
Palsang,[36] but they were close in importance.

Jamchen Chöjé Shākya Yeshé (1354–1435) was the founder of Sera
Monastery. During Tsongkhapa's life, the emperor of China requested
that Tsongkhapa come to Beijing. It was common for great lamas from
the Sakya or Kagyü sects to receive these sorts of invitations, and by
that time Tsongkhapa had become very famous. Tsongkhapa carefully
considered whether it would be more beneficial to go to China or stay

and further establish his system. He decided that it would be better to stay, so he turned down the invitation. A little later a second invitation came, and again Tsongkhapa did not want to go. But this time he sent Jamchen Chöjé in his place, since the emperor seemed to have a sincere wish to learn from Tsongkhapa. Jamchen Chöjé became the emperor's guru and was highly respected in China as well as in Tibet. Later, Jamchen Chöjé returned to Tibet and founded Sera Monastery. In the great assembly hall in Sera, at the center of the altar, there was a life-size statue of Jamchen Chöjé. On the head of this statue was a hat with gold Chinese writing. This hat was the one presented to Jamchen Chöjé by the Chinese emperor, granting him a very high status and official rank.

Sera Monastery had three colleges (*dratsang*): Mé, Jé, and the tantric (*gyü*) or Ngakpa college, which developed corresponding upper (*tö*) and lower (*mé*) divisions, Gyütö and Gyümé. The actual site of the monastery that Jamchen Chöjé founded later became the location of the upper tantric college. In the beginning, there was only one Sera. Then Sera Mé College was established lower on the same hillside. Mé (*smad*) literally means "lower" and here refers to the physical location of the college relative to the rest of the monastery. Shortly after that several other colleges were established, and these eventually all became absorbed into a single college called Tö (*stod*), or "upper."[37] Next Sera Jé was established, and it eventually absorbed Tö, leaving two colleges: Sera Mé and Sera Jé. The word *jé* refers to an exile, someone who has left his home to dwell somewhere else temporarily, or who is not native to the place where he lives. We use the term *jepa* to refer to those of us who are living outside of our native land. We are all *jepa* now.

The founder of Sera Jé College was Künkhyen Lodrö Rinchen Sengé, who lived in the fifteenth century. He had been a very famous scholar at Drepung Monastery, where he had lived for a long time and had numerous students. At some point, he decided to leave with one hundred of his students, setting out in the direction of Sera. Sera already had an assembly hall, and Mé College was already established. When Rinchen Sengé arrived with his students, he established a new college, which was called Sera *Jé* because it was created by exiles. There are some stories that say that Rinchen Sengé left Drepung because of a conflict with other scholars there, but we don't know exactly what happened.

The Mongols had been interested in Tibet all the way back to the time when the Sakya sect held political power. The Sera great assembly hall, which was the place where the monks of all the colleges assembled together, was built in the early eighteenth century by the Mongolian ruler in Lhasa, Lajang Khan. The original Sera assembly hall was smaller, holding maybe one hundred monks. After the construction of the new hall, the old one became the assembly hall of the tantric college, which was established at this same time. Shortly after this the Mongol ruler Pholhané built the Sera Jé assembly hall, and his son built Hardong regional house (*khangsten*) based on the same design.

Monks from Ganden Chönkhor could go to Sera, Drepung, or Ganden, but it was customary to go to Sera because there were several very famous monks from Ganden Chönkhor who had gone to Sera in previous generations and become great men. One had become the Ganden Throne Holder; his teacher had been the abbot of Sera Jé. Another one had become the Sera Jé disciplinarian and then the tutor of Reting Rinpoché, who was regent between the Thirteenth and Fourteenth Dalai Lamas.

It was because of this history that Ganden Chönkhor monks went to Sera. Within Sera, we went to Jé College. On the west side of Tsang there was a monastery called Gangchen and another called Shelkar. The monks from these monasteries typically went to Sera Mé. Jé and Mé drew monks from different territories. The same was true of Drepung and Ganden. If a monk from Tsang went to Drepung, he entered Loseling College rather than Gomang or Deyang. If he went to Ganden, he entered Jangtsé rather than Shartsé. Within Sera, anyone from one of the monasteries in the regions of Tsang—Gyantsé, Phuntsokling, Lhatsé, or Tashi Lhünpo—joined Tsangpa Khangtsen.

23. Entry into Tsangpa Regional House and Sera Jé

To gain entry into Sera Jé's Tsangpa Khangsten, a prospective monk first had to offer tea to the entire assembly. In my case, my uncle was responsible for providing the resources and making the arrangements for this ceremony. I couldn't offer just plain black tea, of course; it had to be good-quality tea churned with butter. I also had to offer some food, at least a good soup. There were around two hundred monks in Tsangpa Khangtsen, so this was very expensive for my uncle. Once I had performed the tea offering ceremony, I was considered a Sera monk.

After entering at the regional house level, one also had to go meet with the abbot of Sera Jé to enter the college itself. There were two kinds of initial meetings with the abbot: one for a newly entering layman who wanted to become a monk and one for a person like me who was already a monk coming in from another monastery.

A layperson who wanted to become a monk went to see the abbot with a senior teacher from Tsangpa Khangtsen and offered a pot of tea, a khatak, and a silver coin. The meeting would be arranged in advance, and the prospective monk was taught the rules and etiquette beforehand so he knew how to behave. When he arrived, he had to wait in a waiting room until the attendant told him he could go in and meet the abbot.

Only the candidate and the sponsoring senior monk were allowed to enter. When the candidate entered the room, he did three full prostrations to the abbot, all the way flat on the ground with arms and legs fully extended. The abbot used this opportunity to check if the man had any physical defects—the monastic code established by the Buddha stipulates that a monk must not have any such problems. Then the abbot asked questions of the candidate and the senior monk. He might ask the candidate directly what his name was, where he was from, what his parents' names were, and other such personal questions. The abbot used the responses to determine if the candidate could hear and speak, and to make sure he was not insane—the monastic code stipulates that a person with such afflictions is prohibited from joining the Sangha.

All of this was an examination, though it didn't explicitly have the form of one. The abbot also asked the senior monk some questions. When he addressed questions to the senior monk, the candidate could not answer, and when he addressed questions to the candidate, the senior monk could not answer. If the candidate tried to answer when the question was addressed to the senior monk, it indicated that the candidate was pushy or a smart aleck. If the senior monk answered when the question was directed to the candidate, the abbot might have thought that the candidate was unable to speak, was deaf, or had some other problem. This was another examination. The hair-cutting ceremony followed this. This is all laid out in the monastic code.

The second kind of meeting with the abbot was for someone like myself, who had already become a monk at another monastery. In that case, the person had to do three prostrations but not full-body ones. He had to offer tea, the khatak, and silver coin, but the examination aspect of the meeting was not required. This would have already been done at the monk's previous monastery, and of course the hair-cutting ceremony would have already been done as well. I had done all this at Ganden Chönkhor.

Thirty or forty scholars from Ganden Chönkhor were at Sera when I arrived, so I had many contacts there. Geshé Lhündrup Thapkhé, who was from the same monastic household as my teachers at Ganden Chönkhor, was there, and he was regarded as something like the leader of the Ganden Chönkhor monks. When I arrived I went to him. Like I had at Ganden Chönkhor, at Sera I would have a fundamental teacher with whom I would stay and who would oversee my education. If a monk from Ganden Chönkhor had a family friend or relative at Sera Jé, he went to that person when he first got to Sera. If not, then he went to Geshé Lhündrup Thapkhé first, and he assigned the new Sera monk a teacher and a place to live.[38] In my case, I went with my uncle to see Geshé Thapkhé, and he said that I should become the student of Geshé Riksal and live with him.

All new monks from Ganden Chönkhor were assigned to one of four teachers: Tri Rinpoché Lhündrup Tsöndrü, Lhündrup Thapkhé, Ngawang Gendün, or Ngawang Riksal. Another important teacher for us was Geshé Chönden, who was a student of Tri Rinpoché. Geshé Chönden was also from the monastic household that was established by Kunyer Tsöndrü back at Ganden Chönkhor. I will talk more about all these great teachers later on.

All the new monks admitted to Sera Jé first lived with a teacher. The new monk would live with his teacher for one month, six months, a year, or even longer. It depended on how the student was doing, how he got on with his teacher, and so forth. At Sera one's fundamental teacher might have been his academic teacher as well. There was no need to seek out another academic teacher right away, because the fundamental teachers were highly qualified scholar monks themselves. Later, as one progressed in his studies, he could seek out another teacher if necessary. At Sera, the system of education led ultimately to the awarding of the geshé degree. The very best of those who completed this were awarded the highest geshé status, called *lharam*. Throughout this process one's teachers were of the utmost importance.

As I recall, I stayed with Geshé Riksal for about six months before I took a small room of my own in the Tsangpa regional house. Of course the newest monks got the worst rooms. They were small, dark, and foul smelling, but I had to stay there, at least for a while. My first room at Sera was nowhere near as nice as my uncle's room back at Ganden Chönkhor.

24. Tri Rinpoché

I'D LIKE TO TALK a little about my main teachers at Sera. These men were instrumental in my education as well as in setting a very good example of how to truly live the monastic life. I'll start with Tri Rinpoché because he was the most famous of the Sera monks who had come from Ganden Chönkhor. It was he who inspired us and gave us confidence that someone from our little monastery could go on to great things. He was an exemplary monk and scholar who served as a role model for all of us, and I feel extremely fortunate to be able to call him one of my teachers.

Tri Rinpoché Lhündrup Tsöndrü was the most senior among the Ganden Chönkhor monks at Sera. He was also the teacher of all the other Ganden Chönkhor scholars that I studied with while I was at Sera.[39] He was a great scholar and was very famous among all the monks of the Three Seats. He was named a first-rank *lharam* geshé by the Thirteenth Dalai Lama. After receiving his geshé degree, he entered Gyümé Tantric College.

As with all the colleges at Sera, there were examinations and other forms of evaluation at the tantric college, and one's progress depended on how well one did on these examinations. There were a number of official positions in the Gyümé hierarchy that led up to the position of Ganden Throne Holder. Tri Rinpoché started at the lower positions in the hierarchy, but he was so brilliant and accomplished that the Thirteenth Dalai Lama quickly moved him directly to lama prayer leader (*lama umzé*), which was the second-highest rank in Gyümé. After serving in this post for some time, he became abbot of Gyümé, the highest position within the college. After that he became the Jangtsé Chöjé, which is the last position before Ganden Throne Holder.

Just beneath the position of Ganden Throne Holder were two positions of equal rank, Jangtsé Chöjé and Shartsé Chöjé. The men who held these positions would be the next two Ganden Throne Holders, one after the other. When I was preparing to come to Sera, everyone at Ganden Chönkhor knew about this great monk. He was a great example for us all, and we were very proud that he was from our monastery. His accomplishments and fame were the primary reason that so many Ganden Chönkhor monks from my generation went to Sera.

When I first arrived at Sera, Tri Rinpoché had just become Jangtsé Chöjé, and shortly after that he became Ganden Throne Holder. This position was held for seven years. The Ganden Throne Holder had several responsibilities while he held this post. He had to lead the morning and noontime sessions during the great assembly of the Mönlam and Tsokchö festivals. During the summer he stayed at Ganden Monastery for a period of two months to train scholars there, as he did at Sera.[40]

Another of the Throne Holder's responsibilities was to give public teachings in Lhasa in the time between the Mönlam and Tsokchö festivals. I went to all these teachings during the time that Tri Rinpoché was Ganden Throne Holder. He was younger than most people who had ever held this position because of the decision of the Thirteenth Dalai Lama to advance him so quickly through the high-ranking posts of Gyümé. He was only about sixty years old when he became Ganden Throne Holder. After he completed his seven-year term in that post, he continued to teach as emeritus Ganden Throne Holder, or Ganden Trisur. During this emeritus period, he taught the complete *Guide to the Bodhisattva Way of Life* in Lhasa.[41] He also taught the *Great Exposition of the Stages of the Path* at another monastery.[42] I received both of these teachings from him.

Tri Rinpoché was a great example for me, not only as a scholar but also as a practitioner of Buddhism. I had a talk with him once when he was

Ganden Trisur, and he gave me some very good advice that I've tried to follow ever since. He said that while a monk was studying and working his way through all his classes, he had to strive very hard and dedicate a great amount of effort to the endeavor. However, it was also important to strive in his practice as well. Tri Rinpoché described the reason for this with an analogy that I still remember. He said that a donkey that has a heavy load has to work very hard to get to the mountain pass, but once he gets there, there is no more climbing to do. Instead, he has to go back down the other side. In other words, study is valuable and important, but not an end in itself. For Tri Rinpoché, after all the studying and hard work, once he became Ganden Throne Holder, there was no more work to do. That goal had been attained, but then what? Therefore one must practice the Dharma along with studying it. At some point there is no more study to be done, but practice remains important all the way to awakening itself.

25. Geshé Losang Chönden

Gen Losang Chönden was very famous as a great scholar and also as something of a *siddha*, or tantric master. He was a very interesting man. He had a long beard and he took snuff. He didn't care about a degree or any government position; he only wanted to live in retreat. I didn't receive any teachings from Geshé Chönden because I was very young at the time when he was still around Lhasa. I did go sometimes to Drupkhang Labrang with others to visit him and pay my respects, but I didn't really get the chance to study with him. Still, I consider him as part of my teaching lineage, and I have great respect for him.

Geshé Losang Chönden was from Ganden Chönkhor. He studied at Sera for some time but did not finish his geshé degree. Instead he returned to Ganden Chönkhor and served as disciplinarian there. Some time after that, the monastery sent him to a nomadic area in the north for a period of several years to give teachings and perform pūjas.

During this time, the new incarnation of the Drupkhang Rinpoché had been discovered and brought to Drupkhang Labrang at Sera. Drupkhang Labrang was a very large and wealthy labrang. Labrangs in general were richer than ordinary monk households. They had money and resources that stayed in the possession of the estate so that it would be there for each subsequent incarnation. Drupkhang Labrang wanted to find an excellent tutor for the young lama. The officials of the labrang asked the Thirteenth Dalai Lama to help in this selection because the Thirteenth Dalai Lama and the previous Drupkhang Rinpoché had a close connection. The Thirteenth Dalai Lama chose Losang Chönden.

Gen Chönden was still away in the north, so someone had to go find him and tell him he had been selected by the Dalai Lama as a tutor. When he heard the news, Gen Chönden was hesitant to go, but since he had been specially requested by the Thirteenth Dalai Lama, he went to Lhasa and became the tutor to Drupkhang Rinpoché.

Gen Chönden was not officially a geshé, and the officials of Drupkhang Labrang wanted him to get his lharam geshé degree and said that they would take care of all the expenses. So Gen Chönden went into the lharam geshé class, even though he had expressed no wish to do so. Just before he was to take his geshé exam, Gen Chönden said that he didn't care about being a geshé at all, but he would stay until Drupkhang Rinpoché got his geshé degree and then leave. Just as Drupkhang Rinpoché was about to become geshé, Gen Chönden fled Drupkhang Labrang in the night on foot.

All of Gen Chönden's students at Sera were worried about him and wondered where he was. Drupkhang Labrang sent horses and food to help in the search. My teacher Gen Ngawang Gendün was chief among the searchers. He looked all over and eventually went to Nenang Hermitage, which was a nunnery near Drepung Monastery in an inaccessible and solitary area. Ngawang Gendün heard that a donkey caravan guide had seen a monk in that area. After more searching Gen Ngawang Gendün found Gen Chönden there and gave him a number of letters from Drupkhang Labrang and various high-ranking teachers and lamas, including one from Gen Chönden's own teacher who was a former Ganden Throne Holder, asking him to return. At first Gen Chönden did not want to return, but finally he gave in since he had been requested by his own teacher as well as other important people.

Gen Chönden said that he still did not want to be a ranked lharam geshé, but nevertheless, he was awarded the second-highest level of the geshé degree directly by the abbot rather than by the usual procedure. In the end, he was awarded tsokram status, with a special degree called *parma*. Parma was a special, additional geshé status granted by the government and the monastery. There were a limited number of geshé degrees awarded in the higher categories, but sometimes the abbot and the government allowed additional degrees to be awarded. A parma geshé had the same responsibilities as the people who attained the normal geshé degree, but he was not ranked and so was not eligible for any of the highest government-granted positions. In the end, Gen Chönden accepted tsokram parma status.

Eventually, Gen Chönden went to southern Tibet, where there were a number of pilgrimage places associated with Tsongkhapa. He stayed in retreat at several of these places for a period of about a year. During this time, Gen Riksal, another teacher named Gen Tharchin, my classmate, and I were participating in the winter session in a region called Jang. I will talk about this session later, but basically it was a special session at which advanced scholars from the great monasteries would gather together to study and debate on Buddhist logic and epistemology. This took place about two days' walk south of Sera. It was also about two days' walk from a small monastery called Chaksam Chuwori, which was near a mountain cliff. The name of the monastery literally means "iron bridge on the mountain." Gen Chönden was in retreat at this monastery, so we decided to visit him there. As soon as we sat down with Gen Chönden, he focused his attention on us two young monks and started asking us very difficult questions on the logical system of Dharmakīrti. We responded correctly, and Gen Chönden said to us, "You young monks know logic very well," even though we had only answered a few questions. Later on, he went back to the area of Ganden Chönkhor and stayed near the monastery at a nice small hermitage up on the hill named Richen Gong, which is where he died.

26. Geshé Ngawang Riksal

MY TEACHER Gen Riksal was also not interested in prestige or official recognition. He was relatively young and he was a great scholar, but being a deeply spiritual man, all he really wanted to do was practice the Dharma. He was tutor to Dema Gönsar Rinpoché and then later in his life to the fourth Phurbuchok Rinpoché. Though he didn't want it, he was awarded lharam status. This was around the time when His Holiness the Fourteenth Dalai Lama was also close to getting his geshé degree, and His Holiness knew Gen Riksal. Eventually Gen Riksal, like Gen Chönden, was given parma status. When the government gave the rankings to the high geshés, His Holiness gave Gen Riksal a number even though his name had not been on the list and he should not have been given a ranking. After this Gen Riksal went into retreat for some time until he was chosen as the tutor to Phurbuchok Jampa Rinpoché. He stayed at Phurbuchok Labrang until his death. One of my students went to the labrang as one of Gen Riksal's attendants. I heard the details of his passing from this student.

One day there was a special event at Sera Jé at which there was going to be a big feast and a money distribution. Gen Riksal told his attendant that he should go to this assembly at Sera, which was a couple of hours away. The attendant said that he did not need to go, but Gen Riksal insisted. Gen Riksal had been feeling unwell for a few days, but it didn't seem like anything serious, and this morning seemed no different than any other. The attendant told us later that Gen Riksal had some tsampa for breakfast but was quiet, and it seemed that he was preoccupied about something. The attendant went to Sera as his teacher had insisted, and when he returned, Gen Riksal had passed away.

I remember thinking at that time about how the first Phurbuchok Jampa Rinpoché had been so famous and respected as both a scholar and a yogi, not only at Sera, but even as far away as Ganden Chönkhor, where we used textbooks written by him. This was very different from the new incarnation. The new incarnation was born into the aristocratic Lhalu family. Because he was still very young at this time, there really wasn't much for Gen Riksal to do. Later, the tutor would be responsible for teaching the child proper behavior and conduct and recitation and so on, but at the time Gen Riksal went to the labrang, the child was still just a baby. The Lhalu family often came and played with the child, bringing toys and many other things. The lama stayed upstairs in his quarters, and the tutor just sat in his room, not having much to do.

It was a great responsibility to train this high lama, whose previous incarnations were so famous and respected. Still, no one ever said it, but I think maybe Gen Riksal didn't like this position. This was right before the Chinese invaded, and there were a lot of rumors and worries, and I wonder if this had something to do with it too. Who knows? Anyway, Gen Riksal passed away unexpectedly, though he was the youngest of my teachers. He wasn't interested in getting a high rank of geshé and all the respect and privilege that entailed. He just wanted to be a simple geshé and a yogi.

These are long stories, maybe not worth telling, but at least they describe something about these teachers who had such a great influence on me, even though they weren't the teachers from whom I received the most teaching. These men were not interested in position or rank. After years of study, they wanted to dedicate their time solely to practice.

27. Geshé Ngawang Gendün

Geshé Ngawang Gendün was also from Ganden Chönkhor and was regarded as a great scholar not only by those at Sera Jé but also by the scholars of Ganden and Drepung. He was very well known by all the scholars of the Three Seats, and he was awarded the number-one rank lharam geshé degree. He held the position of disciplinarian at Sera Jé and also later became the disciplinarian at Gyümé. He probably would have also gone on to the highest positions of the tantric college if it hadn't been for the invasion of the Chinese. Geshé Ngawang Gendün was the teacher of all the younger monks at Tsangpa Khangtsen. He also had many students from the other regional houses of Sera Jé, and he even had students from Sera Mé. I received most of my teachings from him.

At the time of the Chinese crackdown in 1959, Gen Gendün was the tutor to Phurbuchok Rinpoché, a position he took after Gen Riksal had passed away. The people at Phurbuchok Labrang weren't able to flee Lhasa, so Gen Gendün was trapped there. For many years he endured much hardship under the Chinese. Later, the Chinese established a school near Nechung Monastery, and Gen Gendün was made a teacher there. This school taught general education and Tibetan subjects, but it also spread Chinese propaganda.

In those days many people used a two-wheeled, horse-drawn cart to carry things from one place to another. A man named Jampa Trinlé who had formerly been a monk and a student of Gen Gendün had a job driving one of these carts. Jampa Trinlé had also been a student of mine at one time. After he had stopped being a monk, he married a

Nepalese woman and became part of a well-to-do Nepalese family. The Chinese tended to leave Nepalese people in Lhasa alone, so this family was spared from some of the more horrible things going on in those days. Gen Gendün went from time to time to visit and have dinner with this man and his family, though he had to do it cautiously. One day, Gen Gendün told Jampa Trinlé, "Someday, I am going to need to use your cart. When I die, I will need your cart to carry my body off to the cemetery." He said this in a joking way. Soon thereafter, however, Gen Gendün began to feel unwell and died unexpectedly, though he was not very old at the time. Jampa Trinlé did not have the opportunity to follow Gen Gendün's wishes and carry his body to the cemetery, because some of Gen Gendün's students made all the arrangements and took him there themselves.

Later, this remark of my teacher's was understood to have meant something else. After his death, Gen Gendün's reincarnation was found to be one of Jampa Trinlé's children. This was Yangsi Rinpoché. The family had moved to Nepal by that time, near Kopan Monastery where Lama Yeshe lived. It was Lama Yeshe who found the new incarnation.[43] Gen Gendün was also one of Lama Yeshe's teachers, so there was a connection between them. Yangsi Rinpoché stayed at Kopan for a while.

Some time later, I went to visit Kopan and saw Yangsi Rinpoché there. Many Western students were there, and they were teaching the young Rinpoché English and other things. As the senior student of Gen Gendün, I decided it would be better for him to go to Sera for his education. So I sent him to Sera Monastery in southern India, where it had been reconstituted in exile. I was the principal sponsor for his education, but several other of my American students helped pay for the expenses as well. Since I wasn't there at Sera myself, Yangsi Rinpoché was primarily educated by and stayed with my student Gyümé Khensur Losang Tenzin, who now is the Jangtsé Chöjé.

28. Gen Lhündrup Thapkhé and the Pure Monastic Life

EVERYONE FROM Ganden Chönkhor, Lhatsé, Phuntsokling, and the other monasteries in Tsang were students of Gen Thapkhé Rinpoché. When I arrived at Sera, Tri Rinpoché was in Lhasa occupied with his duties as the Jangtsé Chöjé, and was just about to become the Ganden Throne Holder, so Gen Thapkhé was, practically speaking, our senior teacher. He was the one who watched over us, guided us, and advised us. He did this for the students of Gen Ngawang Gendün and for those of Gen Riksal. There were no distinctions made.

Gen Thapkhé did not live in Tsangpa Khangtsen. Tsangpa Khangtsen was on the far western side of Sera; Gen-la lived on the far eastern side. Also on the far eastern side was Samlo Khangtsen, which was mainly made up of people from Amdo and Mongolia. Gen Thapkhé was tutor to an Amdo lama named Khenchen Rinpoché, so he lived in Khenchen Labrang near Samlo Khangtsen. From time to time we went to this labrang to see Gen Thapkhé for teaching and for advice on conduct, behavior, study, learning, and anything else we wanted to know. Sometimes, Gen Thapkhé would come all the way to Tsangpa Khangtsen to check up on all his students.

Even if a student came from an affluent family and had a little money, he was to live simply. Unnecessary material things could cause other people to feel bad or get jealous. After all, all young people are attracted to nice new things, aren't they? Gen Thapkhé looked out for this kind of thing and criticized us if he found it. He usually came unannounced to check up on us, but sometimes we'd have a little warning. Someone would say, "Uh-oh, Gen-la is in such and such's room," and we would quickly check to see if our rooms were in order. Other times we had no warning and he showed up suddenly at our door. If he found anything fancy in our rooms, he teased us in front of the others. He would say, "Oh such and such is so fancy, he has a fine lamp and cushion." Whatever luxurious thing one had, he would make fun of it in a quite humorous way. Mostly he was good-natured about it, laughing and joking, but he always looked out for anything excessive. He was very concerned with these matters. He encouraged us to live simply and seriously, like yogis.

I vividly remember one story that I think illustrates Gen-la's way of relating with his students. One day, close to the New Year, several of my senior students wanted to make sausages. It was the Tibetan custom to make sausages out of sheep's intestines stuffed with blood, grain, fat, onions, and other things. These sausages were cooked in a big pot, and on the New Year they were fried in a pan with oil and onion. Then they were eaten with tsampa. It was very delicious, though I've never seen it outside of Tibet. Making these sausages was a messy and quite awful-looking business.

The sausages were being made in a student's room on the top floor above the temple. It was a large room, so it was a sensible place for making sausages. Everyone sat on the floor and had a plate heaped up with the filling. The intestines were in the middle, and each person was stuffing sausages. As this was going on, someone saw through a window that Gen-la and some other monks were coming quietly toward the building. He said, "Gen-la is coming!" Everybody was covered in this mess and didn't know what to do. Most of them just ran away and escaped. The owner of the room, a monk named Lhündrup Tengyé, was left alone there. He didn't know how to hide the mess, so he took his cushion and put it on top of the plate. Of course his hands and arms were still dirty. Gen-la came in and said, "What are you doing? What do you have there?" There was meat, blood, and intestines everywhere. He looked closely at this monk's face and over at the plate covered with the cushion. Of course he knew what was going on, since it was near the New Year.

Then he said, "Are you alone? Are you all alone or were there others here?" So this monk gave the names of the others, and Gen-la said, "Well where are they now?" The monk was flustered and responded, "They're gone!" Gen-la laughed and laughed. Some time later, we went to get teaching from Gen-la at Samlo Khangtsen. The teaching was in a big room and many students were there. In the middle of his teaching, Gen-la told this story. Everyone laughed and looked at this poor monk who had been left in this embarrassing situation.

Gen-la also made an example out of a classmate of mine named Losang Mönlam. Losang Mönlam was from a wealthy family, and he had come from Ganden Chönkhor as I had. His family often sent him presents like nice clothes, dried meat, good butter, and other luxuries. He liked these fancy things so he was often the object of Gen-la's teasing. One day, again during teachings, Gen-la said that once when he went to visit Losang Mönlam, the furniture was arranged facing south, but the next time his things were facing east. Gen-la said that Losang Mönlam was like a cat moving her kittens around! Of course he did this in a gentle teasing way. Another time Losang Mönlam had bought a shiny brass butter lamp, and when Gen-la came he said, "What is this? Where did you get this?" Of course, he knew where it had come from, but he was again making the point that monks should not be concerned with material things.

This is how Gen Thapkhé related to the students. He didn't scold people harshly. He used humor when he taught. If we had warning that Gen-la was coming, we had time to get our rooms in order, and there was no problem. Then Gen-la came in and sat with us for a little while, joking and laughing. He spent a lot of his time in Tsangpa Khangtsen in that way. He gave advice and told us stories of how great yogis like Milarepa and Gyalwa Ensapa became great spiritual beings. He taught us about the importance of living the pure, simple monastic life.

29. The Monastic Way of Life

AT SERA, there were none of the desirable things of worldly life. From the perspective of most people, our food, clothes, and living conditions probably sound very uncomfortable—rather miserable in fact. But the point of our lives was Dharma. All day and night were dedicated to Dharma activities. That was the purpose of the monk's life. We derived great satisfaction from these things, even from a very young age. Our clothes were filthy and tattered, the food was modest and not very high quality, and the tea was little more than hot water. Everything was very difficult. Even boiling water required work. But the happiness and joy found in religious devotion carried us through.

The monastery was a place of quiet simplicity and monastic discipline. A monk shouldn't have fancy tables, seats, chests, or a decorated altar. A sitting cushion at that time was made of yak leather and stuffed with yak hair or some other kind of hair. That was what we sat on. Our beds were just mats that were brought out at night and rolled back up and put away again in the morning. We also typically had a shabby little table. We bought empty shipping crates and discarded boxes for storing the few books we had. These boxes originally held Indian or British goods that had been brought to Lhasa for sale. Then the boxes were discarded, so they were cheap. Most monks had two or three books in one of these crates. The books were wrapped in yellow cotton cloth and sometimes had a little red edging.

Books could be purchased from the monasteries' printing houses. Each college had its own printing house for the textbooks and other texts that students needed. The government also had a printing house, and there were several other big monasteries in Lhasa, such as Meru and Shidé, that had them as well. There were also private publishing houses. Books were sold at stalls in the market in Lhasa. There were prayer books, philosophical books, and whatever else one needed for one's education or practice. One could find anything he needed if he had the money, but most monks had to save up for a while if they wanted to buy a book.

On top of one's book crate one usually had a simple altar. The altar might have a picture of the Buddha statue in the Jokhang Temple, or of one's teacher, or of some great lama like His Holiness. That was all we had. There were no lights in our rooms of course, but we had a simple oil lamp. Butter lamps were only for offerings on altars; they weren't used for light. Wealthy people would have an ornate brass lamp, like the kind used in India, but we in the monastery could not afford those. Instead, we used a broken cup that had a hole in which oil was put and a wick was lit. We used that lamp for reading. We didn't really need anything more than that.

The kitchen was usually just a part of one's room, though some people had a separate little room for that purpose. We made a simple stove out of the metal bands that merchants used in shipping big packages from India. We wrapped one band around three times to create a little space for fuel. Then we made a simple grate out of three more bands to support a cooking pot. It made the room smoky, but we could boil water in that way with a little metal pot. Next to the stove we kept a clay pot for storing water. In the corner of the room a little enclosure with a hole in it was built to keep cow dung, which is what we used for fuel. That was the whole kitchen.

A monk's support came from some source back home. My support came from my uncle back at Ganden Chönkhor. If a person came from the Lhasa area, it was a little easier for him to get what he needed. But if one was from a distant place, it didn't matter how wealthy his family was—supplies would not be received right away. It took a long time for things to arrive. One was dependent on someone from home coming to Lhasa to bring money or supplies, but they didn't always come when needed, and sometimes they didn't come at all. Sometimes one ran out, so other monks shared with him, or he could borrow for the time being until he received more supplies. The college also provided some support in the form of what we received in the assemblies.

At Ganden Chönkhor, there was always very good tea at the first assembly, with which we ate our tsampa. At the second assembly there was tea and sometimes a very nice soup. Compared to Sera, Ganden Chönkhor had very good food. At Sera, there were thousands of monks, so individually we didn't get much of anything. There was tea at morning assemblies, and we took our tsampa if we had any, but the tea came from the government and was not of very good quality. But of course, the whole point of being there was to study. There were great opportunities at Sera. We were happy just to be there.

Sometimes a wealthy person sponsored the great assembly for the whole monastery, and then we got good tea with butter and also some rice. At the end of the assembly there was a distribution of money. That helped a lot. The sponsor had to assure that he had enough money for all the monks. Some of the officials got more than the rest of the monks. For instance, if the ordinary monks got one dollar, then some of the officials got two dollars, and when the donor made an offering to the abbot on the throne, he may have offered three dollars.

When a money distribution was going to happen, the monks were told in advance, and of course everyone came. Not everyone could fit in the assembly hall at one time, so many would have to sit outside in the stone-paved yard in front of the hall. We sat in rows according to custom. Officials would oversee the distribution, telling monks row by row when they could get their share. The monks outside got their money first, and when they were all finished the monks inside got theirs. It was all very orderly. The money distributions helped because then we could go to the market and get some necessities, but what we received was not enough to support us completely. But again, the reason for being at Sera was for study and the accumulation of merit and virtue. We weren't there to get rich and live comfortably.

As I mentioned above, when I came to Lhasa, I first stayed at Tsangpa Khangtsen with my teacher. Then I got a very small, dark, and smelly room, where I stayed for a while. After that, I got a room in the Mongolian dormitory, which was much better. There were many Mongolian dormitories in Tibetan monasteries because of the former influence of the Mongols prior to the twentieth century. In those times there was a huge monastery in Mongolia that offered basic philosophical training, and many Mongolian monks came to Sera to complete their study. The trip from Mongolia took as long as a year going by camel. For the Mongols Lhasa was considered a holy place, like Mecca for Muslims. The Mongolian dormitories were donated by Mongol kings, queens, or chieftains, and they were very well built.

The Mongolian monks who had already studied back in Mongolia could begin their education at Sera as far along as the Madhyamaka class, which was quite advanced. They had to demonstrate, however, that they had already mastered the earlier materials. They did this by going to the less-advanced classes and defending themselves against the students of those levels. They would then begin their education at Sera in the class appropriate to their level of previous education. As I recall, they couldn't enter any class higher than the Madhyamaka.

During and after the World Wars, the Russians and the Chinese took over parts of Mongolia. After the takeover, the flow of Mongolian monks to Tibet slowed and eventually pretty much stopped. The number of Mongolian monks became fewer and fewer, and the remaining ones got older and older. The Mongolian monks who remained in Tibet received their support by renting out rooms in these buildings. In the old days they had received support from sponsors in Mongolia, but rent was now the only way they were able to support themselves.

There weren't enough rooms in Tsangpa Khangtsen for everyone, so some had to stay elsewhere. This was especially true in the case of the younger monks. Seniority dictated how one got a room in the house.

However, one could also choose to stay outside the regional house. If one wanted more room or a better room, one could stay at one of the Mongolian dormitories. I stayed at a Mongolian dormitory for quite a while. I still lived there when I began teaching, and my students came to me there. I stayed until I became Khamlung Tulku's tutor, when I moved to Khamlung Labrang.

Lhasa was not very far from Sera, maybe four miles or so. It was relatively easy for monks from Sera to go to Lhasa. It was much more difficult for monks from Ganden and Drepung to just go into Lhasa anytime, since they were farther away. Sometimes if monks from Sera heard that there was going to be some big assembly in Lhasa where there was going to be a money distribution, they would go to that assembly and then buy supplies in Lhasa. Many daily necessities were also available at a little market area that was in the plain a quarter of a mile down from Sera. We got matches, butter, onions, vegetables, tsampa, flour, and even sometimes a little bit of dried meat there. Vendors came from Lhasa and other places nearby to sell their merchandise. Farmers came with cow dung that we monks used for fuel. They also sold a type of dried bush that was used as kindling. The vendors sat on the ground or at small tables with their wares. A few had a portable stall with a wooden frame and an umbrella or a piece of cloth that served as a canopy to protect them from the sun. This all took place before noon; after noon the vendors had to leave.

Once a year the vendors had to gather and listen to a speech by the two chief disciplinary officers who had power over the whole monastery. They were like the head administrators or police chiefs. One was from Jé and one was from Mé, and they served for one year. The regional houses took turns providing these officials. The monks of the regional houses voted for a candidate, and the result was passed on to the abbot, who made the appointment. The more senior monk was the more active of the two. These officials were also involved in the government, so they wore special official clothes, had attendants, rode horses, and were given a government seal. Their office served as a connection between the monastery and the government, so they were very powerful. At the annual meeting with the vendors, the chief disciplinary officers came out of the monastery and sat on a raised stone platform. They told the merchants the rules and conditions for selling to the monks. If a merchant didn't come to this lecture, he couldn't sell his goods at Sera. This was all done outside the monastery walls because the vendors could not come inside the monastery. The vendors were both men and women, and women were not usually permitted inside Sera.

Usually we monks had a small amount of black tea in our possession. When we made tea we used just a little bit. Sometimes we would also get a little butter, which was available in the market. For maybe three or five cents we could buy a very thin slice of butter, which was put on a leaf or a piece of paper. Then we would put just a tiny bit in the cup with the black tea. When we drank the tea it had a fine film of butter on top. We blew the butter back as we tipped the cup to drink so we would get just a little taste of the butter. That way we could pour many cups of tea in the same cup and the butter would still be there, getting used up little by little until it was finally gone. That was what it was like day to day. Sometimes we got a larger amount of butter and we would make proper churned tea, which was very delicious. Churning the tea with the butter was a luxury, but sometimes we were able to have tea this way.

Some better-off students sometimes had extra money to shop with in the market outside Sera. There Muslim women sold dried cow or yak meat. A monk would say that he wanted five cents' worth of meat, and the woman would cut a portion off a larger piece with a sharp knife and fold it up in a way that made it look bigger than it actually was. Really, there wasn't much there, but with just this much one could make a good simple soup. If one were too poor to buy all the ingredients, he could get together with several other students and make soup. One person would bring the meat, another would bring some flour for making noodles, and so on, but this was rare.

We students had a sincere motivation and attitude. We were living according to the Vinaya, trying to lead a life of yogic simplicity and nonattachment. We were trying to live purely, and this feeling was very good. Despite how it might sound, this lifestyle wasn't like a punishment. We were always joyful.

30. The Disciplinarian's Lecture

LIKE AT GANDEN CHÖNKHOR, the student's year was divided into a number of semesters and periods in between them. There would be a long and a short semester in each of the four seasons. Each semester at Sera Jé began in the same way. On the first day, a ceremony marked the start of the semester. For the next two days the monks did not assemble in the Dharma courtyard as usual. Instead they went to gather wood from the laity in a tradition called *shinglong*. In the ancient Indian Buddhist system monks went to laypeople's houses begging for food to provide laypeople the opportunity to create merit by offering food. In Tibet we gathered wood in place of this practice.

Some regional houses required all the young monks to do this, while others had different rules, but it was mostly the duty of the youngest monks. During the ceremony on the first day of the session, the disciplinarian assigned different groups of monks different areas in which to collect. On the next day the monks went to the area that they had been assigned from early morning until maybe ten o'clock. They took with them a rope to tie up and carry the wood. Some people would give a few sticks or some brush; others gave nothing. The monks returned by about ten o'clock and brought the wood to a central location. It was supposed to be the monastery's fuel supply, but it wasn't nearly enough. It was really just symbolic.

On the third day of the semester, the whole evening session was taken up by a lecture from the disciplinarian. It was not simply scolding; it had religious significance in that it was similar in content and structure to the stages of the path literature. The disciplinarian had to cover six topics. There was a saying that if the disciplinarian were a great scholar, he would have so many things to say that even if he talked day and night he would not finish his lecture. If the disciplinarian was not such a great scholar, he considered the lecture finished even if he'd said just a few things, as long as he covered all six topics.

During the lecture, the assembly of monks sat on the two sides of the assembly hall with a walkway in the middle. The disciplinarian walked up and down the walkway with his hat in his left hand and gave the lecture. The six topics were:

1. To whom the lecture is offered
2. When the lecture is offered
3. Who gives the lecture
4. The manner in which the lecture is offered
5. How to listen to the lecture
6. The nature of the lecture itself

The first topic, the kind of person to whom this lecture should be offered, referred to those who follow the three collections of the Buddha's teachings—the Sutra discourse texts, the Vinaya discipline texts, and the Abhidharma philosophical texts. In other words, the lecture was specifically for people who lived the ordained Buddhist life. The lecture was to be offered exclusively to them, not to just any kind of people. The second topic, the time that the lecture was to be offered, was always the third day of the session. The third topic, the person who should offer the lecture, was the disciplinarian himself. Not just anyone could offer this lecture. The fourth topic, how the lecture was to be offered, was that it should be offered respectfully to the Sangha. The lecture was not offered in familiar, everyday language but in highly formal language. The first four topics all had to do with the disciplinarian and his duties.

The fifth topic, how to listen to the lecture, helped the students to set their motivation as it is taught in Tsongkhapa's *Great Exposition of the Stages of the Path*. The fifth topic had two parts, which each had further subdivisions. The first part advised the listener on the three ways of listening that should be abandoned. First, you should not be like a vessel turned upside down; you should listen carefully. Secondly, you should not be like a dirty vessel, listening with an impure mind with the intention to criticize or find fault with the presentation. Third, you should not be like a leaky vessel, listening but not retaining anything. Those are the ways of listening that should be avoided.

The second major subdivision of the fifth topic was explained in terms of six perceptions that are based on the well-known analogy of the Buddha as the great physician.

1. You think of yourself as a patient. You regard yourself as sick, in the sense that you are suffering and seeking relief from this suffering. By acknowledging your problem, you begin to seek a solution.

2. You think of the teaching as medicine that relieves suffering. Since the lecture of the disciplinarian was based upon the teachings of the Buddha, we were to regard his lecture as a means to relieve suffering.

3. You think of the teacher as being the doctor. The Buddha is often called "the great physician" because he is the one who can help beings overcome their sufferings. In this particular case, we were to think of the disciplinarian as the doctor who can relieve suffering.

4. You have the conviction that if you put the teachings into practice, you will recover and good fortune will follow. In other words, we were to have faith that the lecture and Buddhist teachings in general are effective and undoubtedly lead to the results promised.

5. You have the conviction that the Buddha is a holy being and is the sole refuge for suffering beings. You feel certain that the Buddha and the Dharma are the only refuge from the sufferings of samsara, the cyclic world of misery. Ultimately, the authority of the lecture came from the fact that it is based upon the teachings of the Buddha himself.

6. You feel certain that by realizing the previous perceptions and

putting them into practice, the teachings of the Buddha will endure in the world. Our motivation for listening to the lecture and for treading the path was to be for the sake of the continued existence of the teachings and for the peace and freedom of all sentient beings.

The sixth topic, the central point of the lecture itself, consisted of the rules and schedule of daily monastic life. Each semester had a different schedule, and there were different rules for those who were first entering monastic life from lay life and for those who were already monks elsewhere but were entering Sera. All these rules had to be discussed.

This happened every semester, so most monks probably already knew much of what would be said in the lecture, although the details may have been different depending on the disciplinarian. If one of the six topics were skipped, however, it would have been noticed.

There were actually two kinds of disciplinarians: the winter disciplinarian and the summer disciplinarian. Each served for six months and presided over all the semesters in those seasons. For the purposes of this division, spring and fall were subsumed into summer and winter. The winter disciplinarian could be either a scholar or a rich monk. Since some of the winter disciplinarians were not geshés, they might invite a geshé to substitute for them on the day of the lecture. Summer disciplinarians all had to be geshés for reasons that will become clear in later chapters, but that meant they gave the lecture themselves.

Whether summer or winter, this lecture was important because it was meant to turn the students' minds to the correct way of thinking and to create seriousness and devotion to the path. It was said that even the abbot and other advanced monks should listen to the lecture from their windows above the gathering place, because great lecturers could give compelling reasons, scriptural citations, and other inspiring advice that could powerfully move the listener's mind in a positive direction.

In the big monasteries, the rules at the regional house level were very strict, but out in the monastery itself, we had to discipline ourselves. We followed the rules out of devotion and dedication rather than just out of fear of being punished. There was no way to keep track of everyone. There were no policemen; discipline had to come from within. If we remembered the purpose of monastic life and pursued it correctly, the results would come. If we didn't have that kind of attitude, there was no point in being in the monastery. It would probably be better in that case to just go back home. If we were there for the right reasons then we would succeed. No one else could do it for us.

There was a saying that went, "For *that* purpose you have come." The disciplinarian reminded us of this in the lecture. He said that we should not waste our time. Going to the sessions in the Dharma courtyard and studying were the means to accumulate merit, clear away obstacles, and develop wisdom. That was what should be done. That was the purpose for which we had come. The lecture helped young people to avoid straying from this. Discipline didn't mean just shouting, scolding, and beating; it was also encouragement and guidance. The disciplinarian had thousands of monks to watch over, but he didn't get personally involved with the enforcement of discipline. Under the disciplinarian there were others with sticks. They gave anyone who misbehaved a lot of hardship.

People from Amdo and Kham in the far east of Tibet came from very far away, and the disciplinarian reminded them that they had not come so far just for fun. The trip was very long and difficult; most had walked for many days, sometimes not even knowing exactly where they were. To a certain extent this also applied to those who came from Tsang. The trip from Kham and Amdo may have taken months, and the trip from Mongolia even longer. There was a very well-known saying about the long and arduous journey to Lhasa from these faraway regions: "You set your sights on the white clouds and measure your progress in steps upon the black earth." There were no compasses, maps, or watches, so there was no way to measure the distance or the time of day. Because the terrain of Tibet is so mountainous, you couldn't really even just go straight in one direction. Sometimes you had to go up a valley to a pass to get over a mountain, and the direction you went might not have been toward your destination at all. At times, you might even need to go in the opposite direction. Keeping your sights on the clouds far off toward the horizon was the only way to keep on track. There were times on the journey when you wouldn't even know whether you had enough food and water to make it. Most people in America these days don't have any idea of what this kind of traveling was like. You had to be very determined and serious to endure the hardships of such a journey.

During the lecture the disciplinarian said, "Having come here from far away, you must keep in mind the hardships that you endured and why you endured them. You have to learn the monastic way of life. Having come to a precious place like Sera, spiritual satisfaction derives from having the right attitude." He made the analogy that the person who had come to Lhasa from those faraway places was like a thirsty person who had crossed a great desert. Having arrived at the place you had sought, you should drink deeply of the teachings and study hard. You shouldn't return home empty-handed, without getting what you came for.

People from nearby in the Lhasa area didn't have to endure the same hardships in order to study at one of the great monasteries there. They had more connections—and distractions—in the city. So in general I think there was a tendency for those who had come from far away to work harder and to better appreciate the opportunities at Sera.

When I came to Sera, it was the first time that I had ever met people from Kham, Amdo, and other faraway places. Even in Shikatsé, the main city in Tsang, the dialect was different from Shang, so it was very difficult indeed for me to understand the people from Kham and Amdo. I had to learn these different dialects in order to debate and talk. There were so many new things at Sera, and many challenges. It was not just the exciting things that I had heard about back in Ganden Chönkhor. The reality was very different.

31. The Curriculum of Education at Sera Jé

THERE WERE FIVE subjects of study in the curriculum of the monastic education system that led up to the geshé degree.[44] First, we studied logic and epistemology based on Dharmakīrti's *Commentary on Valid Cognition* (*Pramāṇavārttika*). It was first approached through a series of elementary logic and debate texts called Collected Topics and took around three years. There were three levels of classes on this material: beginning, intermediate, and advanced.

Second, there was a section on the Perfection of Wisdom literature, which was primarily based on Maitreya's *Ornament of Clear Realization* (*Abhisamayālaṃkāra*) and its commentaries. This section had five subdivisions, each lasting about a year: a junior and senior class on the root text, a junior and senior class on the classical commentaries, and a final perfection class. As you can see, the study of the Perfection of Wisdom literature took a very long time.

Third, the student began the study of Madhyamaka, the central philosophy of Mahāyāna Buddhism. The primary text for this subject was Candrakīrti's *Introduction to the Middle Way* (*Madhyamakāvatāra*), though other fundamental texts were also studied. Students spent two years in the junior Madhyamaka class and two in the senior Madhyamaka class. The same was also true for the study of Vinaya and Abhidharma, the fourth and fifth subjects. Vinaya, the fourth subject, was based on Guṇaprabha's *Vinaya Sūtra*. It dealt in depth with the details of the monastic code established by the Buddha. The fifth and final subject, Abhidharma, was based on the *Treasury of Abhidharma*

(*Abhidharmakośa*) by Vasubandhu, which contains an exhaustive examination of all the categories of existent things, both psychological and cosmological.

After this, students moved into the *karam* class, which was the final preparation for the geshé degree. This class reviewed Vinaya and Abhidharma materials. Most monks remained in this class until their turn came for the geshé examination. The very best students in the *karam* class were chosen by the abbot to move to the *lharam* class, where they would review all the classes of the curriculum. Lharam geshés were the "big geshés"—they were qualified to complete for the high monastic positions in the tantric colleges, which could ultimately lead to one becoming Ganden Throne Holder.

By this point in our education, since we were mostly doing review, the classes consisted exclusively of students. The teacher of that particular class was not generally present. Some of the students were already teaching lower classes themselves by that point. Any given class was composed only of peers.

32. Studying and Teaching at Sera Jé

THOSE MONKS who had begun their study elsewhere and then come to Sera to continue their education may have already studied Perfection of Wisdom, Madhyamaka, and so on. However, there were limits on how far one could progress in the outlying monasteries. Once at Sera, one may have had to start again on the elementary logical texts or one might have been able to jump ahead.

Not every scholar monk who came to Sera completed all the courses and sought the geshé degree. Some people stayed at Sera up through the Perfection of Wisdom or Madhyamaka section and then returned to their own monastery, or perhaps began a period of retreat. Others chose to continue on to the Vinaya and Abhidharma classes. Among the very best students, some chose to go all the way through to the geshé degree and even beyond that to Gyütö or Gyümé, the tantric colleges. The pinnacle of the scholar's path in the Geluk sect, becoming Ganden Throne Holder, required a lifetime of work and study.

Before I went to Sera Jé, I had been studying the second Collected Topics text at Ganden Chönkhor. When I began at Sera Jé I started again on the first text, but my teachers quickly decided that I should move up. I had to get permission from the disciplinarian, for no one was permitted to move up to the next class without first getting permission.

A monk started philosophical study with his main teacher, and later he could seek teachings from other teachers within his regional house. In my case, I began study with Geshé Riksal and then sought teachings from Khensur Thapkhé and Geshé Ngawang Gendün. Each of them had many students and taught many different subjects. In a given day, a teacher might have taught several different classes, like professors in the U.S. do.

Students sought out teachers for instruction on a particular text or texts on a specific topic. *Teaching (petri)* here specifically means being guided through a root text. The teacher read the text with the student and gave oral commentary on it, drawing on several layers of commentarial material. The teachers were not paid, and the college did not assign their teaching responsibilities. If the teacher hadn't completed his studies, he was in classes of his own, so he was very busy. If a group of students only had one teacher, it could be very difficult getting everything covered, so the students would have to get additional teachers to get all the teachings that they needed. Students would learn from many teachers, who would give many different points of view on a given text or subject, which enriched the students' knowledge and understanding.

It was the students' choice from whom they wanted to learn, and it was the teachers' choice whether or not to teach. This was done by a group of students all at the same level, who together made up a class. Sometimes, however, we weren't able to get the teachings requested right away. There was no central schedule that we could count on, so sometimes it seemed like we were always waiting for teachings. We students had to make the requests ourselves, and we had to be very persistent. Once a teacher agreed to give teachings, we went together to the teacher at the appointed time and place. We came to the teacher's room in the evenings with the wrapped textbook on our shoulders.

The first time one came to a teacher, one offered the traditional khatak, silver coin, and tea. After that, one simply came to the teacher's room, left one's shoes outside the door, and entered. The student partially bared one shoulder, held the other part of the upper robe a certain way in the hand, bowed to the teacher, and sat down. Occasionally it happened that a student went alone to a teacher if he were the only one from his regional house, but it wasn't generally done on an individual basis. Sometimes students were able to receive a lot of instruction, but other times they weren't.

It was common knowledge among the students who the good scholars and teachers were, and good students sought out the best teacher that they could find. We had a saying that the best teacher was one who was a great scholar, disciplined, and a good person. If you could find a teacher who was a great scholar and was disciplined, or someone who was disciplined and a good person, that could be all right, but the ideal was someone who had all three qualities. There was no designated faculty—any monk could be a teacher if students requested teachings of them. The monastery did not tell anyone that they had to teach or do any other particular job. The monastery also did not pay teachers. Sometimes students would make offerings such as food, cloth, or flowers out of devotion, but that was all. Teachers taught out of love and compassion, wishing to help good students' development, and students looked up to their teachers almost like fathers. Unlike in the secular Western system of education, at Sera your teacher was more than just your educator—he was your real spiritual guide as well. You treated your teacher with the same kind of respect you gave to renowned lamas.

In addition to academic teachings, teachers also offered general advice and guidance to students. A student could request teachings on things other than the official subjects. Teachers did not generally specialize in a particular subject. If they were already geshés, they could teach any subject. But if a teacher were younger and not yet a geshé, he could only teach the subjects he had already studied. At Sera Jé, for instance, younger teachers could not teach Vinaya and Abhidharma. When students were seeking a teacher, they usually first looked within their own regional house. Better-known teachers would sometimes attract students from outside their regional house as well. One may have had a well-known, senior teacher along with a younger, lesser-known one. Then, if one's senior teacher were not available as often as the student needed, he could go to the other one. This was really the only way to get all the required teachings.

Classes focused on a particular subject, and all the students in a given class would read the same text or texts and debate on that material. Ideally, one would receive teachings on one's subject prior to having to debate on it, but sometimes one would have to wait until the debating had already commenced to get teachings. There were often differences among the students in a class, depending on whether each student were sharp or not, or if he were reading additional texts beyond the basic ones. Also, the different styles and perspectives of the different teachers was very useful later in debate. This system worked well.

By the time I began the Madhyamaka class, I was already teaching others; I must have been about ten years into my studies. People had started asking me to teach, especially students from Tsangpa Khangtsen who had come from Ganden Chönkhor. Then students started coming from other regional houses, and then students who were particularly good scholars started coming as well. As I became more senior I took on more students. I still had to prepare and study for my own class, even while I was teaching Perfection of Wisdom, Collected Topics, or some other subject to others.

33. The Structure of Debates at Sera

A T SERA we had both wet and dry assemblies. The first and most important wet assembly took place in the great Sera assembly hall. Early in the morning, the monks of Jé, Mé, and the tantric colleges all met together. This was the one period of each day when all the monks of all colleges gathered, whether they were worker or scholar monks. This great assembly was what held the whole community of Sera together.

After this gathering, a call went out with the ringing of a gong on the roof of each of the colleges. The scholar monks of each of the three colleges then went to their respective places for the rest of the day of debate, prayer, and study. Sometimes there would be a wet assembly at the college assembly hall a little before noon, but the rest of the day's sessions, the dry assemblies, would be in the dry riverbed area or in the Dharma courtyard.

Scholar monks gathered together at least three times each day for debate: in the morning around 7:00 after the great assembly, again around noon, and again later in the afternoon, between about 2:00 and 4:00. There were two locations where the debating sessions for the scholar monks took place. One was the dry riverbed area that ran through the monastery, and the other was the Dharma courtyard. Most of the debating took place at the riverbed, and this area was used exclusively for that purpose. Occasionally, if the riverbed were unavailable, the sessions would be held in the Dharma courtyard instead. The Dharma courtyard was also used for prayer and recitation during the morning, midday, and late-afternoon sessions. Some debate also took place there after the prayers. Only scholar monks who were still studying the curriculum attended these gatherings. Worker monks did not come to these sessions, nor did senior monks or high officials. Geshés could come if they wanted to, but they were not obligated to attend.

Each morning after the great assembly, a gong was sounded, and the students would first go to their respective Dharma courtyard, where their college's disciplinarian awaited them. At times the abbot would come too. The Sera Jé Dharma courtyard was surrounded by a wall. The ground was covered with smooth white gravel, and it also had some trees. The gravel was replenished every semester, so there was no need for the students to bring a cushion on which to sit. Against the wall was a large stone, which was the abbot's throne. There were also a few other lower thrones for high-ranking lamas. The rest of the monks sat on the ground facing the thrones.

At the morning session when the students were called to the Dharma courtyard, they came running with a great sense of excitement for the debating sessions, which gave the students the opportunity to develop wisdom. Students gathered in their classes. Most of the time, the disciplinarian oversaw the sessions in the Dharma courtyard, and he assigned the topic for that day's debate, but sometimes the abbot would come. When the abbot was there, each class would meet with him before going to the riverbed for the morning debate session. The abbot sat on his throne, and one by one the classes would go before him, bowing three times and remaining kneeling on one knee, palms together. Each class had one person, chosen by the group, who was its leader. The leader had some special responsibilities. The abbot recited a portion of the text that the class was studying. He did this three times, and then the class leader rose up slightly and had to repeat that passage of text back to the abbot. This was a form of examination. Afterward, the class bowed three times and left. After giving every class their lessons, the abbot would sometimes go to the dry riverbed to check on the students' progress. Though the students had run with enthusiasm to the Dharma courtyard, when they left it they went slowly toward the riverbed. This solemnity was a way of showing the preciousness of the time they spent in the Dharma courtyard.

The riverbed came down from the mountain above Sera and ran all the way to the lower monastery wall, bisecting the entire monastery. Sera Jé's assembly hall and Dharma courtyard were on one side, and the general Sera great assembly hall was on the other. Occasionally water flowed in the riverbed, but usually it was dry and sandy. It was surrounded by some bushes and small trees and bordered by a wall. When the students came to the dry riverbed, they sat in a circle around the class leader. The class leader would recite three times what the abbot had said, and the whole class then recited this passage according to a special fixed rhythm. That passage of text was supposed to be the subject on which the students would debate that day, though they didn't absolutely have to use that subject.

There were two forms of debate in the morning session. First, everybody in the class paired off and debated. The class proceeded in this way for a short time. In the second form, one student sat at the head of the class, and the rest of the students sat in two groups with a space between them. Each class level sat in a different formation—the Collected Topics in one, the Perfection of Wisdom class in another, and so on. The student at the head of the class had to defend a particular thesis. The rest of the students would take turns getting up and challenging the first student in debate. All of the classes took these two forms, one after the other.

The students of the different classes met at different spots along the riverbed. The three elementary logic classes met at the lowest spot. Above that each of the four Perfection of Wisdom classes had its own spot. Above this were the two Madhyamaka classes, then, higher up, the Vinaya class, and then the Abhidharma class. At the top of the riverbed were the two geshé classes, where the advanced students prepared for their geshé examinations—the karam class met above the Abhidharma, and the lharam class met at the very top.

When debating, much of what you relied on was the skillful use of logical syllogisms, but you may have also wanted to attack an opponent by pointing out that he had contradicted the explanation of some great master. This only held up if you could recite exactly what that master had said, word for word. If you claimed that your opponent had contradicted some great scholar, the opponent or anyone else listening to the debate could say, "So what exactly did that person say?" If you couldn't quote it, you couldn't prove a thing. You would just end up looking foolish, even if you were right.

This morning session lasted until about ten, at which time a gong was again sounded and the students went to their college assembly hall, where there was sometimes tea. After this came the midday debate session at the riverbed. During this session, the students debated in pairs. At a certain point the class leader left and went ahead to the Dharma courtyard. The students continued debating in the riverbed until the gong would sound from the top of the college assembly hall, at which point the students again ran to the Dharma courtyard and sat in a circle along with their class leader who had gone ahead. Then the Sera Jé prayer leader came and led the students in recitation.

The morning and midday sessions in the Dharma courtyard were usually fairly short. After the midday session, around 1:00 or 1:30, students went home to have tea or tsampa for lunch. Then the gong would sound again, and everyone would return back to the Dharma courtyard for the late-afternoon prayers and debate. This was from about 2:00. All of the sessions in the Dharma courtyard had recitation and prayer, but the late-afternoon session was the most extensive, lasting until around 7:00. The praises of Tārā (*drölma*), the female bodhisattva of compassion, were slowly recited twenty-one times, the *Heart Sūtra* was chanted nineteen times, and there were other prayers and texts that were recited as well. The purpose of these prayers was to clear away obstacles to study. It was believed that there were many hindrances to the study of philosophical subjects, so the prayers, which cleared away obstacles and created merit, complemented the study of philosophy. After the prayers were finished, students called out "*Dhīḥ!*" and a short debate would begin.

All the students of the classes debated, two by two. Particular classes were assigned particular portions of this area, similar to the way it was organized in the dry riverbed.

After the late-afternoon session, around sunset the students from all the classes up to the karam class went home, had some dinner if they wanted, and then used this time for their own individual studies and prayer. These breaks between sessions weren't times for relaxation; they were all used for religious purposes. The time in the early morning was when one would do his own prayers and recitations. The noontime break was usually taken up with reading texts while one had some tea.

The evening session began with the call "*Dhīḥ*!" That signaled the start of the night session debates in the Dharma courtyard. This night-time session was called the *night thesis*. This debating session took the form of one student defending a thesis with all the others challenging him. The disciplinarian made rounds at this session, passing through three times with his lamp. This would go on for at least an hour and a half. After the disciplinarian left, the students could go home if they wanted. Many times, however, debates continued late into the night, with the monks heatedly arguing their subjects. Sometimes even when the rest of the class had stopped or left, two students who were engaged in an important topic would continue to debate fiercely. Others who were around could come listen or even join in, challenging or supporting the debaters.

If one were in the Perfection of Wisdom junior text class or the Madhyamaka junior text class, one would spend all night debating every other night. These two classes alternated. If a monk didn't have to go to one of the night sessions, he had time to himself for reading and study, or would use this time to get teachings on the subject matter he was studying at the time.

The lharam class didn't follow the same daily schedule as the other classes. Lharam monks had their own special rules and regulations. They did not have to attend the general or college assembly hall activities like everyone else. They attended only the debating sessions at the dry riverbed or at the Dharma courtyard. For instance, when the gong was sounded from the roof of the college to call the monks to the late-afternoon prayer session in the Dharma courtyard, those who were in the lharam class went home instead to study until the late prayer session in the Dharma courtyard had ended.

While the other classes were taking their breaks, the lharam class debate session was about to begin. This was still early evening, perhaps sunset or a little before. The lharam students came in through the east gates. The class would stay in the center of the Dharma courtyard with the monks sitting in two rows. The senior lharam class leader would choose one lharam monk as the defender of the thesis and another lharam monk to challenge it. All the remaining monks sat quietly, listening to their arguments. The lharam class leader was also the person who determined the duration of the debates, but they all stayed there until night. While the night debate session was going on, all the other lower-level classes would engage in their own debates positioned around the lharam class. All the other monks would wear their heavy woolen cloaks while debating or in the assembly hall, but the lharam monks did not wear this heavy cloak, except in the winter. They wore only their monks' robes since they only participated in the debate sessions, which were strenuous enough that one didn't need the warmth of heavy robes.

When one finally did leave these night sessions, one went home to study. This was the time that scholar monks could do their homework, which took up the rest of the evening, until around eleven o'clock. A student would be studying root texts but also commentaries and textbooks on the subject, such as those by Tsongkhapa and other great Tibetan and Indian scholars. Every student had to try to read as many of these as possible and also try to memorize them.

It was said in the monastery that once the semester began, the Dharma was continuously being studied, twenty-four hours a day. It was true. Early in the morning there was religious activity in the regional house followed by the early morning great assembly. Then monks went to the riverbed area for debate. A little before noon, the second assembly at the college assembly hall began, and after that monks had to go back to the riverbed area for more debate. Then they were summoned to the Dharma courtyard. The afternoon sessions followed this. The night was filled with the night debate. Finally, the last part of the day was utilized by the students of either the junior Perfection of Wisdom class or junior Madhyamaka class, who stayed in the Dharma courtyard all night until the morning call to the great assembly. This was the cycle of monastic life.

In the midst of all the studying, debating, and so on, one also had to work on eliminating obstacles and generating merit. We had a saying that for every handful of studying there should be a bushel of making merit and eliminating obstacles. In old Tibet, there was a kind of grain measurement device that was a metal box with two intersecting dividers that formed four equal compartments. There was another saying that one's academic study should fill one of the four compartments; the rest of the box should be filled with the cultivation of merit and the improvement of one's ethical and spiritual qualities. Both of these activities were of great significance. The rigorous debates with one's classmates and scholar monks in the Dharma courtyard were causes of the accumulation of wisdom, which dispelled and cleared away wrong views. The elaborate prayers, offerings, and other ritual activities were causes for merit accumulation. A great deal of a scholar monk's time was spent chanting the *Heart Sūtra* and the praises of Tārā and doing other rituals, all of which were very important in making spiritual progress. These activities were done both in the assembly hall and in the Dharma courtyard. These were beautiful things that had to be performed with the right motivation. Both wisdom and merit are essential on the Buddhist path.

34. The Jang Winter Session

EACH YEAR a special session was held outside of the monastery called the *Jang winter session* (*jang günchö*). During this session Buddhist logic and epistemology were studied in depth for a period of about one month. This session was for those scholars who had already completed the elementary Collected Topics classes. Anyone from the senior Perfection of Wisdom class up to the karam class could attend. Those in the elementary Collected Topics classes were not yet prepared to study this material, and those in the junior Perfection of Wisdom and lharam classes were too busy to attend.

The winter session ran from the fifteenth day of the eleventh month to the fifteenth day of the twelfth month and was held at Jang Monastery, which was south of Lhasa near the Nyethang valley. The monastery and the winter session were under the jurisdiction of Ratö Monastery, which maintained it for the purpose of hosting the winter session. Jang had a big temple, a Dharma courtyard, and a large enclosed area, and Sera, Ganden, and Drepung each had their own buildings there. Though Jang was very busy and crowded during this winter session, for the rest of the year it was mostly deserted except for the caretakers.

Many scholars from Drepung, Ganden, and Sera came to the winter session. All the monks from Ratö Monastery came to this event, and some came from another monastery called Dakpo Ngari, which was also south of the Lhasa area. These monks hadn't always come to the winter session, but as the session gained in fame, its size also grew.

There was an interesting legend about Jang Monastery. It was said that there was a logic scholar monk who had died there and been reborn as a strange creature who was called Bongbu Sotsik. This creature was said to be half man and half donkey. It wore a woolen scholar's cloak and had the hooves and teeth of a donkey. It was said that this creature would try to take scholars away during the winter sessions. In fact there were a few instances of scholar monks who had disappeared or been carried away to distant mountains or rivers during this session. So people were a little bit afraid of this creature.

Every day when evening prayers were finished, all the scholar monks would gather in a circle in front of the temple courtyard before they proceeded eastward toward the Dharma courtyard for their evening debates. The head of Ratö would then stand in the middle of the circle, and a monk with a big torch would shine the light on everyone's faces to make sure that none of us was Bongbu Sotsik. Then the monks would recite some short prayers and then clap three times. The purpose of the claps was also to show that none of us was this creature—since it had hooves for hands, its clapping would have been instantly recognized. Because of this legend, many monks were hesitant to stay alone in their rooms or walk by themselves. We scholar monks would often joke among ourselves, saying, "Geshé-la is coming! Geshé-la is coming!" *Geshé-la* was the respectful nickname for Bongbu Sotsik.

The Jang winter session was very fruitful. Its subject was exclusively logic and epistemology. The texts studied were Dignāga's *Compendium on Right Cognition (Pramāṇasamuccaya)* along with its autocommentary and the Seven Treatises by Dharmakīrti.[45] We also studied commentaries by Tibetan masters and textbooks that clarified the more difficult points. Throughout the session monks from the different monasteries competed with one another in debate, which greatly helped to clarify things. Each monastery had its own unique textbooks, so one would encounter a range of different interpretations based on these different perspectives. This kind of study and debate really helped the scholar monks develop a deeper and more nuanced understanding of the subject.

The schedule for the Jang winter session was similar to the semester schedule at Sera. There were at least three debate sessions every day. During the early part of the day, monks from different monasteries debated with one another. Later in the day there were also debates among the individual colleges. During the evening session in the Dharma courtyard, two monks would be selected from among the scholars of Sera, Drepung, and Ganden to sit on a high throne. These two monks would be challenged by all the other scholar monks for the entire session. I attended the Jang winter session five or six times, and in those five or six years, I sat three times as the defender of the thesis in the evening session. It was very difficult but also very exciting.

Students really didn't get much sleep during this winter session. When we weren't debating, we spent the evenings studying so that we could do better the next day, and even though this was difficult, we felt that it was good for us. This session gave us scholars the precious opportunity to study the fundamental logic and epistemology texts that were not studied during the regular semester. It was also exciting to have so much contact with monks from different monasteries.

After the Jang winter session, a special one-day examination ceremony was held at Sera in honor of the returned scholars. The event was sponsored by the monastery and held in the Dharma courtyard. It was attended only by the abbot, the disciplinarian, the scholars who had attended that year's session, and the entire lharam class. The examination served two purposes. One was to examine the returned students on their improved understanding of the texts and their debating skills. The other was to recognize them for their hard work in completing the winter session. Special tea and soup were served, and the scholars were given their portions of any money donations or offerings that they may have missed during this period. There was also a short debating session between the newly returned scholars and the current year's lharam geshés. Two or three lharam geshés would act as the challengers of the thesis, while the winter-session students had to sit and defend.

35. The Honor of Being Named Rikchung

THE FIRST YEAR of the Perfection of Wisdom junior text class was a period of intensive debating and examination. The class was quite large, having from twenty to as many as sixty students. As I recall my class had about thirty or forty students. During the first semester of this class, as noted above, the students had to spend all night in the Dharma courtyard, taking turns presenting and defending a thesis. This class and the first-year Madhyamaka class took turns doing these overnight sessions, with each class staying up every other night, and the class wasn't allowed to leave the Dharma courtyard until the call for the morning great assembly. Every year following these intensive sessions, the disciplinarian chose and ranked eight young monks for a special honor called *rikchung*.

During the summer, in the sixth Tibetan month, this group of rikchung monks stood up in pairs in the Jé College assembly and engaged in debate for four days. The first monk recited a thesis in a kind of chant, and then the other debated with him—one was the proponent of the thesis, and one was the opponent who challenged it. The disciplinarian assigned which role each monk took. There were specific subjects that were dealt with in these debates, such as the three turnings of the wheel of Dharma and buddha nature. We were given these topics well in advance.[46]

It was a great honor to be named as one of the rikchungs. These monks had an elite status and were accorded great respect. It didn't matter very much if you were ranked first or second among the rikchungs; all eight got special treatment. Once granted rikchung status, a monk was considered a senior monk, and from that time on, everyone recognized him as a great scholar. The disciplinarian did not choose the rikchungs according to regional house—only by merit. In any given year, one regional house may not have had any rikchung students while another may have had two or three.

Toward the end of the semester prior to the summer semester in which the rikchung debate occurred, the disciplinarian announced the rikchungs at the riverbed area. There was a small Tārā temple halfway up this area, in front of which the disciplinarian had a stone throne. On this day he first called the student leader of the junior Perfection of Wisdom class and assigned him the topic for debate, as I've explained already. Then he called out the name of the first rikchung; this person was ranked number one. The disciplinarian then gave him his subject for the rikchung debate. Then everyone waited to hear who was ranked second, then third, all the way through to the eighth rikchung.

I was named rikchung when I was about twenty years old. Being named rikchung brought some privileges within the monastery. For instance, in the regional houses there were obligations called "freshmen duties," where young students were assigned to the many jobs that needed to be done in the monastery. All the regional houses had to give some students to do these jobs. Once one was granted the status of rikchung, one was exempt from these jobs and from that of being the regional house teacher who monitored the monks and the temple. That was the rule in Tsangpa Khangtsen, in any case. From the time I was named rikchung, I was exempt from all these kinds of jobs. I wouldn't have to do the shopping, keep the money for the regional house, or serve as the kitchen supervisor. I was setting out on a different path.

There was also a lot of work that went with the honor of being named rikchung. I had to read and study a lot in order to be ready for debating in the assembly. I had to be prepared to respond to a positive answer, a negative answer, or a follow-up question from my opponent. I never knew exactly what he would say, so I had to be ready for every possibility. My opponent in this debate was from Trehor Khangtsen, which meant that he was from Kham. Even if one's debate opponent were from the same regional house, one never knew exactly what the other person was going to say. There was always a great deal of practice that had to be done. One had to go with someone else to a secluded place to practice, making sure that the opponent could not hear. Sera Jé had two Dharma courtyards, one on the east side and one on the west. The rikchung student from the western Dharma courtyard would go to the east side of the monastery, where there was a grassy area with a stone path. The rikchung student from the eastern Dharma courtyard would go to the west side of the monastery near the mountainside. In my case, I went to the east side of the monastery to the grassy area to practice. My rikchung teacher Gen Samten and another rikchung student went along too, and my teacher taught us the subject matter for the debate as well as proper debate techniques. Of course during this time I had regular classwork to do in addition to preparing for this debate, so I was very busy.

Before the rikchung student did his debate in the assembly, he had to go to every class from his own first-year Perfection class on up and debate there on the thesis he had been assigned. I remember that I went together with my opponent and another monk who had been chosen as *rikchen*, a higher honor that came later in the curriculum, to these other classes to debate with the students there. We sat down in the defender position, and the monks in these classes would put a question to one of us, turning to the next if the first couldn't answer. So the first day we would go to our own Perfection of Wisdom junior-text class, then the senior-text class, then the junior auxiliary topics class, and so on, up through the Madhyamaka, Vinaya, and Abhidharma classes. In some cases we had to do this in more than one session in a day. Whether or not the debater were able to defend himself in all these classes, and he wasn't likely to do so when pitted against the more senior scholars, he had to go every single day until he had defended himself against the scholars of all the classes, win or lose. Even though these debates were on the subject that we were studying at this stage, these sessions were very hard because senior monks would ask very difficult questions.

Between the semesters in this period, the rikchung students had to go to a session at each of the different regional houses and again defend their thesis against all those scholars. There were courtyards in the regional houses with stone thrones where the rikchung students sat. The scholars of each regional house would debate with the rikchung students. First the senior monks would challenge them, and then the junior monks would take their turn. Tsangpa Khangtsen's courtyard was small, so we had to go to another bigger regional house's courtyard for this.

There was also a ceremonial obligation involved with this stage. Each of the rikchung students had to offer a meal to his teacher and to the disciplinarian of the college, which was a financial burden for poor students. The disciplinarian represented the Dharma protector of the monastery, so the meal offered to him was very elaborate and ceremonial and could not be combined with the offerings to others. This meal took place in a special room set up for him according to traditional rules. The meal offering to other guests, one's teachers, and so forth was less elaborate and less rule bound, but it was still done according to established customs.

There were also special obligations for the reincarnate lamas who were named rikchung. They had to make an offering of tea and soup to the whole college assembly and offer some money to all the monks of the college. Lamas had to make extensive offerings like this four times altogether: when they first entered the monastery, at the time of rikchung, at the time of rikchen, and when they were granted their geshé degree. This was very expensive, but generally the labrangs had the resources for this. Some years there were lamas among the rikchungs, some years there were not. Everyone in the college was of course more enthused when there were!

The actual debate performance in the Sera Jé assembly went on for four days, with two rikchung students debating each day, once in the college morning assembly and again in a later assembly that was held during this period. The whole college gathered for this event. For this debate, the rikchungs had to dress up in their finest robes and sit in a special place of honor at the head of the assembly. The proponent would chant a lengthy thesis, and then the actual debate began. Both monks removed their outer robes and began the debate, which went on until the disciplinarian said that they were finished. The whole thing was done according to a strict ceremonial method. If the proponent did something with his hat, the opponent had to do the same, in a kind of imitation. In one sense I enjoyed this, but in another it was very stressful and difficult. My assigned topic was the path of preparation or *jorlam*, the second of the five paths toward awakening. For the debate ceremony, my debate position was that of defender of the thesis. Since there was a great amount of honor in having been chosen as one of these rikchungs, word got around to all the monks of the monastery, and in my case it was known back at Ganden Chönkhor too. I suppose that must have made my uncle happy.

36. The Higher Honor of Being Named Rikchen

AFTER COMPLETING the rikchung debate in the assembly, one went on to the second year of the Perfection of Wisdom root texts; then to the first and second year of the Perfection of Wisdom commentaries; then to the final Perfection of Wisdom class; and then on to Madhyamaka. After the Madhyamaka class, reincarnate lamas often went through the Vinaya and Abhidharma classes more quickly than others, so when they got to the karam class, they were younger than the other students at that level. Lamas would typically get their geshé degree at a younger age than ordinary monks, which makes sense of course from our perspective. Lamas are the reincarnations of great beings from the past, so they have previous lives' experience and knowledge. For most people, however, it took close to twenty years to get the geshé degree.

At Sera Jé, Vinaya is studied after Madhyamaka, and Abhidharma is studied last, but other monasteries have their own systems. For instance, at Drepung Vinaya comes last. The karam class at Sera, where students reviewed Vinaya and Abhidharma, was made up of students of mixed age, because it had students who had just finished the Abhidharma class and students who had finished in previous years. One stayed in the karam class until the abbot called him to move up to the lharam class or until his turn came to get his geshé degree in the monastery.

Students in the karam class could be awarded the honor of *rikchen*. This worked basically the same way as rikchung, where one was selected and ranked, but now one's opponent came from Sera Mé rather than from within Sera Jé. The Sera Mé disciplinarian chose the four students from Mé, and the Sera Jé disciplinarian chose the four from Jé. The rikchen debate ceremony took place during the seventh Tibetan month. It was held in the Sera great assembly hall. During the first early morning session, all the monks were given some khapsé. The Sera khapsé were very famous and very delicious. At the second great assembly everyone was given tsampa. In the hall, the Jé monks sat on one side and the Mé monks sat on the other. Out in the courtyard everybody mixed with everyone else, but in the assembly hall they were divided. During major event periods like this one, not all the monks could fit into the assembly hall, so many would have to sit outside in the courtyard. The monks who sat outside received tsampa and khapsé and any money offered but no tea.

While the ranking of the rikchungs did not have great significance, in this stage, one's ranking was very important because this would determine one's geshé class and thus whether one would end up as a "big geshé" or a "small geshé." The big geshé degrees were granted in Lhasa by the Dalai Lama's government, and one would have to compete with scholars from all the Three Seats. If one became a small geshé, the degree was granted by one's own monastery alone. Small geshés did not have the same prestige or opportunities as the big geshés.

All of these decisions were made by the disciplinarian. He held a lot of power. As I've mentioned, there were two kinds of disciplinarian, the winter disciplinarian and the summer disciplinarian, both of whom were appointed by the abbot. Each ruled for six months. The winter disciplinarian could have been either a geshé or a rich monk, but the summer disciplinarian had to be a geshé and a great scholar because he had the responsibility for naming and ranking both the rikchungs and the rikchens. This disciplinarian would of course have been rikchung and rikchen himself.

Like the rikchungs, once a student was named rikchen and given his debating topic, he had to go to all the other classes to defend his thesis. Since at this point the rikchens would have studied all the subjects, they were asked questions on the topic of whatever class they were visiting, not just their own debating topic. The rikchen students also had to defend their thesis at the regional houses in a session between the semesters. They did this at the same time as the pairs of rikchung students, but there was only one rikchen student, because only half of the eight rikchens were from Jé college and the other half were from Mé and they would be doing this in their college along with their rikchung. The Jé rikchen and the Mé rikchen practiced on opposite sides of the monastery, again so that neither knew what the other would say.

The rikchen debate was held in the Sera great assembly hall. All the monks attended. There were two debating sessions for every pair, so each debater had one session to act as the defender of the thesis and the other to act as the challenger. The two rikchens took turns being the proponent or the opponent. One day the Jé rikchen would start, and the next day the Mé rikchen went first. During this debate the assembly was very loud, the monks on each side cheering in support of the debater from their college.

If, for instance, the student from Jé quoted something from one of Tsongkhapa's texts or from one of the Indian pandits to back up his argument and the Mé monks didn't accept this, they would heckle out loud, "Whaoo, whaoo." It was usually senior, more knowledgeable monks who started this, but then all the monks from that side would join in. This was a way for all the monks to cheer for their college. For the debaters, this was unnerving, but on the other hand, all the laughing gave one some time to think of a response. This was typically not done to reincarnate lamas. The disciplinarians of Jé and Mé sat at the head of the front rows of the assembly, and whoever was the elder of the two had the authority to stop the debate. The two students had to continue until they were told to stop. The two sergeants-at-arms also sat there by the door, but they were not in charge of these events.

The best students, the ones who had received a high ranking as rikchen, would be selected to move from the karam class to the lharam class. Once one was advanced to the lharam class, he was accorded great respect, but he also had to be very seriously dedicated to his final studies.

Since I was named as first rank among the rikchen, I was able to move into the lharam class.

There were special customs to be observed when one was about to enter into the prestigious lharam class. The new student performed an offering ceremony called the *shukja*, which means "tea for entrance," for all his fellow lharam classmates. This ritual took place in the Dharma courtyard before the lharam evening debate session began. The offering to all of the students in the lharam class consisted of a fine strong butter tea, a khatak, and yogurt. The yogurt was the last thing offered, as this was considered auspicious. When one was finally awarded the lharam geshé degree, there was a second offering ceremony. This was called the *tenja*, which means "tea for departing." This offering was made at the end of each year by that year's lharam geshé degree recipients, just before the Tibetan New Year celebrations began. The new lharam geshés offered tea, a khatak, yogurt, dried fruits, and a silver coin to each of their class-mates. These offerings were also considered auspicious. I was able to offer the *shukja* ceremony to my classmates, but I never got the opportunity to make my *tenja* offering because of the Chinese invasion.

This period of the scholar's education required intense study, and he would use every opportunity to read as much as he could. Even though all the monks from the Three Seats were supposed to go to Lhasa in the second month for the Tsokchö festival, some of us advanced students would stay behind to do intensive text memorization retreats (*petsam*). In these retreats one would do intensive memorization of philosophical texts like the root texts of the great Indian masters. When he had memo-rized these, he read the commentarial materials. These retreats were typi-cally done by a group of maybe two or three monks. One monk would cook the morning meal while the others recited. After the meal, each would begin to memorize verse by verse. Then in the evening he would recite what he had memorized until he went to bed. In the morning he would start memorizing again right away, then have breakfast, and so on, continuing like this for several days or even weeks. This was a very good opportunity for intensive study because most of the monks were gone and it was quieter than usual. The fact that so many people were gone, however, also made it necessary for there to be a kind of security force. There were some laypeople who worked for the monastery as security guards. These guards walked all around the monastery in the evening and beat a drum as they patrolled. This was supposed to be for the protection of all those unattended rooms. When I stayed behind during these periods, the monastery was nearly silent except for the sound of the drums.

37. The Different Grades of the Geshé Degree

THE PEOPLE in the karam class followed the same daily routine that they had in the other classes—they went to the riverbed, the courtyard, and so forth. They primarily debated Vinaya and Abhidharma. The students in the lharam class were exempted from some of the daily activities. They debated on all five subjects, but they also tended to emphasize Vinaya and Abhidharma. This time was also an opportunity to learn about these subjects in more depth and detail, because like everyone else, the lharam students had to wait until their turn came for the granting of the geshé degree. This could take up to ten years at Sera Jé because only two or three lharam geshé degrees were awarded each year.

When a monk was moved up to the lharam class, it was already assured that he would be a big geshé, either a lharam or a tsokram geshé. Students in the karam class who were going to be moved into the lharam class were ranked before they were actually moved. In my karam class there were twenty or twenty-five people. From among these, four or five were selected by the abbot to go to the lharam class. Two or three of these would become lharam geshés, and the others would be given tsokram status. Both degrees were awarded by the Dalai Lama's government officials in Lhasa. The highest, most prestigious, lharampa geshé degree was awarded during the Mönlam festival at the beginning of the Tibetan New Year. The tsokrampa geshé degree was awarded during the second month of the year at the Tsokchö festival.

The monks in the karam class who were not advanced into the lharam class received their geshé degrees from the monastery. At Sera, they were called *lingsé*, which means "within the monastery domain." These were the small geshés. The small geshé candidates had to wait in karam class until their turn came to get their geshé degree.

Some stayed in the karam class a long time, others got out quickly. Generally only eight geshé degrees were awarded each year: two lharam geshé degrees in the winter, two karam geshé degrees in the spring, two karam in the summer, and two more karam in the fall. Unless one was advanced to the lharam class, which was a much smaller, more exclusive class, he may have had to wait a long time before getting his geshé degree. The order in which these karam monks received their degrees was determined by their class ranking. With only six karam degrees granted each year, it could be that one was stuck there for a long time. If a monk didn't want to wait for his turn to come around to receive the geshé degree, he could leave and go to some other monastery, enter retreat, or travel around. This would be the end of his progress through the monastic education system; he would have an excellent philosophical education by this point. In addition, he would have gained expertise at many things, and he could be a highly respected teacher or lama at some monastery.

When I was in the karam class, I was ranked first in my class. One could be named rikchen more than once, and generally one wasn't moved up to the lharam class until one had been named rikchen at least twice. In addition to determining whether one would be a small or big geshé, one's ranking among the rikchens also determined how long one would have to wait to be awarded the degree. When I was in the lharam class, I knew that I would be the first one in the class to get the degree because I was the number-one ranked rikchen. The class leader of the lharam class and the top-ranked rikchen would go first. After these two, the next two highest-ranked rikchens would go the following year, and so on in order, until the whole class had been awarded their degrees. And one's ranking as rikchen in his own monastery didn't necessarily mean he would be ranked the same in the final competition. When he went for the examination during the Mönlam or Tsokchö festivals in Lhasa, he would be competing with other scholar monks from all of the Three

Seats, not just his own monastery. That was the system of Sera Jé. I can't say anything about the system at Drepung and Ganden, but it was probably similar.

At the time when I was in the karam class, a number of excellent scholars had just graduated from the lharam class, passing their geshé exams during the Mönlam festival. The abbot decided that there were a number of good scholars in my class, so he moved four of us into the lharam class right after the first time we were named rikchens. So by the abbot's own hand, some of us were given lharam status and some of us were given tsokram status earlier than was customary.

The order of rank of geshés for Sera monks was lharam, tsokram, rikram, and then lingsé. The intermediate-level *rikram* geshé degree was exclusive to Sera Monastery. The monks who were awarded the rikram geshé degree spent some time in the lharam class, but they did not get the same high-level degree as the lharampas and tsokrampas. Just before the Mönlam festival there was a short, seven-day period when the monks from Sera went to the Ramoché Temple, where a famous Buddha statue was housed.[47] The monks who received their geshé degrees at the Ramoché Temple during this time were called *rikrampas*.

38. The Conferring of the Geshé Degree

THE ATTAINMENT of the geshé degree was considered one of the most important achievements in one's spiritual life. It brought great honor and satisfaction, not only for oneself but also for one's family back home and for the many supporters and sponsors who had offered assistance through the years.

There were three stages to the geshé examination: one at the Norbu Lingkha, one within the monastery, and finally an examination in Lhasa, where one would debate with all the other great scholars of the Three Seats. In the summer the students of the lharam class went to the Norbu Lingkha. The entire class stayed there, and the candidates who would receive their degrees in the following year were examined, entirely in debate form. Since this was where His Holiness stayed in the summer, one might be able to see him before or after the actual debating. During the debating he was in the palace observing from behind a curtain. The principal observers and judges of this debate were *tsenshaps*, the high geshés who had been selected to be the young Dalai Lama's debate teachers and partners. These monks were chosen from among the best geshés of the Three Seats. Sera had two tsenshaps, one from Jé and one from Mé; Drepung had three, one each from Loseling, Gomang, and Deyang; and Ganden had two, one from Jangtsé and one from Shartsé. All together there were seven tsenshaps. These men had government appointments, and they stayed with the Dalai Lama in the Potala in the winter and the Norbu Lingkha in the summer. The Dalai Lama was educated in the same general way as all geshés, but he never experienced debating and learning with other children or young people. He was always with these old geshés, so he really had the best possible education.

During this time at the Norbu Lingkha, the candidates had nice rooms and meals provided by the government. In one sense it was very pleasant, but it was also very frightening and tense because they were being tested by the tsenshaps. The tsenshaps had the authority to decide that someone who had been sent there was not good enough. They could send the person back to the monastery, telling the abbot that the person was not ready and that someone else should be sent forward. Even if the abbot had chosen a monk as lharam, the tsenshaps could overrule this and send him back. It didn't happen often, but it did sometimes happen.

Next, there was a ceremony at the monastery level, which was called the *geshé damja* or the "geshé thesis ceremony." This was the official occasion on which one was granted the title of geshé by the monastery, regardless of which ranking one had attained. There were seven or eight such ceremonies within the monastery every year—one ceremony for each of the degrees awarded. Each scholar monk who was to be awarded the degree, whether lharam, tsokram, rikram, or lingsé, had to go through this stage.

Early in the morning of the day of the geshé damja, the student had to debate against all the great lamas, elder geshés, and senior scholar monks of Sera Jé. In the afternoon session, the student had to debate with all the monks in the karam and Abhidharma classes. Finally, in the evening session, he was challenged by the scholars of the rest of the classes of Sera Jé. In all of these sessions the candidate took the role of the defender of the thesis, defending his position against all who came forward. The whole evening session he was challenged by the students of every class, from the senior-level scholars down to those of the Perfection of Wisdom junior text class. If the candidate were a tulku, then the evening debating session would conclude earlier, but otherwise this would continue late into the night.

By the time one went through the geshé damja, he would have accumulated a lot of wisdom. One didn't just study and debate, however; one also had to make substantial offerings for the accumulation of the merit side of the bodhisattva path. Between the morning and midday debating sessions, at around eleven in the morning, an extensive prayer ceremony was held in the Sera Jé assembly hall. During this ceremony, each candidate had to offer an elaborate and expensive feast to the entire college assembly. This could be quite costly, since Sera Jé had a few thousand monks. Long before this event, one had to accumulate a lot of money and make all the arrangements. All the monks of Sera Jé were offered butter tea, money offerings, and a very delicious rice and butter porridge called *geshé damja thukpa*, which was only served on this occasion. The rice was cooked and mixed with very rich butter, dried apricots, dates, and sometimes meat. When prepared, it was so thick that it was served with a big scoop and the scoops were heaped up in the bowl so that it looked like an ice cream cone. This was a very special treat for all the monks.

This offering ceremony was a major financial burden, but if one were ranked first or second, then people would come forward to sponsor this offering. So there wasn't much of a problem for a highly ranked lharam candidate, even a poor one, because there was always a crowd of people who wanted to help pay for this. There was a huge amount of merit in this for the donor, too. However, if the candidate were not so highly ranked, he had to take care of this offering himself, which could be very difficult for the monk. So you see, if one did not put every effort into one's studies, there were hardships at every step of the process.

My uncle knew the costs of making this elaborate offering. He wrote me a letter about what to do if I were advance to the level of becoming a geshé. He said, "Don't be stupid. We don't have the money, so you should leave Sera right away and return to Ganden Chönkhor." I think this indicates just how much of a burden it was to arrange and pay for this event for one individual scholar. I wrote back to my uncle reassuring him that since I was at that time already the tutor to Khamlung Rinpoché, the Khamlung Labrang would take care of everything, so he did not have to worry. As I got closer to my geshé damja ceremony, two students of mine, one from a wealthy ordinary family and one from a very wealthy government official's family, also wanted to sponsor my geshé damja ceremony, so I was all set.

If the Chinese had not invaded, I would have had this elaborate ceremony in Tibet. But, this was not the case. My geshé damja was held in India after our escape from Tibet. This was a very difficult time for us Tibetans. All my sponsors and their arrangements no longer existed. Even the delicious Tibetan butter rice was not available in India. Instead it was replaced by simple bread and tea. I was upset to lose the opportunity for a normal geshé damja.

For lharam geshés the last stage of the geshé examination and awarding of the degree took place during the Mönlam Festival. The candidates were again tested, this time in the courtyard outside of the Jokhang Temple in Lhasa, in front of all the scholar monks of the Three Seats, the abbots, and the tsenshaps. There were three sessions of examination: morning, noontime, and afternoon. In the morning the subject was logic and epistemology; at the noon session it was Perfection of Wisdom and Madhyamaka; and in the evening it was Vinaya and Abhidharma.

In these examinations, the candidate sat alone. The nearest audience was made up of all the abbots. The tsenshaps watched from above on the balcony of the Dalai Lama's room. The senior abbot from Drepung Monastery was in charge, and he would judge how well the candidate did. He gave a ranking and turned this over to the tsenshaps, who also ranked the candidates. Finally this was given to the Dalai Lama. There could be some change in the ranking. The tsenshaps could change the ranking of the abbot, or the Dalai Lama could change the ranking given by the tsenshaps, though this was very unusual. In the end, the Dalai Lama affixed his seal to the ranking of each candidate. The top ranked was sometimes from Sera, sometimes from Ganden, sometimes from Drepung. Of course there was the possibility of taking sides on the part of the abbot or the tsenshaps, and someone might get an unfair advantage depending more on his monastery affiliation than on the quality of his scholarship. Someone from Ganden might say, "This year we should be number one, Sera got number one last year." This kind of thing was always going on, but in the end, the final ranking was given by His Holiness, and people respected his decision.

This examination was very harrowing for the person being examined. All the abbots were there, as were the senior geshés, the lharam geshé candidates from one's own class, and hundreds of other students. Anyone was allowed to interrogate the person being examined. Of course, if the candidate were from Sera Jé, it was unlikely that anyone from Sera Jé would challenge him, but many monks from Ganden and Drepung would come up to do so. They would ask him hard questions, and it was unpredictable what would be asked. The only thing that mattered then was what words came out of one's mouth.

There was a Drepung disciplinarian who oversaw the process of who was allowed to come up to debate with the candidate, and of who had to sit down and wait. Other than this crowd control, however, there was no restriction on who could challenge the person being examined. In the earlier sessions, many younger students came to challenge the person being examined on the subjects of logic and epistemology and Perfection of Wisdom and Madhyamaka. The evening session was the time for examination on Vinaya and Abhidharma, and that was when the abbots, other geshés, and senior monks would ask questions. The younger people were finished but still stayed to watch. Everyone wanted to see how the person answered.

One learned a lot at these examinations about how to ask questions and how to answer. A challenger could stand up and recite some passage from Nāgārjuna or some other great philosopher, and then he would say to the person being examined, "Please explain—what does this mean?" Another challenger might give an arcane technical term and ask the candidate to define it. Sometimes the candidate would have a good answer, and sometimes he had no answer at all. All kinds of things could happen. If the person gave a wrong answer, then everybody else who came up to challenge would ask the same question just to stump the candidate. The person being tested just wanted to forget that question, but it would continue to be brought up: "You said such and such before, now are you sure...?" So the candidate had to be very careful of what he said. All the other scholar monks were just waiting to find something to trip him up.

I remember very clearly going to these geshé examinations to listen to the questions and answers and to challenge the person being tested myself. This was a very exciting time, and it was enjoyable for those of us not being tested. But of course the real purpose of these examinations and of the whole education system leading up to the geshé degree was to cultivate wisdom. This wasn't just some worldly kind of competition. The whole method of debate had much significance. Various gestures and symbols were used in the debates. The clapping together of two hands was symbolic of the unification of method and wisdom, crushing wrong views. The movement of the left hand downward represented pushing negativities down, and the movement upward of the right represented increasing good qualities. At the start of the debate, the challenger called out *Dhiḥ*. The right hand represented the method side, and the left hand was the wisdom side. So all of these gestures had spiritual significance. But in truth, sometimes you had no thought of the symbolic meaning of what you were doing—you just wanted to beat the person in debate.

Even though the Three Seats were huge, it was well known among all the scholar monks who the good scholars were from each monastery. We were in competition with each other at the Jang winter session and at the Mönlam and Tsokchö festivals. But even though we were in competition, some of us were also good friends. For instance, my teacher Geshé Ngawang Gendün was a close friend of a great scholar from Drepung, a geshé who escaped to Dharamsala and later became abbot. He and my teacher were very close friends. During the Jang winter session they would invite each other for tea or a meal. What started as a competition could later become a close relationship.

It was the advanced scholar monks who tended to know each other across monastery lines. With the size of the monasteries, you might think it was almost impossible to know monks from other monasteries, but at our level we actually had a lot of contact. The big geshés from each monastery even had opinions about who should be ranked highly in the other monasteries. Then again, when we saw all the thousands of monks in Lhasa during Mönlam, we didn't know who was from Drepung and who was from Ganden.

After all the candidates had been examined, at the end of the Mönlam festival a large government assembly was held upstairs at the Jokhang Temple. The Dalai Lama would be sitting there on his throne. Next to him were khataks and complete new sets of monks' robes, each with a pandit's hat and a lot of money. These were in individual piles, and they symbolized the degrees to be awarded. The candidates sat outside, waiting. Someone came to the door and read out the name, monastery, college, and ranking of the top five candidates. All the candidates would come inside and offer a khatak to the Dalai Lama, surrounded by many government officials. His Holiness would give his blessing and then present the top five monks with their degrees and these gifts of clothes, money, tea, and so on. When a monk emerged from the Jokhang Temple carrying these things, he was now a government-recognized lharam geshé, with the ranking granted by His Holiness himself.

This was how it was in Tibet, but I didn't actually do my examination until we were in India, so my experience was somewhat different. I would have received my geshé degree in the Mönlam festival in 1961, just one year after coming to the lharam class, but the war started and prevented this.

39. Gyümé and Gyütö Tantric Colleges

THE TWO TANTRIC COLLEGES were called Gyütö (Upper Tantric College) and Gyümé (Lower Tantric College). These names did not indicate that one was superior and one inferior but rather referred to their physical location. These names also referred to a time in the past when these two institutions were located outside of Lhasa. Gyütö was originally in Tsang, and Gyümé was originally in Kham. Tsang is at a higher elevation than Kham, so this was the sense in which they were "upper" and "lower," and the names remained even after both were moved to the Lhasa valley.

Even if one were not a great scholar, it was possible to enter into the study of tantra. Monks who wished to enter either of the two tantric colleges fell into one of two categories: those who had already earned their geshé degree, called *completion-stage students* (*dzokrimpa*); and those who did not have their geshé degree, called *generation-stage students* (*kyérimpa*). These two names correspond to the two stages of meditation in tantric practice; the generation stage is the preliminary level to the completion stage. Not having earned the geshé degree did not prevent one from going to the tantric colleges, but it did affect one's status there and what position one could ultimately attain.

Among the completion-stage students, only the lharam geshés had a chance at the high monastic positions granted by the government, such as lead commentary reciter (*ṭīkā kyorpön*), abbot, or Ganden Throne Holder. The disciplinarian positions at the tantric colleges could be held by a geshé or by one of the generation-stage students. If I remember correctly, they alternated between the two. But the positions beyond this were only for lharampas. There was a series of examinations that determined whether one would earn the highest positions in Gyümé and Gyütö. Only the very greatest scholars would be considered for these positions.

Within the highest positions of the colleges, one would start as the lead commentary reciter, then become the lama prayer leader (*lama umzé*), and then finally become the abbot of the tantric college. In a sense, the lama prayer leader was the most important of the positions in the tantric college. Ordinarily, a prayer leader, or *umzé*, is the person who leads the chants in the assembly hall. He would have a good strong voice, but would not necessarily be a great scholar or master. But the lama umzé at Gyümé was different. The person who held this position was really in charge of the whole tantric college. He was the one who presided at the head of the assembly of Gyümé. He was the ritual master, the greatest scholar, and was more like an abbot than someone who just led the chanting. All the students at Gyümé, all the way up to lama umzé, were bound by a very strict code that was over and above the monastic code. Their whole lives were very rigidly controlled. They couldn't wear luxurious clothes or shoes, they couldn't ride on horseback, and they were bound by other similar rules. They were more like yogis.

The position of Gyümé abbot was held for three years, though the abbot was not really even part of Gyümé anymore, since he was no longer bound by the strict code of the tantric college. He could ride in the Dalai Lama's procession on important ceremonial occasions and participate in other high official capacities. He was no longer involved in the day-to-day activities of the tantric college. After this three-year tenure, the abbot of Gyümé then attained the position known as Dharma Master of Jangtsé, or Jangtsé Chöjé. The abbot of Gyütö attained the title of Dharma Master of Shartsé, or Shartsé Chöjé. Although Jangtsé and Shartsé are also the names of the two colleges of Ganden Monastery, these two positions do not have anything to do with the running of these colleges. The Jangtsé Chöjé lived and taught at Jangtsé College and the

Shartsé Chöjé lived and taught at Shartsé College, but these positions went beyond any involvement in educational or administrative matters. The Jangtsé Chöjé and Shartsé Chöjé ascended by turn to the Throne of Ganden, which they held for seven years each.

Like the Jangtsé Chöjé, the Throne Holder of Ganden didn't have anything to do with the government's ceremonial events or any other mundane duties. He was beyond all this. The Ganden Throne Holder was the direct successor of Tsongkhapa, and he was regarded as almost as high as the Dalai Lama himself. I remember once when I was young and had first come to Lhasa, I attended some major government event. At that time the Dalai Lama was still very young, so the regent was still ruling. The regent and the Ganden Throne Holder were both there in the room on their thrones, and the two thrones were the same height, which indicated that they were of equal standing. This demonstrates how greatly respected the Ganden Throne Holder is by Tibetans.

The small geshés did not have these opportunities in the tantric colleges. At best, they could be disciplinarian for four or six months at the tantric college. Otherwise they were just tantric lamas. Still, they would have a thorough knowledge of sūtra and tantra, and they could be abbot at some other monastery or be a great lama. After all, all the Geluk monasteries in Tibet, especially those with an academic curriculum, wanted an abbot or teacher who had been educated at one of the Three Seats.

40. The Reting Affair and Other Troubles

THERE WERE TWO times when my life was disrupted and it became impossible to focus on study and practice. One was when the Chinese cracked down in 1959. The other was in the time before the Chinese came, during a period in the mid- to late-1940s when tension grew and then erupted between Sera Monastery and the central government of Tibet. These problems were connected to conflicts between two regents, Reting Rinpoché and Takdrak Rinpoché.

Reting Rinpoché was said to have done many miraculous things even before he was discovered to be a tulku. Before he was born, the Nechung Oracle predicted that Reting Rinpoché would be born near an elephant-shaped cliff. He was born in the southern part of Tibet into the poorest class. One story was that when Reting was very young, his parents had put a clay pot on the stove to make some simple soup. His mother went somewhere nearby to beg for something to eat, so Reting was alone at home. Eventually the clay pot started to boil over, and the boy didn't know what to do. He had a type of shoe that was fastened to his foot with a piece of cord. So he took this cord, cinched the clay as easily as if it were leather, and tied the mouth of the pot closed. This was a very widely known story. Later, the Thirteenth Dalai Lama took this pot to the Potala, where it was regarded as one of the treasures of the Potala.

Another story was about a large upright stone that was near Reting's house. Reting was seen pushing sticks right into the solid rock as if it were mud. Someone asked him what he was doing, and he said, "This is for them to tie up their horses when they come." It so happened that the party sent to recognize him as the next incarnation of Reting Rinpoché was coming that very day. He knew before they arrived that they were coming. This stone could be seen even after the Chinese had taken over. One time when I went to the south on a pilgrimage, I saw this stone myself. There were no sticks left when I saw it, but there were still holes in it from where they had been stuck in. The sticks were gone because people who had come to see the rock had taken them as blessed objects. The stone was covered with offerings of butter and khataks, but someone showed the holes to me. A short distance from this there were a small child's footprints in solid stone. It was said that Reting Rinpoché made these footprints in solid stone as if it were only mud. From these stories one can see why we thought that Reting Rinpoché was not an ordinary being. I actually saw the elephant-shaped cliff, the footprints in stone, and the holes left from the sticks Reting Rinpoché pushed into stone when I went to southern Tibet.

Reting Rinpoché was selected as regent after the death of the Thirteenth Dalai Lama. By that time Reting Rinpoché was a student at Sera Jé, so during those years Sera Jé became very influential. Reting Rinpoché was quite young at the time that he became regent, yet he was the one who oversaw the search for and discovery of the new incarnation of the Dalai Lama. Later, when the Dalai Lama needed a tutor to help him learn the prayers and rituals that start one's education, Reting selected Takdrak Rinpoché, an older man and a great scholar from Drepung Gomang. Takdrak Rinpoché and another great scholar named Geshé Sherap Gyatso had been chosen by the Thirteenth Dalai Lama to revise and correct the numerous mistakes in the printing blocks of the Lhasa Old Shöl edition of the Kangyur. That was a big responsibility, and the people entrusted with this task had to be great scholars. Much later, Geshé Sherap Gyatso went over to the Chinese side and was put in charge of Amdo under the Chinese. In any case, Takdrak Rinpoché was a great scholar, and Reting Rinpoché had some connection to him through empowerments and teachings received from him. Takdrak was like a guru to Reting.

After several years as regent, Reting Rinpoché wanted to resign temporarily, so he offered the regency to Takdrak. By this time Takdrak was very old, but Reting Rinpoché wanted someone accomplished and skilled to fill in for him. This was in 1941. Reting was supposed to return as regent after three years and serve until the time that His Holiness was old enough to rule. There has been some disagreement about what exactly took place during this transfer of power, but this is how we heard it at Sera. It's hearsay, I know, but I believe it was true. Takdrak was very old, so it made sense that he would only have to be regent for a short time.

Takdrak was from a small hermitage far down in the south. During the time when he was regent, Takdrak's home hermitage was repaired and expanded. This was done with government help because Takdrak was like the king. They improved his residence for when he visited, and the monastery itself was also expanded and improved. This all happened within three years' time. During this time Takdrak Rinpoché's labrang manager (*chanzö*) was very powerful in the government. Other new people were also appointed to high positions and became very powerful. Just like here in the U.S. when a new president appoints new people to the government, when some of Reting's appointees left, they were replaced by Takdrak Rinpoché's appointees. Some of these new government officials began criticizing Reting and his administration, saying that they were corrupt and immoral. In 1944 Reting came back and tried to resume his position as regent, but the government didn't allow it. Reting returned to his monastery, disappointed. This was one of the main causes of Sera Jé's dissatisfaction with the central government in Lhasa, and it began a period of increasing conflict between Sera Jé and the government.

Another problem arose that contributed to this uneasiness. As I've explained, monasteries owned parcels of land where laypeople lived and worked. The laypeople received a portion of the grain that they harvested, while the rest belonged to the monastery. This kind of estate, both the land and the place where the workers stayed, was called a *shika*. A shika had a strong connection to its parent monastery. Sera Jé owned a shika in Phenpo. Nearby there was another shika that was owned by a high government official who belonged to a part of the government called the Yiktsang.[48] This man was a very high monk official and was also from the Gomang College of Drepung, the same as Takdrak Rinpoché. Shortly after Reting was turned down from resuming his position as regent, some kind of conflict occurred between these two shikas. I'm not sure what it was about, but there was a fight, and someone from the monk official's shika was killed.

The death was blamed on the people from the Sera Jé shika, and further accusations were made about Jé College. There was already some rivalry between Takdrak's people and Reting's people, and this incident made it worse. Eventually the government got involved, and it chose to punish Sera Jé. The government arrested and imprisoned the people from Sera Jé's shika who were accused of the killing. I don't really know all the details, but in any event there were quite a few people associated with our college who were imprisoned, including the monk administrator of the shika. The government also accused the college itself of wrongdoing.

As the Mönlam festival approached in 1945, Sera Jé made what I think was a bad decision. The abbot at that time was Geshé Ngawang Gyatso, who was from Trehor Khamtsen and was a very great man. I heard that Geshé Ngawang Gyatso, or Geshé Ngagya-la, as we called him, was a classmate of Reting Rinpoché when the latter was at Sera Jé. Reting Rinpoché was the one who had appointed Geshé Ngagya-la as abbot. The abbot was always appointed by the Dalai Lama or by the regent in his place. Geshé Ngagya-la was a very proud and principled man. He told the government that while they could bring those who were guilty to trial, at least some of the people in prison were innocent, so they should be released. He said this several times. Finally, he said that if the government did not release these people, the monks of Sera Jé would not come to the Mönlam festival that year. This was an especially important Mönlam because it was to be the first one publically attended by the current Dalai Lama.

The Mönlam festival started and two or three days went by. The Sera Mé monks went, and most of the tantric college went, but the monks of Sera Jé did not go. Jé was the biggest part of Sera, and we were told by the abbot not to go so we stayed, though with much apprehension. Finally, the government responded by releasing the prisoners. After that, we were told that we would be going to the Mönlam festival early the next day. We were told to line up in the morning and go peacefully into Lhasa. Nearly the whole length of the road from Sera to Lhasa would be filled with monks going to Mönlam. This was also the day that His Holiness's procession was going to the festival, so we were told not to make any trouble. This procession was a very big ceremonial event. It included His Holiness, of course, and all the great lamas and officials were elaborately dressed and rode on horseback. The abbots of Sera, Drepung, and Ganden also rode on horseback in the procession. The Mönlam festival continued without incident, and the Sera Jé abbot looked like he was the big winner in this conflict with the government. Shortly after that we went to the Tsokchö festival. At the same time, however, the government called in the soldiers from all over Tibet: from Tsang, from the south, and from everywhere else they were stationed. They were concerned about what the Sera Jé monks would do when they took their next steps against the monastery. They had decided to remove the abbot from office.

A few months later, in June, the abbot was supposed to go to a meeting at the Norbu Lingka with the other abbots and the government. The abbot, suspecting what was going to happen, said that he was sick and needed to take sick leave. He received permission from the government not to go to the meeting, but shortly thereafter, the government said that if the abbot could not come, then he would be relieved of his position. There is a special robe that is given by the government to the abbot, and the government said that if the abbot were not going to come to the meeting, then he should return this robe to them.

Remember, the abbot was appointed by, and was a friend of, Reting Rinpoché, and Reting was no longer in power. Takdrak Rinpoché was regent at this point, and he was from Drepung, so the abbot's, and Sera Jé's, standing with the government was not very good. His Holiness was still very young and didn't have anything to do with any of this. If the abbot did return the robe, then he would be just an ordinary person, and the government could arrest him at any time. It was more complicated with an abbot. This was a government position, and the government couldn't easily take any action against him while he was serving in this capacity. They were hesitant to go too far as long as this was still the case. There was also the possibility that the monks would fight the government.

The abbot was very clever in his response. He began to move his things from the labrang where he lived to one of the small dormitories of his regional house. He moved his things little by little at night. Then, before the government or even the monks of Sera Jé knew anything about it, he left the monastery and headed for Kham. He left in lay clothes by horse along with his manager. For three days, neither the monks nor the government even knew that he was gone. Then the government sent another order that he should report to the government, but when the messenger looked for the abbot to give him this order, it was discovered that he was already gone. The government sent soldiers after him. We heard that the army almost caught him, right at the border at Chamdo. Just as the troops were almost upon the abbot, he crossed over into China. Eventually he went completely over to the side of the Chinese because of this fight with the Tibetan government. There were some strange things happening back then.

With many more soldiers now in Lhasa, the government sent a letter to Sera Jé listing people who were supposed to report to Lhasa. The people on the list were all high officials of Sera Jé. The abbot and disciplinarian were not on the list, but other high officials, like the business officers and so on, were. Most of them were monastery administrators, but some were geshés. Throughout this period, there was a growing tension between Sera Jé and Sera Mé. We were all in the same monastery, so the Sera Mé monks knew what was going on in Sera Jé. It would have been difficult for the government to find out who was involved in this incident at the shika, where the man had been killed, by themselves, and we heard that Sera Mé was collaborating with the government and giving them information. Many in Sera Jé thought that Mé should be supporting Jé rather than siding with the central government.

After the government announced the list of the high monk officials of Sera Jé, these monks were ordered to come to a meeting with the government officials. The Sera Jé people eventually went, and as soon as they arrived in Lhasa, they were taken by the army and locked in prison. They never came back. When we heard that all of them had been captured, people were upset, but there wasn't much that we could do about it. The monks of Sera Jé talked heatedly about this among themselves. Some wanted to fight, others said we should not.

After all this happened, many Sera Jé officials, including geshés, were expelled from the monastery. They were beaten and either put in the custody of some noble family or exiled to a faraway location. Some were sent away for a few years, some were sent away forever. The government appointed a new abbot, Geshé Tendar, who was Mongolian and a very good scholar. Many Sera Jé monks did not like Geshé Tendar because of the way that he came to be abbot, and because he was a supporter of the regent Takdrak. Despite the bad feelings of many Sera Jé monks, nothing much happened for a while, but then, a year and a half later, things went from bad to worse.

Sera Jé had a large stockpile of old British guns. Künphel-la, a very powerful and influential government official, got these weapons from the British during the time of the Thirteenth Dalai Lama. The weapons were stored in a large building next to the Sera Jé assembly hall. After Künphel-la died, the weapons remained in the possession of Sera Jé. During the Tsokchö festival of 1947, Geshé Tendar, the new abbot, went to a meeting in Lhasa and was told that Sera Jé should not have this stockpile of weapons. After all, they said, Sera was a monastery not an army camp. The government said that they would take the guns and Sera Jé would be given a shika or something in compensation. The government's primary reason, of course, was to make sure that the Sera monks did not have access to weapons. It was well known that many of the monks of Sera Jé were upset, and it was feared that they might do something in retaliation against the government. The abbot, Tendar-la, agreed that this was sensible. When the Sera Jé monks heard that the abbot had agreed to this, some of the dopdops got so angry that they wanted to kill the abbot.

On top of all this, these events were happening at the same time as the culmination of the conflict between Reting Rinpoché and the government. There were a lot of rumors being circulated about Reting Rinpoché. Letters accusing Reting of various misdeeds were being sent to Sera. These rumors suggested that Reting was conspiring with the Communist Chinese and other such things. The monks of Sera Jé thought that the government was the source of these rumors and that they were made up and false. There were some high lamas and officials acting as mediators between the government and Sera Jé, and these mediators advised that we should just remain peaceful. Many of the monks just wanted to fight. A letter from the government came saying that the monks should behave. Finally, the government decided that Reting should come to Lhasa and be tried by the government court. In 1947 they sent soldiers to capture Reting. He was arrested and brought to the Potala, where he was imprisoned. He was not allowed to see either Takdrak or the Dalai Lama. Of course this angered the Sera monks even more.

Sera thought that the government was going to kill Reting, which it seems turned out to be true. The abbot Tendar-la seemed to support the government arrest of Reting Rinpoché, which further angered the monks, and some of the monks had a meeting and decided to kill the abbot, who they called a dog. That night, they killed him. The abbot's manager tried to stop them, and he was killed as well. Of course this made the situation much worse. This was a terrible time for Sera Jé.

This caused everything to burst. The Sera Jé monks said that if the government were going to imprison lamas and put monks in jail, then they had nothing further to lose. Even if the government were to completely destroy Sera Jé, the monks would fight. A war started between

Sera Jé and the government. Sera Jé monks stationed themselves on the hill above Sera, and the army fired their guns at the monastery. The monks returned fire. We couldn't see anything for all the smoke and dust. Until the smoke cleared, we didn't know how much of the monastery was left. There were several battles over the course of about a week. We scholar monks could not study during this time. Everything came to a halt. Those of us who did not want to fight stayed in our rooms and hid, though we had to be careful to appear to support our monastery. If we went out, we had to carry a long knife or a little pistol to make it seem as if we wanted to fight, too. We couldn't say that we didn't want to fight—this would have caused trouble. It was safer just to stay in our rooms. I was in hiding through most of this.

In the end, of course, the government won and took over the monastery. Soldiers were all over the monastery with their guns. Tsangpa Khangtsen was at the edge of the monastery, and soldiers had rounded up monks there. Some of my students helped me by letting me stay with them in another dormitory. Both my teacher Gen Riksal and I were thinking that when this thing was finished and we had lost, the soldiers would come and we would be killed. We thought that death was imminent. We didn't know anything about war. We thought that when one side lost then everyone on the losing side would have to die, so we prepared to die. We had no idea about such things. Soon after Reting Rinpoché was captured, it was said that he was not well in prison. A few days after this war, we heard that Reting Rinpoché had died in prison. At the time, of course, I was angry that Takdrak Rinpoché, a great lama, could let these things happen. The letters from the government said that Reting Rinpoché was bad, but we thought that this was all false. But who knows?

For a while, the situation was very bleak. In a sense, this was all very bad for the Buddha's teachings and for Tibet—these events, but even more so later when the Chinese came. But looking back now, I see that the events of that time removed many obstacles, making it possible for Tibetan Buddhist teachings to endure and for the Dalai Lama to remain in the world. Now his teachings are spreading everywhere, to places where they never had before. Maybe this is a result of the obstacles being cleared away back then.

41. Being Named Tutor

BECAUSE OF the controversies and the many horrible things going on in Lhasa, my uncle urged me to come back to Tsang. He wanted me to come back for good and said that I should sell whatever few things I had and return to Ganden Chönkhor. He thought I should leave Lhasa not only because of the difficulties there but also because he was getting old and eventually would need my help. In the end I did go back to Ganden Chönkhor and stayed there for about a year. It was just about long enough that I should have been removed from the regional house and college rolls at Sera Jé, but Gen Thapkhé told the officials that my name should be left on the list as an auspicious sign that I may return. My teacher told me that he had requested this and said that for the time being I should do as my uncle said and stay.

While I was staying at Ganden Chönkhor my uncle remained healthy, and I received a number of letters from my students at Sera asking me to come back. These letters were helpful. They changed my uncle's mind about my returning to Sera. Seeing these letters, my uncle said that for the time being he was still healthy and didn't really need me there to take care of him. He said that if he became ill or too old to support himself, then he would send for me, but in the meantime, it was a waste to keep me there when there were students at Sera who needed me. He said that it was better for me to go back. It was his decision, and I followed his advice.

It was not long after I returned to Sera that I was chosen to be Khamlung Rinpoché's tutor. When that happened, I wrote to my uncle and told him that from then on the labrang would provide everything I needed so he wouldn't have to send me support anymore. This made him happy. It had always been in the back of my mind that if my uncle became too old or sick, I would have to go back to Ganden Chönkhor and take care of him to repay his great kindness to me. But once I was chosen as a tutor, my uncle told me that I no longer had to worry about that.

When young tulkus entered the monastery, they moved into the labrang, and a tutor needed to be selected for them. The tutor was selected by the labrang officials. They made this selection based on divination and consultation with others. In the case of Khamlung Tulku, Trijang Rinpoché was consulted. Trijang Rinpoché was one of His Holiness's two tutors and a very famous lama in Lhasa. It so happened that the previous incarnation of Khamlung Rinpoché was a relative of Trijang Rinpoché. Therefore, when the new Khamlung Tulku came to Sera and it came time to select a tutor, the officials of the labrang went straight to Trijang Rinpoché. There were a number of scholars under consideration, but Trijang Rinpoché chose me.

When the labrang asked me to be Khamlung Rinpoché's tutor, my first thought was, "I can't be a tulku's tutor!" At that time Trijang Rinpoché was a tsenshap, so I went to see him at the Norbu Lingkha. He gave me very good advice and some presents. Then I had to accept. I suppose it was my humility that made me hesitant before. I thought that I should just be teaching other regular people but not a tulku. I knew that I would have to move to the labrang, and I didn't know anything about how things worked there.

When I became Khamlung Rinpoché's tutor I was not yet geshé, though I was at the level of the Vinaya or Abhidharma class, so quite far along. This was just after the conflicts between the government and Reting Rinpoché. This was an inauspicious year for me. In the Tibetan calendar system there are cycles of twelve years, and certain years of a person's life are considered inauspicious. As I've mentioned, I was born in the pig year, just like His Holiness, so both of us have the same inauspicious years. His Holiness was thirteen at this time, so I must have been twenty-five.

Khamlung Rinpoché stayed at his own place in Phenpo until he came to Sera and I was selected as his tutor. I lived at Khamlung Labrang from that time on, up until we left Tibet. It was a very nice situation at the labrang because the living conditions were much better than the average monks' accommodations. The tutor lived upstairs with the Rinpoché. Being a tutor was a great honor and demanded great respect, but it also carried serious responsibilities and obligations.

I was the only teacher of Khamlung Rinpoché, and while I was teaching him I was teaching many other people as well, especially students from Tsangpa Khangtsen. From the student's perspective, it was important to get as many teachings as possible, so one would ask for several sessions. But most teachers were teaching several classes, and each class wanted teachings on their particular subject. This took away from the teachers' own studies. When I was in the lharam class, which was very demanding, I had to balance the requests of the students with my own needs. There were constant educational demands at this time, and I had to take care of the lama too. He was very young when I first became his tutor, so he couldn't understand anything too complicated. But I had to teach him the proper behavior for a monk and a lama, and I gave him Dharma teachings as well. It was also my job to do the scolding and deal with other parental responsibilities.

42. Finding Time for Practice

A LOT OF THE TIME that I spent at Sera was taken up by study and proceeding through the various classes that led to the geshé degree. As demanding as that was, however, it was not all that I was doing. Throughout the time that I was going to my classes I was also receiving more informal teachings on spiritual and ethical matters from my teachers. I often received teachings and spiritual advice from my teachers Gen Thapkhé Rinpoché, Ngawang Gendün, Gen Ngawang Riksal, and even Tri Rinpoché. It is important to stress that while philosophical learning was a major component of one's education, this was only one part of the discipline and training of spiritual life. We monks were not just trying to compete to gain a great education for its own sake, or for fame and privilege. We were also working on our spiritual development. After all, that is the true purpose and intention behind the monastic life.

In Nāgārjuna's text, *Letter to a Friend (Suhṛllekha)*, he discusses the eight goals of worldly life. He says that people strive: (1) to gain wealth and financial security; (2) to avoid poverty; (3) to have pleasant sensations; (4) to minimize or avoid physical pain; (5) to surround themselves with other people and situations in which they receive praise and positive words; (6) to keep away from those who do not speak well of them and avoid hearing any criticism; (7) to cultivate fame and a positive reputation so that even people far away hear of their good reputation; and (8) to avoid a bad reputation. These kinds of things are always in the minds of people whose goals are only concerned with this world and this life.

Spiritual life looks beyond these concerns. When a person sets his sights on spiritual improvement, these worldly goals are no longer the focus. A spiritual person does not concern himself with wealth, comfort, flattery, or fame, nor does he worry as much about avoiding their opposites. In some ways, having a spiritual goal makes the unpleasant side of these goals easier to endure. And to some degree, experiencing, for example, poverty and physical discomfort can actually be beneficial to spiritual progress. On the other hand, a person who is trying to live a spiritual life must be especially cautious not to be concerned with flattery and fame. Those can be real hazards for spiritual aspirants. As it says in some of the stages of the path literature, even if someone is living far out in the wilderness in a cave, he may still be thinking about his fame and repute in the town. Though it is a subtler obstacle, the spiritual person has to remain on guard to avoid this kind of thinking.

A spiritual person should be able to endure hardship because he sees the greater value of the spiritual goal. Even people in worldly life are able to do this kind of thing to some degree. For instance, if a person is seeking fame, she will be willing to work very hard and even do without some things in order to attain her goal. Similarly, someone might undergo some short-term suffering in order to gain better overall health. Even in the midst of suffering one can remain happy knowing that it is for some long-term purpose or goal. The spiritual person is able to live in poverty and discomfort because his purpose goes beyond these worldly concerns. This is what I mean when I say that even when we were living in conditions that most people would see as unbearable, we were not unhappy. Because of our higher purpose, we were actually joyful. Of course, I'm not saying that everyone in the monastery was like this. I'm not saying that there were no conflicts between people or that bad things didn't go on in the monastery. Of course these things happened. That is human nature. However, we tried to rise above such things because of our sense of the spiritual focus and purpose of our lives.

The theoretical framework of meditation was learned when one was studying the Perfection of Wisdom from the *Ornament of Clear Realization*. One learned actual methods for meditation from great lamas such as Trijang Rinpoché and Ling Rinpoché, who were His Holiness's two tutors, or from His Holiness himself, who would give teachings on the stages of the path or something similar, as well as empowerments. These teachings were given from time to time in Lhasa or in one of the monasteries. When one heard about this kind of thing one could go, but it was a personal matter. It was not part of the monastery's role at all. In some cases even if one wanted to attend something like this he had to get permission first. If it were in the middle of a semester, he may have had to miss an outside teaching. But if outside teachings or empowerments fit into one's schedule, it was good if one tried to attend them.

As I've mentioned, in each season there were two semesters: a short one and a long one. In the summer there was a long semester that lasted about a month and then another, shorter semester that lasted about fifteen days. The same was true for the fall, winter, and spring, and in between these semesters there were short breaks. It was possible to attend major teachings and empowerments in between semesters, and monks could even give up a semester if a teaching were important enough to them. It was also possible to do a retreat in between the academic semesters. These periods were perhaps one month at the longest, but more commonly one would do a retreat for only a week or two. In the big monasteries like Sera, one could do this without getting permission from the monastery, but at the smaller monasteries like Ganden Chönkhor, monks would have to get permission. Scholar monks often had to use these breaks to do text memorization retreats. Other times, one would use this time to do a retreat on a tantric practice like Vajrayoginī or on the stages of the path or something similar.

Other than in these periods, our daily life as a scholar monk at Sera during the semester didn't allow much time for anything other than our studies. There was a little time in the early morning and sometimes in the evening to use for the prayers, rituals, and other practices associated with spiritual development, but we always had to practice this kind of thing on our own time. Otherwise a monk spent all his time being a student.

43. Phabongkha Rinpoché and His Legacy

VERY SOON after I arrived at Sera, Phabongkha Rinpoché was teaching the *Great Exposition of the Stages of the Path* in the assembly hall of Sera Mé. In between the Dharma courtyard sessions I would go watch the teachings from the balcony. There were monks from Sera, Ganden, and Drepung, as well as nuns and even laypeople there. Anyone who wanted to could come to these teachings. At the end of the teachings Phabongkha Rinpoché gave the permission for the practice of White Mañjuśrī, a practice from the *kriyā* class of tantra.[49] Generally, *empowerment* refers to those high empowerments required for highest yoga tantra (*anuttarayogatantra*) practices, but a permission (*jenang*) gives you the authorization to do the *sādhana* of a particular practice.[50] In other words, a permission is a lower level empowerment. Once you've received a permission, you have to recite the mantras of those deities every day afterward.

White Mañjuśrī was a very important practice for scholar monks at Sera, Drepung, and Ganden. Students sought out this practice as a method for sharpening their minds, since reciting Mañjuśrī's mantra helps develop wisdom. I heard a story about a monk named Jamyang Karpo who was not very sharp when he began his studies. He did a retreat on White Mañjuśrī and became very intelligent. In fact, he wrote a commentary on Jé Rinpoché's *Essence of Good Explanation.*[51]

While Phabongkha Rinpoché was teaching at Sera, someone asked him to give the permission for this practice and he agreed. At that time I was new to Sera, but everyone said, "Oh! White Mañjuśrī! We have

 དང་དགའ་རྫུན་ཆོས་འགོར།

Shang Ganden Chönkhor prior to the Cultural Revolution.
Photo courtesy of the author.

Sera Monastery in 1936. Photo by Hugh Richardson.

*Geshé Lhündrup Thapkhé
when he was abbot of Sera Jé.*

Geshé Ngawang Gendün.

*Tri Rinpoché Lhündrup
Tsöndrü.*

*Geshé Sopa and the lamas in his care in India, before
departing for the U.S.: Geshé Sopa, Khamlung Tulku,
Sharpa Tulku, Lama Kunga, attendant.*

Photos courtesy of the author.

Tibetan refugees at the Indian border in 1959. Tsewang Choegyal Tethong (wearing a white hat) stands in the center of the photograph, holding young Gönsar Rinpoché's hand. Khamlung Tulku (holding a white hat) stands to the right. Geshé Thapkhé (carrying a pack) stands at the far left of the frame. Geshé Sopa can be seen in the background between T.C. Tethong and Gönsar Rinpoché.
Photo by Marilyn Silverstone.

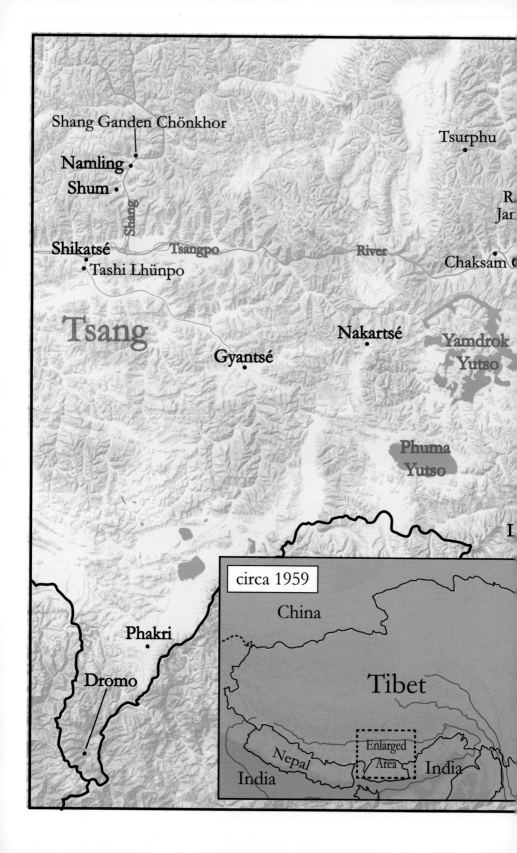

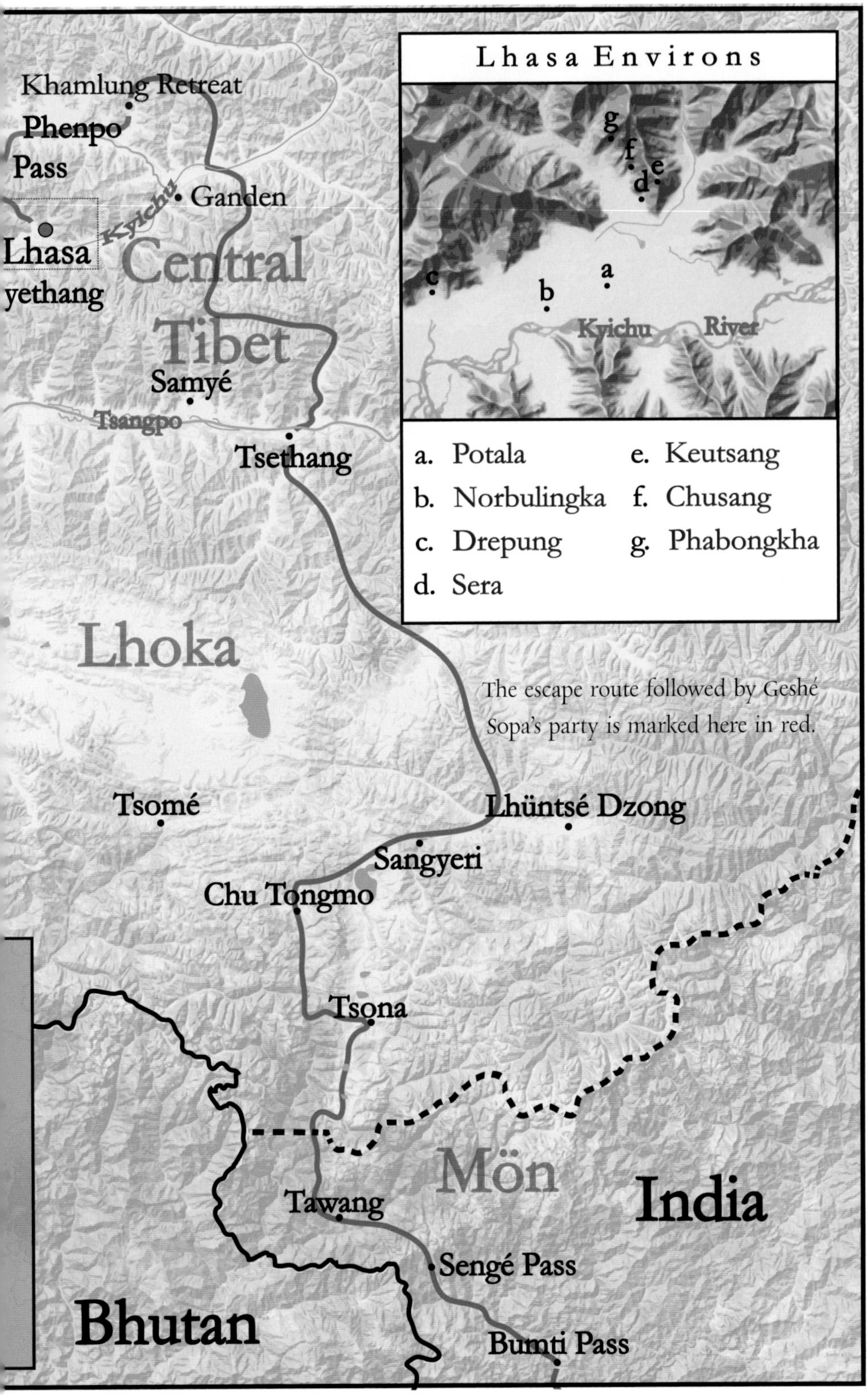

Lhasa Environs

a. Potala   e. Keutsang
b. Norbulingka   f. Chusang
c. Drepung   g. Phabongkha
d. Sera

The escape route followed by Geshé
Sopa's party is marked here in red.

Khamlung Retreat
Phenpo Pass
Lhasa
Ganden
Central Tibet
yethang
Kyichu
Samyé
Tsangpo
Tsethang

Kyichu River

Lhoka

Tsomé   Lhüntsé Dzong
Sangyeri
Chu Tongmo

Tsona

Mön   India

Tawang
Sengé Pass

Bhutan   Bumti Pass

Geshé Wangyal in New Jersey with Khamlung Tulku, Lama Kunga, Sharpa Tulku, and Geshé Sopa, 1963. Photo by Vytas Valaitis.

The recent arrivals with the Dalai Lama's brother Thubten Jigme Norbu, 1963. Photo by Vytas Valaitis.

*At the Lamaist Monastery in New Jersey: (left to right)
Lama Kunga, Geshé Sopa, Khamlung Tulku, and Sharpa Tulku.
Photo courtesy of the author.*

4 Tibetan Monks Fly Here to Study English

Four traditionally garbed Tibetan Buddhist monks arrived here yesterday to study English for two years at a monastery near Farmingdale, N. J.

They will return to India, where they have been living in exile from Chinese Communist occupation of their remote homeland since 1959.

Chosen for the study mission by the Dalai Lama, spiritual and temporal ruler of the ancient country, they traveled from New Delhi to New York by way of Paris on a Pan American jet airliner.

The monks, or lamas, were greeted at New York International Airport by Tubten Norbo, the Dalai Lama's elder brother, who has been here for several years.

The four—Tsangpa Lhundup Sopa, 37 years old; Thartse Kunga Gyurme, 25; Khamloong Tulku, 18, and Sermay Tenzin Tinlay, 14 — stepped from the plane clad in maroon shawls, saffron and gold shirts, dark brown skirts and Western shoes.

𝔈𝔥𝔢 𝔑𝔢𝔴 𝔜𝔬𝔯𝔨 𝔈𝔦𝔪𝔢𝔰
Published: May 3, 1962
Copyright © The New York Times

Jeffrey Hopkins teaching English to Lama Kunga, Khamlung Tulku, and Geshé Sopa, December 21, 1963. ©Bettmann/CORBIS

Geshé Sopa with Kenneth Morgan and his wife. Photo courtesy of the author.

Geshé Sopa with Richard Robinson and his wife.
Photo courtesy of the author.

Geshé Sopa and Elvin Jones. Photo courtesy of the author.

Geshé Sopa's first public teaching in Bucks County, Pennsylvania, 1968.
Photo courtesy of the author.

Professor Geshé Sopa's
first year on the
University of Wisconsin–
Madison campus, 1969.
Photo courtesy of the author.

Geshé Sopa with Lama Yeshe in Madison, 1975.
Behind them, Elvin Jones washes dishes.
Photo by George Propps

His Holiness the Dalai Lama and Geshé Sopa during the 1981 Kālacakra initiation
in Madison. Photo courtesy of the author.

A group photo following the Kālacakra empowerment, 1981. Photo courtesy of Kalleen Mortensen

Song Rinpoche, Lama Zopa Rinpoche, and Geshé Sopa at the cremation ceremony for Lama Yeshe at Vajrapani Institute in Boulder Creek, California, in 1984. Photo by Åge Delbanco.

Geshé Sopa meets with Khensur Lhündrup Thapkhé during his 1987 visit to Lhasa. Photo courtesy of the author.

Geshé Sopa greets His Holiness the Dalai Lama in Madison, Wisconsin, 1989.
Photo by Kalleen Mortensen.

End-of-semester photo of Geshé Sopa's last university class, 1996.
Photo courtesy of the author.

Geshé Sopa's retirement party, 1997: (front row, from left to right)
Dr. Morgan, Khamlung Tulku, Geshé Sopa, Geshé Thapkhé, attendant,
Sharpa Tulku, Yangsi Rinpoché, Jangtsé Chöjé Losang Tenzin.
Photo courtesy of the author.

Geshé Sopa, B. Alan Wallace, His Holiness the Dalai Lama, and Thupten Jinpa visit
Richard Davidson at the University of Wisconsin–Madison in 2007.
Photo by Jeff Miller / University of Wisconsin–Madison.

The new temple at Deer Park Buddhist Center in Oregon, Wisconsin, 2008.
Photo by Martín Chávez.

Geshé Sopa
teaching in 2009.
Photo by
Kalleen Mortensen.

to go!" so I went too. But even before the permission ceremony, I was going almost every day during my lunch break to listen to Phabongkha's teachings. Usually I went home for lunch, but during this period I skipped lunch and went to Sera Mé instead. I was completely amazed at Phabongkha. He would sit there on the teaching throne, short but fat. He had a very pleasant teaching style; he was always teaching with jokes. I very much wanted to get teachings from him, but I was still a new student, so I couldn't do the whole stages of the path course. But I was very happy to receive the permission to practice White Mañjuśrī. Much later, but still while I was in Tibet, I did a one-month retreat on White Mañjuśrī.

The White Mañjuśrī permission was the first real tantric initiation that I received. Strictly speaking I suppose that it was my second initiation, since I had gone to a Kālacakra empowerment when I was very young. But at that point I was just trying to grab whatever I could get. I didn't really even know what I was receiving. When I received the permission to do the White Mañjuśrī practice, I had a much better sense of the significance and purpose of what I was doing.

I'd like to take a little time to talk about Phabongkha Rinpoché and some of the controversy that has arisen lately about him and his teachings. During his lifetime Phabongkha traveled all over the country giving teachings. When he was young but already very well known and respected, Phabongkha Rinpoché traveled all over the country teaching. After the Sera Mé teachings, he was invited to some of the big monasteries in Kham. There were many places in Kham that they called monasteries, but the so-called monks there had long hair, drank alcohol, had wives, and were doing all kinds of questionable things in the name of tantra. Phabongkha went there and gave many teachings on the *Great Exposition of the Stages of the Path* and other such teachings. As a result, many of these monasteries turned into pure Geluk monasteries. Not everyone saw this as a good thing. Some people said that Phabongkha was poisoned on this trip but that he was able, through his spiritual power, not to succumb to the poison. It was said that this was what had led to his becoming very fat and dark skinned while in Kham, even though he had been thin when he arrived. When he went to Kham again later in his life, he never returned. He went back soon after his teachings at Sera Mé, and a little later we received the news that he had died.

Among the Nyingmapas, Kagyüpas, and so on, there were many who did not like Phabongkha and what he was doing. Phabongkha strongly discouraged any practices that were not based on a pure monastic foundation, so his teachings seemed critical of some of the other sects' practices. In any case, many monasteries became Geluk during this time, and even those that did not began to observe the monastic vows more purely. Unfortunately, this also began a time of increased antagonism between the Gelukpas and members of the other sects. Phabongkha was only concerned with teaching the Ganden system of Tsongkhapa, which is said to be pure like polished gold. Jé Tsongkhapa carefully examined and analyzed the Indian Buddhist teachings, refuting what needed to be refuted and establishing clearly what needed to be established.

This is similar to what Atiśa did at the beginning of the second propagation of Buddhism in Tibet. Atiśa stressed the importance of pure monastic discipline and ethical restraint, and he was opposed to wild things going on in the name of tantra. Tsongkhapa was also concerned with this pure observance of the Vinaya. Most of Jé Tsongkhapa's writings were on tantric subjects, but he emphasized the ethical and monastic foundations of these practices. Phabongkha was trying to reestablish these pure Tibetan Dharma teachings, which had deteriorated in many places, just like they had in ancient times after Langdarma. This kind of thing had to be refuted by the Kadam system a thousand years ago. By Phabongkha's time, the Geluk system, which is considered the descendant of the Kadam system, had degenerated in some places, so Phabongkha was trying to revive it.

Phabongkha's emphasis on the pure teachings of Tsongkhapa included practices connected to an exclusively Geluk Dharma protector, Dorjé Shukden. After seeing the degeneration of the monastic system in Kham, Phabongkha wrote some ritual texts to Shukden, including the life-entrusting (*sokté*) ritual, which includes a smoke offering and other things. The idea of these ritual texts of Shukden is to spread and strengthen the pure teachings and destroy wrong views and practices, so their language and imagery tends to seem rather sectarian and aggressive. This has caused a lot of bad feelings with the other schools. Of course, the real objects of refutation here are wrong views and the unethical behaviors that such views cause, not the other schools themselves, but that is probably not so easy to see from their perspective.

His Holiness has publicly stated that he is against the worship of Shukden. Beginning in the 1970s, His Holiness began to have misgivings about the worship of this protector. He did extensive research into the history of this protector and his worship and, based on what he learned, decided to discourage people from this practice. This was consistent with the position of the Thirteenth Dalai Lama as well. Since the loss of our nation, His Holiness has advised against anything that divides Tibetans, and that is his main point here. It is not necessarily a criticism of Phabongkha or of the teachings of Tsongkhapa; it is more a matter of creating harmony and mutual respect, bringing people together. His Holiness has spoken out against the worship of Shukden because it can be seen as the rejection of Tibetan Buddhist ideas and practices other than the Ganden system. In earlier times, there was rivalry between people from different parts of Tibet, such as those from Kham or central Tibet, and there was also rivalry between the different sects, such as between the Geluk and the Nyingma and Kagyü. But after the exile, His Holiness has had to bring the people of all these sects and regions together.

The problem is that many Gelukpas have this practice as part of their religious commitments. The worship of Shukden was widespread in the Lhasa area. Phabongkha was the most famous lama of his generation and his principal protector was Shukden, so if his disciples did any protector practice it was that of Shukden. Nearly all the monks at Sera Mé had Shukden as their protector. Phabongkha also had many disciples at Sera Jé and Drepung. Most of the high lamas from Drepung and Sera were disciples of Phabongkha. Shukden's ritual was not done in the assembly at Sera Jé, but many monks did it privately. Before the occupation, this was not necessarily a problem, but because of the divisive nature of the language of the practice, it has become more harmful. Thus, despite the fact that many Gelukpas have the propitiation of Dorjé Shukden as part of their practice, His Holiness has requested that people discontinue this practice. This has created controversy.[52]

These days, there is much violence being done in the name of religion. I believe that every religion has some unique good qualities to offer, but it seems that too often people use religion as the justification for harming others who don't think as they do. This is sad, and it should be resisted, no matter whether it's among Buddhists or between Christians, Muslims, Hindus, or whatever. Religion should never be used to harm people or justify discrimination and hatred toward others. For our part, we Tibetans need to be united and supportive of each other regardless of sectarian differences. These are not times for division. His Holiness's remarks about the worship of Shukden are based on his examination of historical sources and are motivated by this desire for unity and peace.

44. Teachings from Other Great Lamas

I RECEIVED MANY TEACHINGS, permissions, and so on, while living in Tibet, but I can't recall everything exactly, so I'm recounting here only the things that I remember for certain. I also received others later when we were in exile, but in this chapter I will give only those that happened in Tibet.

One thing I am absolutely sure about is that I received my bhikṣu vows from Phurbuchok Jampa Rinpoché. Monks from Sera and other places sought out Jampa Rinpoché for this because he was so famous and well respected. The Vinaya stipulates that one can't take the full monks' vows until the age of twenty, so I know that I was twenty years old when I took these vows.

TRI RINPOCHÉ LHÜNDRUP TSÖNDRÜ

I received many teachings on the stages of the path from Tri Rinpoché, both during the time he held the position of Ganden Throne Holder and after. During the time when he was Throne Holder, Tri Rinpoché was obligated to give teachings on the short stages of the path texts in the period between the Mönlam and Tsokchö festivals. In these periods, I received teachings on the *Easy Stages of the Path* written by Panchen Losang Chögyen and its commentary and the *Sacred Words of Mañjuśrī* written by the Fifth Dalai Lama. After Tri Rinpoché had become emeritus Throne Holder, a noble family requested a teaching from him, which he gave at a big temple in Lhasa called Meru. There were a lot of geshés and lamas at this event. I really enjoyed these teachings. Later another noble family requested a teaching on the complete *Guide to the Bodhisattva's Way of Life* by Śāntideva. All of these texts contained many wonderful things to practice.

TRIJANG RINPOCHÉ

Over his lifetime Trijang Rinpoché, the main disciple of Phabongkha Rinpoché, became a very famous and respected lama. After completing his geshé degree, Trijang Rinpoché began to teach many stages of the path texts, like Phabongkha had done. Later, he became a tsenshap, and then he was selected as junior tutor to His Holiness. Ling Rinpoché had been selected as tutor first. "Junior" refers only to the order in which Trijang Rinpoché became tutor; it doesn't imply any difference in status or importance. Indeed, Trijang Rinpoché was older than Ling Rinpoché, and he was also more well known. He was the son of a government official, and he was from a noble family. He was well connected with people in power, and he was a direct disciple of Phabongkha. He had received everything that Phabongkha had taught. I received the stages of the path text *Liberation in the Palm of Your Hand* from Trijang Rinpoché, which was a record of Phabongkha's teachings that Trijang Rinpoché had edited. He taught this at Sera Jé.

Later I received the empowerment of Vajrayoginī, along with the Cakrasaṃvara empowerment and the teachings on the practice. For the practices of highest yoga tantra, one has to receive the empowerment before one can receive the teachings; without the empowerment one is not allowed to hear the teachings. In this particular case one has to receive the Cakrasaṃvara empowerment in order to get the Vajrayoginī empowerment. After the empowerment one can get the teachings and all the details, which is what I did. Later, in Lhasa, I received the permission for the *Hundredfold Collection of Ratnasambhava* from Trijang Rinpoché. This is a collection of hundreds of mantras of Tārā and other deities. There are many such collections, and this is one of the most famous ones.

LING RINPOCHÉ

Ling Rinpoché was the more reserved of His Holiness's two tutors. He had more of a yogi's personality. Even when he had the position of tutor to His Holiness he was very humble. I received a number of teachings and empowerments from Ling Rinpoché while we were still in Tibet. Ling Rinpoché gave the combined empowerments of Guhyasamāja, Cakrasaṃvara, and Vajrabhairava, along with their commentaries.[53] The commentary was based on that of Geshé Sherap Gyatso, the great lama from Amdo. This particular empowerment and teaching took about a month. It was given in Lhasa just before I entered the lharam class. This was fortunate because once one enters the lharam class, he is not allowed to participate in any of these outside teachings. Instead he is restricted to intensive study of the curriculum leading to the geshé degree.

This kind of empowerment has certain requirements that must be met before one is allowed to attend. One must have studied stages of the path and must have a great dedication to doing that practice. One cannot receive teachings or do the practice until after getting the empowerment. These high empowerments are restricted; they are not public. They can, however, be attended by monks, nuns, or laypeople. Some lay practitioners had a very good education and background. They had listened many times to stages of the path teachings and so on.

DRAKRI RINPOCHÉ

Drakri Rinpoché was a disciple of Phabongkha Rinpoché and a very famous lama from Sera Jé.[54] The name Drakri refers to his hermitage place of that name. From Drakri Rinpoché I again received the empowerment of Vajrabhairava. There are several forms of Vajrabhairava, and as I recall the one taught at this time was the solitary hero form. At that time I also received the empowerment of the severance (*chö*) practice.[55] Some Khampa lamas had requested this empowerment. At that time many people were doing this practice, so when I heard that Drakri Rinpoché was giving this empowerment, I wanted to go and see what this severance empowerment looked like. Unfortunately, I didn't really have time to study or practice it at that time, but at least I received the empowerment. I also received the permission to practice the long-life White Tārā practice, and the scriptural transmission (*lung*) of the collected works of Tsongkhapa and his two principal disciples, Khedrup and Gyaltsap. Such a scriptural transmission provides a connection with the reciting teacher and provides a link for the student all the way back to the author himself.

HIS HOLINESS THE DALAI LAMA

Though I received many more teachings and empowerments from His Holiness later in exile, in Tibet I received a teaching on Tsongkhapa's *Three Principal Aspects of the Path*, which were a preliminary to an empowerment of Kālacakra. When a lama gives a public empowerment like this, he has to teach some stages of the path first, so this is what His Holiness did. This was at the Norbu Lingkha Palace when His Holiness was nineteen or twenty years old. At that time he had both tutors so it must have been quite late in his time in Tibet. Shortly after this His Holiness went into exile.

45. Vajrayoginī Retreat at Phabongkha Labrang

D URING THE BREAKS between sessions at Sera Jé, scholar monks had more time to focus on their own practices and sometimes even go into a short retreat. Usually it was not suitable to do this in the monastery, so one would go to some retreat center nearby. Sometimes a monk would do this alone, but other times he would go together with someone he knew who was also doing the same practices. Performing the *tsok* worship was also done in this way.[56] This was all done on an individual basis; there were no organized groups or anything like that. If one knew a friend or classmate that would be doing tsok, then they could get together to do this, but most of the time one did this kind of thing alone. One also had to know the dates for these rituals, because they weren't publically announced or scheduled. Even if one did get together with others for a group tsok in the monastery, the group was not allowed to play the bell and drum in the ritual. The ritual had to be done quietly. If someone in the monastery were sick and one wanted to do a ritual, one had to go to the disciplinarian and get permission to use a gong, bell, or whatever was needed in the ritual. Otherwise this kind of thing was prohibited in the monastery. It seems like here in the West, everything is done right out in the open and people make as much noise as they can. But at Sera these tantric things were personal and secret.

I did one retreat on Vajrayoginī while I was still in Tibet, and I did it in Phabongkha Rinpoché's own room at Phabongkha Labrang. At that time Phabongkha had passed, but he had stayed there in the past. The place was in the charge of a man who was Phabongkha's former secretary.

He had given up being a monk and married, but he was put in charge of this place. He had a wife but no children, as I recall. I had known him from the time that I became Khamlung's tutor.

Earlier, one of my students and I had wanted to do a text-memorization retreat, so we rented a small house near Phabongkha Labrang at Chusang Hermitage for this purpose. There were many such places near Sera. They were usually small monasteries founded by some great lama where the lama's disciples gathered to be with their teacher. These places were usually a little bit removed from the city and other populated areas, located high up in the mountains. They often had vacant rooms that could be used by people who wanted to do a retreat. They typically did not require any rent, and even if they did, it was a very small amount, so monks had many places available to them for retreats. Tibetan people were very good about providing monks these opportunities. The exception to this was in the availability of rooms in Lhasa during the Mönlam Festival. Some people took advantage of monks then.

During our retreat at Chusang, we got up early in the morning and did our daily prayers and rituals. Then we spent all day memorizing texts. In the evening, after dark, we would recite what we had memorized. We had two rooms in this place. I stayed in one room and my student stayed in the other, and he did the cooking for us. Several days after we arrived, the caretaker of Phabongkha's hermitage came there and talked to us. Having been Phabongkha's secretary, he was well acquainted with and admired scholar monks. After that he came to visit several times; it seemed he liked us. He asked us what we were doing, where we were from, and all that kind of thing. Another time he came and brought us an offering of food. We, however, never went to his place. We would never have even thought to go there, though we were very nearby. This hermitage was not the kind of place regular people would just visit. In addition to the fact that it belonged to Phabongkha, this labrang was a very beautiful place. It had three stories, with a garden and trees and those kinds of things. In any case, I got to know this man on this first text-memorization retreat. Later he came to Khamlung Labrang at Sera and visited me there. By that time we were on friendly terms.

Some time later, I decided that I would do a Vajrayoginī retreat. I told this man what I wanted to do, and mentioned to him that I thought the place where I had been before was good, but in case it was not available, I asked if he knew any other places in that area. To my surprise, he told me that I could use one of the rooms in the labrang. Not only that, he said that he would arrange everything and be my assistant for the retreat. The Vajrayoginī ritual includes a lot of extensive torma offerings and other complicated rituals. I didn't know much about this sort of thing, but this man was an expert on such matters, having done this for Phabongkha many times. When I came for the retreat, he let me use Phabongkha's room on the top floor. He even gave me Phabongkha's own seat and table to use. The room and furniture were very nice, and the room had a good Vajrayoginī thangka and other religious items. I felt extremely fortunate to have this. He provided all the offering objects, as well as all the food for me and two of my students. I didn't have to spend a cent. Of course at that time Khamlung Labrang would have provided this for me, but I didn't need to ask for it. So every day I would sit there in Phabongkha Rinpoché's room. The retreat went very well. This man took care of all the offerings and even took the offerings out for the hungry ghosts in the evening.[57]

Sometimes in the afternoons when I was in between sessions he would come to talk to me. He didn't ask me the basic stages of the path questions; he was interested in more philosophical things. One day he came to me with a question about impermanence. He said, "How can it be said that everything is impermanent and momentary when these things here in this room seem to me to be constant?" The table in the room in the labrang was made of walnut wood. It was very shiny and of good quality. It surely seemed to be permanent and stable, not impermanent and fleeting. He said, "How can we say that this is momentary?" He knew that I was fairly well known as a person with expertise in philosophical matters. In a way he was playing with me, but he was also seriously interested in this question. So I asked him, "This table was once new. Is it new now?" He said, "No, it is some years old." So I said, "Well then, this table is getting older. How did it get older? When did it start to get older? Did it suddenly get older or did it gradually begin to get older? Last year's table is different than this year's table. Where is last year's table? Is it gone?" I said, "There was a time when this table was fresh and new. The first moment, this table was fresh and new. The next moment, was it exactly the same or had something changed? Did this table get older little by little, moment by moment, or did it all of a sudden get older at some certain point in time?" He thought for a minute and finally said, "Yeah, yeah, yeah," laughing. At that moment it seemed that he really had some feeling and grasp of impermanence.

The next day he told me that the previous night, he had meditated and felt a strange kind of feeling thinking about what I had said—a sensation of warmth in his body, which almost brought him to tears. He felt that he'd really attained some deeper understanding that he had not had before, no matter how much he had listened or heard. Apparently, this was just from our casual, almost joking conversation. He finally got it.

From that time on this man was very devoted to me. He served me very well for that retreat, and it was a really good experience for me. I guess this attendant of Phabongkha really did attain some kind of realization from our talk. That was a good feeling for me. I didn't talk about what had happened; only a couple of people knew about it. Shortly after this I entered the lharam class, so I didn't have an opportunity to do a retreat like this again for a very long time.

46. What I Gained and Lost in Becoming a Tutor

WHEN I MOVED to Khamlung Labrang and no longer had to worry about material concerns, when everything was provided for me and I had a comfortable life, the wonderful feeling of humility, simplicity, and spirituality changed. This wasn't necessarily bad, but there was definitely a difference. In some sense, the way I had lived earlier, in hardship and simplicity, was more satisfying. At that time I could utilize my difficulties as a way to develop merit and virtue through patience and renunciation. Some of this sense was lost when I became a tutor. I had good food and nice tea all the time, a nice bed with soft cushions, and all that kind of thing. My job was to train this young rinpoché, to teach my students who came to learn, and to go to lharam class and do all the things that led up to the geshé degree. Before, when I was younger, there were none of these things. I just lived this pure, simple life, and it felt worthwhile. All the hardships that I faced were combined with a virtuous attitude, and so life was not unhappy but joyful.

The Three Seats were famous throughout the nation, and Sera Jé was known everywhere—and I was right in the middle of it, studying with great teachers and living a wholly religious life. I didn't learn how to succeed in worldly affairs; that never even entered my mind. I was striving for a religiously successful life. Khamlung Labrang was not a big labrang, but when the time came for me to receive my geshé degree, I knew they would provide as much as they could. Several of my students were the sons of government officials from noble families, and some of them also offered to provide for my needs during the geshé ceremonies.

I had another student from Tsang who was from a very wealthy family, whose older brother was the merchant officer for Tashi Lhünpo Monastery in Shikatsé. This student also said that his family would provide everything for my geshé examination. By this point there wasn't much of anything for me to worry about financially; I was well set.

Other things changed as well. My life was no longer focused exclusively on studying. By this time I was teaching many people. I tried to emulate Gen Thapkhé's way of teaching and the way that he related to the students. Even though I was living at Khamlung Labrang, I would go to Tsangpa Khangtsen to see the students as Gen Thapkhé had done for us. Gen Thapkhé was a great role model. He didn't have to come to the regional house and sit and talk and give advice, but he did. As I began this new part of my life, I thought back to the visits we made to him at the labrang where he lived. The labrang was very wealthy. They had a huge building with many servants, and Gen Thapkhé lived way upstairs with the lama, in very nice, beautiful rooms. Sometimes when we went there for teaching we'd watch as the labrang offered Gen-la tea. That tea was of excellent quality, golden colored and made with very good butter. When he drank it he'd swish it around in his mouth and savor it. We would watch this and think how wonderful that must be. Of course, we didn't know what Gen-la himself thought about it. Anyway, he didn't have anything worldly to worry about. After years and years of hard work, these things were taken care of. Of course Gen Thapkhé's own teacher, Gen Losang Chönden, had a life like that at Drupkhang Labrang, but he fled it. I thought about these things as my own situation changed, when I became the one sitting there as a tutor to a lama. Then I was the one living in comfortable circumstances, drinking good tea.

I can't really say that I wished that I could go back to my simpler life, but I developed a greater respect for that time. I looked back on it joyously, rather than thinking that it was miserable and feeling thankful that it was past. It was an important part of my training. This change also gave me an even greater appreciation for the kindness of my uncle who had made it all possible.

47. The Dalai Lama Takes Power
and the First Exile

A S I'VE MENTIONED, Tibetans believe that there are certain years
in one's life when there is an increase in hindrances and obstacles.
During those years some bad things may happen, or the person may
get sick or even die. These bad years come in twelve-year cycles, so the
thirteenth year is one, and the twenty-fifth, the thirty-seventh, and so
on. The year of the problems at Sera was when I was twenty-five and His
Holiness was thirteen. Twelve years later, when I was thirty-seven and
his Holiness was twenty-five, the Chinese army completely overthrew
the Tibetan government and began the extermination of our culture.
That was 1959. That year was when both His Holiness and I fled to India
as refugees. This great tragedy had really started almost ten years before,
though few of us saw it coming.

His Holiness took leadership of Tibet in 1950, the same year Chinese
Communists first came into Kham and took the city of Chamdo. The
Khampas fought back, but they were greatly outnumbered and were
eventually defeated. After that, many Khampas fled and came to Lhasa.
Fighting was going on in the border areas like Kham and Amdo, and the
People's Liberation Army was making inroads into Tibet, but in Lhasa
things went on pretty much as usual. We monks were studying and
debating as if everything were normal. Ordinary people weren't worrying much. Even later, when Kham was basically lost and more and more
Khampas were coming to central Tibet with stories of the real methods
of this Chinese "liberation," Lhasan people didn't seem to have much
fear or worry. They thought, "Lhasa is safe, it is a sacred city. They will

never be able to come here." This was naïve, but at the time nobody realized the power of the Chinese Communists. The Khampas kept pouring
into central Tibet. They were collecting provisions, horses, and weapons
to fight the Chinese and trying to get young people to help in the fight.
These Khampas had experience with the Chinese, so they knew how
they really were. The Khampas had plans ready for when the Chinese
got to Lhasa, and they were ready to escape to India or someplace else.
For the rest of us, however, it wasn't until 1959 that we realized the real
nature of our "liberators" and the power that they had.

Those in the government knew better. Shortly after Chamdo was
taken by the Chinese, His Holiness left Lhasa and went south to Dromo,
close to the Indian border. He stayed in Dromo for almost a year, ready
to escape to India if necessary. He took with him some government officials and gold and other provisions. They had more time for these kinds
of preparations then than they would later when His Holiness finally
left Tibet for good in 1959. At this point the Chinese had not yet come
to central Tibet, but it was assumed that they were on their way, so His
Holiness left for Dromo.

The day that His Holiness left for Dromo was during the period
that all the scholar monks from Sera, Drepung, and Ganden were at
the intensive logic session at Jang. That was where we heard the news
that His Holiness was leaving. I remember that the weather that day
was very bad, very strange. It was windy and, ominously, there was a lot
of dust coming down, like a rain of ashes. The whole sky was filled with
dust and ash, and it looked dark and hazy. I had never seen weather like
that before.

We knew that His Holiness would be coming right past Jang as he
went south because the road from Lhasa passed by the foot of the mountain, so we watched for His Holiness's procession. Finally we saw some
horses and soldiers passing by, so many monks ran down to the road and
did prostrations, trying to stop His Holiness from leaving, pleading for
him not to go.

Everyone in the procession was wearing lay dress—silken robes,

Mongolian clothes, and that kind of thing. No one was wearing monks' robes. Some government officials who were dressed up in regal clothing approached the monks who were trying to stop His Holiness and told them that he was coming next. In fact, His Holiness had actually come first in the procession wearing a chuba, which is what just ordinary people wear. His Holiness and his tutors were riding on horseback, and they were all bundled up and covered because it was winter and very cold, so no one could tell that it was them. They had passed by before the monks could get down to the road to try to stop them. Soon more government officials passed by on the road, and finally everyone had come and gone, and there was no Dalai Lama. He was already long gone. The officials knew that they had to pass the winter session monks, and they knew that the monks would cause problems. And the monks did try to stop him, but failed.

The place where the monks had tried to stop His Holiness was Upper Jang, and after the procession had passed there, they had to go over a pass at Lower Jang. The procession stopped there for a while, and we heard that His Holiness got very upset about this trick and cried. He ordered government officials in Lhasa to go to Jang and make offerings to the winter-session monks. The officials came the next day and offered a big feast and gave each monk a large amount of silver coins—I think it was fifteen coins each, which was a lot of money. His Holiness sent a message that asked that we do certain prayers and rituals such as the praises to the Twenty-One Tārās and a long-life ceremony to protect him and help him return safely. This was supposed to keep us from trying to chase after the procession. We all accepted these offerings and tried to pray and do the rituals, but we were too upset. People were crying. We didn't know what to think. It seemed like our country had become empty. After all that, no one could really concentrate on his studies or debating. We could not read, we could not study, and the debating yard was nearly empty. Nobody went there. There were things that we were supposed to be doing, but no one felt right.

After His Holiness left for Dromo, the prime minister, Lukhangwa, was put in charge in Lhasa. He was a very old man then, but he was also very strong willed. When the Chinese came, they did not like him at all. He was very stubborn and unyielding in his dealings with them. Lukhangwa was the lay ruler and the main person in charge. The monk ruler, Losang Tashi, was a very good man as well, but that period was very sad. Everyone thought that His Holiness was not coming back. We monks also had different opinions about it, though I don't remember now what my feelings were at the time. We heard that while His Holiness was there at Dromo, he received a message from Jawaharlal Nehru, the prime minister of India, who said that His Holiness shouldn't come to India but should go back and talk with the Chinese. Nehru said, "If you leave, then your country is lost." Some people in the Tibetan government thought His Holiness should leave, others thought he should not. The government at Dromo was divided on this. Finally, however, they decided to go back to Lhasa.

48. Gen Lhündrup Thapkhé Is Appointed Abbot of Sera Jé

WHILE LUKHANGWA was prime minister, my teacher, Gen Lhündrup Thapkhé, was appointed as abbot of Sera Jé. My teacher was a great scholar and teacher, and instead of being Sera Jé abbot, he should have been progressing through the ranks of Gyümé Tantric College. He should have been the lama umzé, then abbot of Gyümé, then Ganden Jangtsé Rinpoché, all the way up to Ganden Throne Holder. Instead, Lukhangwa made him Sera Jé abbot. This position had a lot of political aspects and involved working closely with the government, but it was not much use in terms of becoming a religious leader.

Lukhangwa gave my teacher an excellent reason why he should accept this position. Lukhangwa told my teacher when he went to see him after his appointment that he realized that my teacher was on the path to Ganden Throne Holder, but that position, though greatly respectable, did not impact very many people. He said that if my teacher were to instead become Sera Jé abbot, he would benefit many more people. Lukhangwa said that up to that point, my teacher's life had been very valuable, and his taking on of the abbot position of Sera Jé would make it continue to be valuable. So with this advice and encouragement my teacher accepted the position.

Usually the abbot of Sera Jé or one of the other monasteries was a geshé but not necessarily one that was the type to be able to progress through the tantric college's ranks up to Ganden Throne Holder. There was a precedent though for my teacher's being made abbot. In the Thirteenth Dalai Lama's time, a monk who was abbot of Gyümé Tantric College had been appointed abbot of Sera Jé instead of progressing toward Ganden Throne Holder. Still, my other teacher, Geshé Ngawang Gendün, was a little bit upset about this, saying, "They've taken our teacher away. This is no good. It's as if they've made him a territorial governor, a job that is just hard work." The abbot had to go to meetings with the government about policies and that kind of thing, so Ngawang Gendün was upset that our teacher had been diverted from religious pursuits.

Gen Thapkhé told us later, however, that given the circumstances, with His Holiness gone and so forth, he was not upset. Also, this move was for Sera Jé. For some time, there had been problems between Sera Jé and the government over Reting Rinpoché and the murder of the Mongolian Sera Jé abbot. After that Takdrak Rinpoché had appointed a new abbot from a very wealthy Khampa family who was not very well educated and was clearly one of Takdrak's supporters. As a result of all these things, many Sera Jé monks had bad feelings toward the government. To be fair, though, the Khampa abbot had done good things too. He once said, "I am not a scholar and do not have the capacity to be one," so he invited Trijang Rinpoché to give a teaching at Sera Jé on Phabongkha's *Liberation in the Palm of Your Hand*. It was thought that this would help appease the Sera Jé monks and calm things down. This was very good. However, the appointment of Gen Thapkhé—a great scholar who was greatly respected by all the Sera Jé monks—restored the line of legitimate Sera Jé abbots. Lukhangwa was very smart in doing this. It really helped.

49. A Gradual Transformation

His Holiness returned to Lhasa in the fall of 1951. The Chinese had already come to Lhasa by that time, and more Chinese troops continued to arrive regularly. Lhasa cautiously welcomed them. The Chinese said that they had come with peaceful intentions. They said that they had come to "liberate" us and that there were two kinds of liberation: aggressive and peaceful. They said they wanted to help Tibetans, bringing material things, a new government, and so on. However, they also said that Buddhism in Tibet was archaic and oppressive. Still, for nine years the Chinese didn't make any drastic changes. The Tibetan government continued on, and His Holiness was still in charge, going about his business.

Up until that time, there were no roads to get from China to Tibet. There was no way for trucks or buses to get there, so the Chinese army first came by foot. On the way they handed out a lot of Chinese money to people. The money was a kind of silver coin called a *dayuan*. Poor people and beggars lined up to get this money. People were also hired to work to build the road between China and Tibet. They received something like a salary, though it was in Chinese money. The Chinese say that they helped Tibetans in this way, but of course they had other motives too. For a little while these poor people liked the Chinese, thinking that it was wonderful to have a job and money. I heard later that Mao Zedong's idea was that it would be easy to win over Tibetans with these coins and then later switch to paper money. There was no such thing in Tibet up to that time, just real silver money. It went on like this for a long time, and as the road was built, more and more trucks and buses full of Chinese troops came to central Tibet.

Near the larger cities, the Chinese requested land from the government to construct some buildings, or they requested existing government buildings, which they were given. Slowly, around the cities, especially Lhasa, the Chinese built big military camps. They also built structures near the big monasteries like Tashi Lhünpo. At that time we didn't know what these buildings were. Were they military buildings, buildings for ordinary people, or what? For nine years, little by little they kept building things, and more and more Chinese people came. Eventually they established a National Assembly that included Chinese representatives as well as Tibetans. Finally they said that we didn't need a Tibetan army anymore; the Chinese army was enough. So the Tibetan government slowly dissolved the Tibetan army, and the Chinese army replaced it. The government started to run more like the Chinese system, changing little by little. At some point they even wanted to put the Chinese flag in the Potala area, which people didn't like. Tibet came to be more and more under Chinese rule and the Chinese way of doing things. It continued this way right up until the time that His Holiness left.

Though the Chinese invaded Kham in 1950 and the Khampas had been fighting them ever since, most Khampas didn't flee to the Lhasa area until after the Khampa uprising in 1957. Everywhere they went the Khampa fighters forced people to join them and fight, and they gathered horses, guns, and whatever else was available. They never stayed long in one place. They would be one place one day, and the next they would be gone. This became important later when the Khampas took control of the south because this was the route that His Holiness took to escape. In 1959, the Khampas had temporarily driven the Chinese from that region. All of us who escaped did so through this Khampa-controlled area.

The Khampas also came to Tsang, especially around the Ganden Chönkhor area. They wanted to get the guns that were stored at Shang Ganden Chönkhor. In earlier times, the Dalai Lama and the Panchen

Lama had a bodyguard regiment: five hundred men in Lhasa to guard the Dalai Lama and five hundred near Tashi Lhünpo to guard the Panchen Lama. During the Thirteenth Dalai Lama's time, there were some problems between him and the Ninth Panchen Lama, and in the end the Panchen Lama left Tashi Lhünpo, and the Lhasa government took control of the area. To facilitate this there was a central governor's office near Tashi Lhünpo, and the Lhasa government controlled this area of Tsang from this office, maintaining the cache of guns that had been used for the bodyguard regiment. A few years later, when it was believed that the Panchen Lama would return to Tashi Lhünpo with Chinese troops, the Lhasa government had to get its guns out of there, so they were put in this storage area under Shang Ganden Chönkhor.[58] At that time, in the mid 1930s, Shang Ganden Chönkhor was not within Tashi Lhünpo's jurisdiction but was strictly allied with the Lhasa government. Most of the rest of Tsang, however, was under Tashi Lhünpo's governance.

The Khampas knew that there was this store of weapons at Shang Ganden Chönkhor, so one day they showed up there. This was in 1958. The monastery was up on the hillside, but down below by the river there was a garden area that also belonged to Ganden Chönkhor that was surrounded by a fence with a gate. The Khampas went there and summoned Ganden Chönkhor's officials: the abbot, disciplinarian, and so on. When the officials got there, they were taken prisoner, and then the Khampas went into the monastery and took all the weapons. After they took the weapons they left. I was at Sera when this happened, but I heard about it later. Ganden Chönkhor did not freely offer these weapons to the Khampas, so the monastery did not get in trouble with the government.

After that the Khampas went to another place in Tsang and engaged in a battle with the Chinese, killing many of them. They escaped into the north, then came back and fought in various places. They fought on the move like this, never staying in one place for very long. Eventually they ended up in the far south and established their headquarters there in the Tsethang area. Gaining control of the area and of the road that went from Lhasa to India, they drove the Chinese out of that area and made possible the Dalai Lama's escape. These people called themselves the Army Protecting the Teachings. Though they were warriors, they were fighting the Chinese in order to preserve the teachings of the Buddha in Tibet.

50. The Tenth Panchen Lama

IN THE THIRTEENTH Dalai Lama's time, the Lhasa government controlled both central Tibet and Tsang. As I mentioned, there had been some conflict between the Lhasa government and the one at Tashi Lhünpo in the mid 1930s, and the Ninth Panchen Lama had left Tashi Lhünpo, gone to Mongolia, and then to China. Later, he wanted to return. The Panchen Rinpoché's advisors sent a message from where they were in Amdo to the Lhasa government stating that they wanted to go to Tashi Lhünpo, bringing Chinese troops. The request was rejected. The Tibetan government said that if the Panchen Lama wanted to come with his own people that was fine, but he could not come with Chinese troops. He never was able to return, and he eventually died in exile in 1937.

To my knowledge, the Panchen Lama's labrang found the reincarnation according to the traditional methods. The Tenth Panchen Lama was born in Amdo, near where the Dalai Lama was born. Their ages were almost the same. The Tenth Panchen Lama didn't come to central Tibet until after the Chinese invaded. The Chinese tried to exploit the conflict between the Dalai Lama and the Panchen Lama and use the Tibetan people's respect for the Panchen Lama to their advantage. As a result, for a little while after the Chinese came the Panchen Lama was very powerful, though he was still very young at this time. Many Lhasan people did not like the fact that the Panchen labrang sided with the Chinese. I remember when the Panchen Lama first came to Lhasa with Chinese officials. This was in 1952. For a few days the Panchen Lama and his people were in the Dalai Lama's palace in Lhasa at the Jokhang guarded by Chinese soldiers. Despite the circumstances, many Lhasan people lined up to see him since he was still regarded as a great lama.

I went to see him since many monks from Sera, especially from Tsangpa Khangtsen, were going. In addition to the many Chinese bodyguards, there were Tashi Lhünpo's own bodyguards and other officials from the Tashi Lhünpo government there. The Panchen Lama sat on a high throne as any high lama would do. All the Chinese were wearing white facemasks that covered up their mouths and noses, and the Panchen Lama wore one too. The Dalai Lama never did such a thing. Some people spoke negatively of the Panchen Lama for this. I guess the Chinese thought that Tibetans were dirty and smelly. I remember that I myself didn't like that the Panchen Lama was wearing this mask. I didn't have any actual interaction with the Panchen Lama at this time. I was just an ordinary monk. The Panchen Lama stayed in Lhasa for almost a month altogether, and then he went on to Tashi Lhünpo. Tashi Lhünpo was very powerful for some time. The Chinese wanted to have a Tibetan leader who was on their side, and they played the old animosities between the Panchen and Dalai Lamas to their advantage.

Later the Chinese turned against him. In fact, he was kept under house arrest for years in Beijing during the 1960s, and he was not seen publicly in Tibet again until the end of the 1970s. After that, he regained some of his power, but he still refused to just go along completely with what the Chinese said. I met with him in the late 1980s when I visited Tibet. He died in 1989, and some people said that his death was not natural. People said that he was poisoned by the Chinese for his criticism of their administration. I don't know that it is true, but this is what I heard.

51. Debating the Dalai Lama

THOUGH HIS HOLINESS had already taken leadership of Tibet by the end of 1950, he didn't take his geshé examination until 1959. Shortly afterward, things got much worse, and His Holiness fled to India. Interestingly, everything came to a head right after His Holiness finished his education.

Most of us never saw His Holiness except during special times like at the Mönlam Festival, but during the time of his geshé examination, we got to see a bit more of him. Usually he was surrounded only by his tutors and the tsenshaps. His tutors taught him, and the tsenshaps debated with him. The tsenshaps trained him in philosophical methods. This name *tsenshap* has a special meaning in relation to His Holiness. For regular geshés, the ceremony where they receive their degrees is called the *geshé mingtak* or the *granting of the name*. The word *ming* is the non-honorific form of the word *name*. For His Holiness and other high lamas, the granting of the title uses the honorific form of *name*, which is *tsen*. One who serves (*shap*) in the granting of the title of geshé for His Holiness is thus called a *tsenshap*.

The Dalai Lama had to follow the same curriculum leading toward the geshé exam and master the same five subjects as all the other scholar monks. For regular monks, debating took place in the academic sessions at the monasteries as I've explained. But the Dalai Lama, who did not attend sessions at one of the monasteries, did his debating at the Norbu Lingkha in the summer and at the Potala in the winter. Rather than learning with his peers, his debate teachers and partners were the tsenshaps, so he learned from the very best scholars of the three great monasteries. He learned from different monastic textbooks depending on the monastic affiliation of the scholar he was studying. Because of this, the Dalai Lama received a broader education than the average scholar monk.

At the time of his geshé examination, the Dalai Lama had to go to each of the Three Seats: first Drepung, then Sera, and then Ganden. At each monastery, he defended his thesis against the abbots and other high scholars who asked him questions. He also had to get up and debate with these scholars. The final examination took place during the Mönlam Festival, when all the monks of the Three Seats came to Lhasa. Each of the Three Seats selected several scholars to ask His Holiness questions in this examination.

During the Mönlam Festival there were three wet assemblies and three dry assemblies each day. In the morning the Dalai Lama had to go to a place in Lhasa called Sungchöra. This is also where the Ganden Throne Holder gave teachings during Mönlam. This place had several levels. The Ganden Throne Holder and the abbots sat on the highest level, the geshés who were receiving their degree that year sat on the next level down, and the rest of the monks sat on the huge stone floor. During the morning dry assembly His Holiness had to defend his thesis there on the subject of logic, mostly on the works of Dharmakīrti. At noontime His Holiness had to answer questions on Perfection of Wisdom and Madhyamaka in the big outer courtyard of the Jokhang Temple, which is called the Khyamra. Finally he was examined on Vinaya and Abhidharma at the same place in the evening.

Every college at each of the Three Seats had to select scholars to examine His Holiness in the morning, noon, and evening sessions. The scholars asking the questions in the morning tended to be younger, though they were still advanced scholars. During the noon session they would be intermediate-level scholars, and in the evening session the interrogators would be the abbots and the old geshés and lamas. In the case of Sera Jé, the abbot selected the monks for this task, and I was chosen to be one of these examiners. Once we were selected, we had to prepare ourselves. We didn't know exactly what the subject would be until it was almost time, but we would know the general area based on which session we were doing. Since I was doing the questioning during the noontime session, I knew that the topic would either be Perfection of Wisdom or Madhyamaka. It wasn't necessarily the case that scholars in the Madhyamaka class, for example, would be assigned Madhyamaka subjects. It was simply a matter of the abbot selecting good scholars, regardless of their class. That was a truly wonderful experience for me. Being chosen was a great privilege, but it was also intimidating. I didn't want to look foolish in front of all those great scholars and, of course, in front of His Holiness himself.

On the day of the debate, all the great scholars from the Three Seats were there, as were government officials, the abbots of Sera, Drepung, and Ganden, the tsenshaps, and His Holiness's two tutors. And there I was, debating in front of all these people. I asked His Holiness questions, and he had to respond. It was not easy. There is some film footage of this session at the Khyamra. I can be seen debating His Holiness, though my face is not shown. The camera was behind me facing His Holiness, so you can only see me from the back. You can't tell that it is me, but I remember it, and I can recognize myself. It was just coincidence that I was the one who got filmed; not everybody who debated there was recorded.

I had to dress up for this event, so I had to borrow a good robe from one of my students because I didn't have anything all that nice. I didn't have to wear the silken kind of clothing that high officials and some lamas wore to debate His Holiness, but we ordinary monks had to at least wear good-quality, new robes. In our normal lives we wore pretty rotten clothing. That kind of thing was just not important. As the debate began we had to wear the outer robe a certain way then shift it to another way. Finally, we folded it down around the waist, and the actual debate started. That was the traditional, ceremonial way of doing it.

My debate topic was the Perfection of Wisdom literature, and I was assigned to ask His Holiness about the subject of the buddha nature. In Mahāyāna Buddhism, it is said that although everybody has the potential to become a buddha, that potential is usually sleeping. Through study and learning, this potential can be awakened, and this is called *awakening the lineage*. There are many sūtras on this subject, and it is discussed in Maitreya's *Uttaratantra* in many passages.[59] I recall that it was one of those passages that formed the basis of my question to His Holiness. His Holiness reminded me a couple years later that this was the question that I had put to him during his exam, and we joked about it a little bit. Then he said that since I had done this, I had to go to America to awaken the buddha lineage there.

52. The Tibetan Uprising of 1959

FOR ALMOST nine years things had been changing slowly in Tibet, but especially for those of us engaged in intense study, the change was so gradual that it was easy not to notice what was really happening in central Tibet. The Seventeen-Point Agreement had been signed in 1951, and on the surface it didn't look that bad. I think it was always the Chinese plan to bring changes bit by bit, in stages, and eventually completely do away with His Holiness's authority and the Tibetan way of doing things. We heard about the Seventeen-Point Agreement, but we didn't know much about the details. Most people didn't know what exactly was in this agreement, but they said that there were some things about it that would eventually cause a lot of trouble for Tibet. Of course, by the mid 1950s, we also knew what had happened in Kham and Amdo, where many people had been killed and the Dharma itself was under attack. Although so far Lhasa had been relatively peaceful, we assumed that the Chinese authorities would slowly change their methods and do the same things in central Tibet as well, though we didn't see it until it was too late. His Holiness's powers became fewer and fewer, and more and more power was held by these "People's Assemblies."

Our lives in the monastery did not change that much during these years, though there was a pervasive sense of uncertainty and fear. One of my classmates in the lharam class was the tutor to Phakpa Lha, who was a high lama and became very important in the later days of Tibet's history. Every day I sat next to Phakpa Lha's tutor, and he would tell me quietly that the Chinese were not to be trusted, that they had no intention of allowing Tibetan culture to remain as it was. He said that they would never allow Tibet to be independent. They would eventually just take over, and eventually we would be completely absorbed into China. When people talked about Tibet's autonomy within China, he never believed it. According to him, it was not possible for things to end that way. He knew these things because he was in a much better position than most of us to see the way that the Chinese did things. The manager of Phakpa Lha's labrang, the lama's older brother, was a government official under the Chinese who would eventually be killed by a mob of Tibetans during the uprising at the Norbu Lingkha.

In order to understand the uprising, we have to understand what led up to it. Several days prior to when everything erupted, Chinese officials had invited the Dalai Lama to a performance of a dance company at the Chinese army camp. The thing that set people off was that the Chinese officials said that His Holiness did not need to bring any Tibetan security personnel or bodyguards. I don't know if this is exactly what they said, but this is what we heard. Usually when the Dalai Lama went somewhere, he went with his bodyguards and a number of Tibetan officials. But this time the Dalai Lama was told to come without them. The Chinese said that they would provide security.

By this time in 1959, the Dalai Lama's powers had been greatly reduced, and the Tibetan people were very upset about this. The Chinese hadn't thought this out very well because when the message came, it spread all over Lhasa. Everybody knew about it and thought that it was a trick. They thought that the Dalai Lama was going to be taken prisoner or harmed. On the day that the Dalai Lama was supposed to go to the performance, March 10, 1959, thousands of Lhasan people went to the Norbu Lingkha and blocked his way, pleading for him not to go. They had the palace completely surrounded, and only Tibetan government officials were allowed in or out by the crowd.

The crowds were extremely angry, not only at the Chinese, but also at Tibetans who were cooperating with the Chinese. At some point that day Phakpa Lha's labrang manager, the Tibetan official working for the

Chinese government, arrived at the Norbu Lingkha. I heard that he came riding a motorcycle, wearing a Chinese uniform, a helmet, dark glasses, and a white mask covering his mouth like the Chinese often wore. Someone got angry and threw a stone at him. He was knocked down and more stones were thrown, and eventually the mob killed him. The crowd outside the Norbu Lingkha didn't want messages from the Chinese going to the Dalai Lama, and they thought that this man was the one delivering these messages. I heard that after he was dead, the crowd dragged his body around with a rope, shouting slogans. They dragged him all the way to Shöl, in front of the Potala. From this point on, people got more and more agitated. They were shouting that Tibet was a free country and that the Chinese should leave. This was the beginning of the Tibetan uprising.

As I said, I was close to the tutor of this labrang, and we knew that something was going to happen this day. At Sera, once we heard about the labrang manager, we wondered, "Now what is going to happen? What can we do?" We were very fearful that the Chinese would do something, but we had no idea what that might be. Usually lamas lived at their labrangs, but Phakpa Lha was such a high official that he actually lived in quarters within the Sera assembly hall with his tutor and other people who worked for him. Within a day of this event, Phakpa Lha left Sera and sought protection in the Chinese camp. Then the people associated with Phakpa Lha's labrang all left and did the same. Other Tibetan officials who had been cooperating with the Chinese also took refuge with them at this time.

Now there were two sides among the Tibetans. Those Tibetans who had been working with the Chinese were in danger, so they had to go to the Chinese for protection. On the day that the labrang manager was killed, I was visited by the servant of Phakpa Lha's tutor. He came with a khatak, some silver Tibetan coins, and a message from my friend saying that he had to leave Sera and go to Lhasa. He had to go with the lama; it was his duty. The message asked me to pray for him. That was a very upsetting situation. All over Sera things were a mess. Nobody was studying. Everyone was talking about what was happening. We wondered where His Holiness was and what was going to happen next.

For almost a week, a huge crowd stayed outside the Norbu Lingkha day and night in order to protect His Holiness. The uprising also spread into Lhasa itself. Tibetan soldiers were circling around, and people were practically living out on the streets, calling for the Chinese to leave. Things just kept getting worse, but the Chinese did not strike at the people yet.

After a few days, the Chinese army fired several shells at the Norbu Lingkha. On March 17th, His Holiness, his tutors, his family, and some Tibetan government officials quietly left the Norbu Lingkha at night. The south gate of the Norbu Lingkha was right by the Lhasa River. I heard that His Holiness and the others with him dressed up like Tibetan soldiers, carrying guns and so on. They went to the south gate at night, acting like they were on lookout patrol, and nobody noticed them. That was how they escaped. For days everybody, including the Chinese, thought that His Holiness was still in the Norbu Lingkha, but he was gone. I got a message with the news a few days later, and soon thereafter all of Sera discovered that His Holiness was gone. He was probably already in the south somewhere, having traveled day and night on horseback.

By this point negotiations were already going on between the Tibetans and the Chinese. The Chinese were saying that the people should disperse, but the Tibetans were saying that the Chinese should leave. The Chinese said that if the Tibetans did not disperse and go home, they would start shooting and shelling. They sent up flares that lit up everything at night. One could see this even from Sera. For a couple of minutes at a time, everything could be seen, so the Chinese could find where the Tibetans were gathering. The Tibetans were trying to get weapons together, and the Chinese were also preparing to fight, even though they said they were negotiating.

On the twenty-fifth day of the Tibetan month, we performed a tsok ritual at the labrang. After the ritual we stayed up for a while talking, so we got to bed very late. Early the next morning, at maybe 2:30, these huge Chinese guns starting firing. They were shelling the Norbu Lingkha, thinking His Holiness was still there. We could hear machine guns and see the flash of the huge guns going off, but we didn't know who was shooting what. The Chinese were very skillfully keeping under cover. It seemed like no matter how much the Tibetans would shoot, it was as though there were no object there. The Chinese were firing at the Potala and the Norbu Lingkha and at every place where Tibetans were gathered. We could see all this from Sera. This went on from 2:30 a.m. until light. We waited and waited for the morning. It was a very long wait. We thought that after it all ended and we saw the results, everything would be gone. We had seen and heard these big guns being fired at the Potala all night, so we thought that there couldn't possibly be anything left.

Finally at sunrise we could see the Potala from the back, and it looked like there was no damage. The golden roof was still there, and the red palace and everything was the same. We were so happy and surprised. Then the Chinese tried to play a trick on us. All the firing stopped around daybreak, and then nothing happened until maybe 8:00 a.m., when someone came to Sera and said that the Tibetan army had won and that we should just stay there peacefully because there was nothing to worry about anymore. It was delivered by a Tibetan messenger, but it was a trick. The message had actually been sent by the Chinese because they didn't want the monks to come to Lhasa. If the monks from Drepung, Sera, and Ganden were to come to Lhasa, the Chinese would have had big problems. So the message said, "Please just stay there peacefully; everything is fine now." This worked for a little while. Everyone was relieved and thought that this was wonderful. For a little while longer nothing happened at Sera.

The shelling started again around 8:30 a.m. They were shelling the Potala and other places in Lhasa. Chinese and Tibetan forces were shooting back and forth, so there was constant noise. By this time, some Sera monks had gone down across the big open plain toward the Potala, approaching from the back. They knew that there was a stockpile of weapons there under the Potala. Many Sera monks were able to get these weapons, which they intended to use to fight the Chinese. But the Chinese found out about this by the time that the monks were on their way back to Sera. When the monks had almost reached the wide sandy area just outside of the monastery, the Chinese started shooting at them with machine guns.[60] The Chinese didn't fire on Sera itself, just the monks who were coming back with the weapons. By this time we had already left. When the firing had started again, we decided that we had no choice but to leave Sera, at least until the worst was over.

53. Deciding to Leave Sera

KHAMLUNG RINPOCHÉ had a hermitage and a family home in Phenpo. Because Khamlung Rinpoché was a lama who had connections to the government, there were some horses at his home in Phenpo that were used for official business. The two best horses had been sent to Sera some time back by the people at the hermitage. At that time Khampas were going around taking good horses from people to use in the fight against the Chinese, so the horses were sent to us at Sera to keep them from being taken. We kept the horses at a stable near Khamlung Labrang in Bati Khangtsen. When the uprising occurred, we felt that there wasn't much choice so we decided to escape, temporarily, on these horses and go to Phenpo to Khamlung Rinpoché's place there.

There was a monk official in Bati Khangtsen who was a communist. He didn't like the Tibetan government because he was one of the officials who had been involved in the problems between Sera and the government. He had been sent away to jail but had since returned. He often spoke out against the Tibetan government. I had heard some of the things he said and didn't like him much. During the uprising, this man was sending pro-communist messages around the regional house. When we went to get the horses, he figured out that we were leaving and threatened me. He said that he knew we were leaving and said, "Are you taking Rinpoché to Phenpo? That is a bad idea. When you come back the monks will have had their revolution, and it will be very dangerous for anyone who has left. It's better for you to stay; it will be safer." I didn't believe the things he said, but I was still a little worried.

After this man left, we decided to do a divination to help decide whether or not we should leave. We needed to go to Tsangpa Khangtsen to do this. This was a little dangerous because Tsangpa Khangtsen was on the far west side of Sera, a long way from where we were at the time, and we did not want to call attention to ourselves after this man had made this threat. So Rinpoché and I cautiously went to Tsangpa Khangtsen to do the divination. Tsangpa Khangtsen relied on the Dharma protector Chamsing, who was one of the important Geluk Dharma protectors, along with Palden Lhamo and Hayagriva. We went to Chamsing's shrine to do a divination called a *senril*.

This divination is done by making two perfectly round balls of dough of equal weight. Inside each ball of dough, one puts a small strip of paper. On each strip, one writes one of the two things between which he has to decide. The balls of dough are then put in a large Chinese-style cup with long handles, and one does Chamsing's prayer and ritual before his shrine, making requests for guidance. The cup is then rolled slowly in one's hands until one of the two balls comes out of the cup. The answer in that ball is the outcome of the divination, and this is what one should do. Rinpoché and I made the dough balls, and on one of the pieces of paper we wrote "stay" and on the other "go." That was risky, wasn't it? Depending on our karma the result could have been "stay," and we would have stayed. My entire life would have been different! But we went before Chamsing, did the ritual, and the answer came out "go," which meant we would go to Phenpo.

We returned to the labrang and quickly made preparations. We didn't collect many provisions, just enough for that one night, because our intention was to go to Phenpo and stay away for just a little while until things settled down. Then we would come back. So we left most everything there, taking only a little food and clothing. I think we left the Chinese a fortune. This was a little dangerous because many monks in Sera would probably not have wanted us to go. By this time my teacher Gen Thapkhé was now emeritus abbot and was in retreat at Keutsang Hermitage behind Sera. He did not escape because he was in an inaccessible place, and there was no way to contact him, no way of letting him know what was going on. We weren't able to talk to him or get his permission or anything. We left while he was still up there. That was very difficult emotionally.

We took the horses to the west side of Sera near Tsangpa Khangtsen, where there was a place for horses and other animals to drink. We pretended that we were just taking these animals to drink. Then slowly, cautiously, we continued on, hoping not to attract attention. We headed toward Phenpo Pass, which would take all night to cross on horseback. We had gone a little farther to the west, to a high place that overlooked Sera and the valley, when the Chinese started firing on the monks who were returning to Sera from the Potala. We had just left when this happened, and we could see and hear it in the distance. For a little while we couldn't even see Sera Monastery because of all the dust and smoke from the Chinese machine guns.

54. The Beginning of the Exile

THAT EVENING we reached the bottom of the mountain pass. It was already dark. There was a little village at the foot of the mountain, and we stopped at a family house, made some tea, and had a brief rest. While we were there, a group of people came from a nearby hermitage, maybe Drakri Hermitage. It was Gönsar Rinpoché and Geshé Rabten, accompanied by Gönsar's mother and some attendants.[61] They said they had gotten a horse at a nearby retreat place that was connected to Gönsar Labrang. All they had was this horse and a very small amount of food, and they were dressed in just simple clothes. They weren't prepared for a journey any more than we were, but they were happy to see us. We told them that we were going to Khamlung Hermitage, and they suggested that we could go together across the pass. So we had tea and a little food and then set off.

We had two horses, so a couple of us rode but the rest had to go on foot. It took the whole night to go over the pass. The next day around noon we came down on the other side, where Khamlung Rinpoché's family home was. We went there and visited for a little while. There was storytelling, tea, and some food. While we were there we got word that there was some shooting going on at a nearby monastery, Phenpo Ganden Chönkhor.[62] We decided that it wasn't wise to stay there. We left and continued on to Khamlung Hermitage, where we stopped again. The hermitage was part way up a mountain, past the valley. We planned to stay there until things in Lhasa settled down—at least that's what we thought at the time.

We stayed at Khamlung Hermitage for four or five days, and it was actually very enjoyable, all things considered. Every day we had good food and nice rooms, and Geshé Rabten and Gönsar Rinpoché were also given nice rooms. While we were there, many monks and lay Tibetans who were fleeing Lhasa came through that area. It seemed that Lhasa must have been completely lost with so many people leaving. People were heading south to where the Khampas were camped. There was a crossing on the Tsangpo River where one could take a big boat to get across, and the Khampas controlled this crossing.

We stayed there at Khamlung Hermitage relaxing and enjoying ourselves until a friend of the Khamlung Labrang manager arrived. He said to the manager, "You are still here? I thought you would have gone by now. The situation is very bad. You should be preparing to leave. You should not stay here. It is urgent that you leave now. You see all those people coming from Lhasa? The city has been lost, and soon the Chinese will come here too. You must leave." Again we had one night to prepare to leave. This time we planned for a longer journey. We had horses and some mules. We all wore lay clothes, chubas with a heavy wool lining under an outer layer of cloth. We also dressed to appear more fearsome than we were. Some carried pistols, and everyone carried at least a long knife. This time we also brought a lot of food. We had tsampa, meat, and butter. Some of the servants of Khamlung Labrang came, and some laypeople came too. This made us a rather large group, fifteen or sixteen people, starting out. We thought that we might not be able to stay together if we encountered the Chinese, so we each carried enough provisions to keep ourselves from starving for a while in case we had to run on our own.

In order to go south we first had to go north and cross a mountain pass. When we stopped for the night, someone on horseback came from Khamlung Hermitage and said that now things had calmed down in Lhasa. He said that Sera Monastery was back in operation, the monks were doing prayers and rituals, and the Chinese were giving out money. In fact none of this was true—it was just more Chinese deception. They sent out these messages to keep people from leaving. We were several days away from Lhasa by that time. It is frightful to think about now, but we almost went back. We discussed it among ourselves, and Gönsar Rinpoché said that a little farther south there was an estate that belonged to his mother, who was some kind of government official. There was a big house there where we could stay. The Khamlung Labrang manager said, "Well, maybe it will be good to go back later, but for the time being let's continue on to this estate. We can visit the pilgrimage places in the south. We have gone this far, so let's continue." So that's what we did.

Every day, however, things seemed to get worse and worse. More and more people were coming out of Lhasa. Some were on horses and some walked. Many of them had guns or knives and everyone wore chubas, whether or not they were really laypeople. Monks did not want to be recognized as monks. We came to another mountain pass and then to the Tsangpo River, which is where the Khampa-held territory began. Since we had two lamas and two tutors in our group, the Khampas seemed to respect us, so they let us pass right through. They could have held us up for a long time, but they immediately let us go. They were giving other people trouble. They were taking horses and weapons and telling some of the young people, "You should stay with us." They said, "The Buddhist teachings are almost gone, so you should dedicate yourself to protecting them." It seemed that their intention was to protect the Dharma.

In any case, the Khampas let us pass through. We then came to a place called Döndrup, in the Tsethang region. This was a major center connected with the government where there used to be an ancient kingdom. There was another river there, and the Khampas controlled that crossing too. They were stopping everyone before allowing them to go on toward India. Here too they were forcing young men to join them to fight the Chinese, but they let our party through. From there we had to pass through a narrow area below a mountain in which there was a huge cave. A group of Chinese soldiers had been driven from this territory and had holed up in the cave. They were stuck there, trapped by the Khampa fighters, but they had machine guns, and sometimes they would shoot at people traveling by. For this reason, the Khampas said that this route was dangerous, but fortunately the day that we went through it was quiet. We passed without problems, and then we came to a town where there was an estate that belonged to a nobleman that our labrang manager knew. We stayed one night. There was also a Khampa camp there, where we had to check in. Here, we lost two of the young servants that were with us. The Khampas would not let them go on. They were forced to join the Khampa resistance.

55. A Brief Respite and the Long Journey out of Tibet

THE REST OF US continued on. We crossed another mountain pass and a long plain, and then came to another pass. When we came down the other side, we arrived at the estate of Gönsar's mother. It was a long way from the last place we had stopped. We were told that we could stay there as long as we wished. It was a very pleasant place, and we were quite comfortable, enjoying the stay. We had been there for a couple of days when again we suddenly received bad news. Farther down the valley was a place called Lhüntsé Dzong, which was a territorial government center where many Tibetan soldiers and Khampas had gathered. The governor of Lhüntsé Dzong was a friend of Gönsar's mother. He sent a message that said, "Don't stay there a moment longer. You should leave immediately and go to India. The Chinese will come either today or tomorrow, and once they've reached this territory, you may be stuck. You should leave right away." We had thought that this was going to be the place where we could stay until things calmed down. We had planned to stay there for a while, go to the pilgrimage places in the south, and then go back to Sera. But once again we had to quickly get our things together and flee. The labrang provided us with some food, clothes, money, and other things that they had prepared, and we left again.

This time we were headed to a place called Tsona, which was a broad valley. Beyond that, across another pass, was Mön, an area that spanned both sides of the border with India east of Bhutan. We stopped to have some tea late in the day before going over the pass to Tsona. While we were there we met some people who had come from Ganden, including an old lama named Dzamling Rinpoché. Later we would be roommates in India, but this was our first meeting. While we were sitting there having our tea, we saw some people coming over the pass on their way back from Tsona. They said that the Chinese were coming to Tsona either that very day or the next. The Chinese had already conquered Lhüntsé Dzong and other territorial centers in that area, and many Tibetan soldiers had been lost. Now the Chinese were ready to move on to Tsona. We were trapped. Now we were in a serious quandary. What should we do? We could either go back toward Lhasa with these people or go on to Tsona. We went to Dzamling Rinpoché to ask what his group was going to do, thinking that maybe we should follow them. The lama did a divination and said, "If we go today, there will be no problem, it will be all right. We are going." So our manager said, "Let's go with them," and we went along with them toward Tsona.

This route was the best way out of Tibet. We hadn't heard of any people dying on it, though some animals had fallen from cliffs along the way. There was another route on which many people had died. This other route was much longer and more difficult. If we hadn't taken that lama's advice and had gone back, we would have had to take this other route. It would have required going much farther east and then down to India. Part of the route led down to a huge river that had a long rope and wood bridge. The bridge was very narrow, and in parts it actually touched the water. The bridge was mostly just rope, and one had to have good balance to stay on it. Sometimes the water was so high that it rushed right through where one had to walk. This was where many people had died. The other route, the one that we were taking, was less dangerous, and it was the same one that the Dalai Lama had taken. Many people chose this route for this reason.

After finishing our tea we went across the mountain pass and traveled a long time across the plain of Tsona. Finally, we reached the foot of the next mountain pass, where there was a big empty house. The family had already left because they heard that the Chinese were coming. We knew this because the family had left a message saying so. The message also said that if anyone else came through, they should take whatever they could use. There was a lot of dried meat, tea, and butter in the house. This was a very good development, and it was very kind of these people. We made tea there and cooked dinner and ate. After dark, we left to go over the pass. We had a very nice time at that house, but we were there at just the right time. We heard later that the Chinese got there the next morning.

That night we climbed up into the mountains and had to spend the night there in a rocky place. It was very cold. The next day we went on. The entire crossing was covered in snow, and we traveled on the snow all day. There was no visible path, and it was very hard to tell which way to go. If we went one way, we would end up in Mön, which was in Indian territory; but if we missed that and went a different way, we would end up in Samyé, which was in Tibetan territory. Some people who crossed this mountain thought they were heading toward Mön but took the wrong path and ended up in Samyé and were caught by the Chinese. It was hard to tell which direction was which, and we really didn't know where we were going, but fortunately we went the right way.

Even though it made our travel difficult, the bad weather actually saved us from another danger. The Chinese came flying over us in an airplane, but the snow and wind were blowing so hard that it was difficult to see. We could hear the plane going over, then circling around and coming over us again. If the sky had been clear, we would have been easy to see against the snowy mountain, but luckily the Chinese could not see down to the ground. We heard them go over a few times, but finally they gave up and left. That was a perilous moment, but we didn't get caught.

We had a lot of difficulty that day. Khamlung Rinpoché, the manager, and I and a few other people were on horses. We had dark glasses that we brought from the labrang, so the glare from the snow was not too bad for us. But others were walking on the snow all day without protection. It was said that you had to shield your eyes somehow, or later when it got dark you would have snow blindness. We were fortunate to have dark glasses, but for the others it was difficult to find anything to cover their eyes. Some people took protection cords or strips of red cloth and partially covered their eyes. The people who had long hair untied it and used that to partially cover their eyes, which helped a lot. But this made walking on the snow even more difficult, so some of them gave up and pulled their hair back or took off the other things they were using to cover their eyes. This didn't cause them much trouble while it was light, but when night came and we got to a dry place to stop for the night, their trouble started. We couldn't get to a town or a safe stopping place, but we found a flat, dry rocky place to stop and have some tea and food. That night, these people's eyes started to swell. They became painful and watered constantly, and eventually swelled closed. The next day we had to wait almost the whole day for them to get better. Slowly they improved and could see a little bit, and we could go on. That was one of the worst times on the trip.

The next day we came down into the Mön region. First we came to a very deep, steep valley with a river rushing through way at the bottom. These valleys were very narrow and difficult to travel. There wasn't much of a path, and there were evergreens and other kinds of trees everywhere. We had horses and mules, which had to go very slowly. We went down, down, down, and finally came to a place where there were rhododendron trees with lush green leaves and beautiful flowers. The poor horses were so hungry that they started eating these leaves and flowers on the way, but they were poison. The horses' stomachs swelled up, and they began foaming at the mouth. They couldn't walk at all. There was a local Mön remedy for this. Normally one would give the horses tea leaves with honey, butter, and some other things, and it would help—but we didn't have all those things at the time. The horses couldn't go on and we couldn't stay there, so we had to leave the horses. We unloaded the sick animals and put the things that they were carrying on the horses and mules that weren't badly affected. Those loads got heavier and heavier. Then we went on. That was very upsetting. The suffering of these animals was terrible.

At some places there were portions of the trail that were very narrow, with one side right up against the cliff face and a sharp drop-off on the other side. In some places the path was too narrow for it to be passable, so there would be a kind of small wooden bridge. The horses and mules were heavily loaded so it was very difficult for them to walk across. One mule was carrying a silver pot and some other valuable things that we had brought with us that stuck out from the side of the mule's pack. As the mule went across the bridge these things rubbed the rock wall and tipped the poor mule off the path, and it fell way down below. After that, we unloaded the animals whenever we came to such a narrow passage. We led the animals across and then brought the things over from the other side of the bridge. We had to do this many times. We would go down, down, down and come to a river. We'd cross this and then go back up the other side, where there would be more of these little bridges that we had to walk on when the path was too narrow. At some places, after crossing the river, we would have to climb up a little. There wasn't any good path there, but the Mönpas had made a kind of ladder by carving notches into a log. How were we supposed to take the horses up these ladders? Some of the animals couldn't climb up alone, so people would try to lead them. Two people would go up to the higher place and pull the animal, and several others would push the animal from behind. In this way some of them made it up these makeshift stairs. Others just could not do it, and we had to leave them behind.

Later on we saw some of these horses, including some of the ones that had been poisoned, in the possession of some Khampa soldiers in Mön. Perhaps the Khampas had treated the horses, or maybe they had just recovered. Either way, we recognized some of our animals, but there wasn't anything to do about it at that point. We couldn't ask for them back. At least the animals hadn't died.

Finally, we came to a place called Chu Drangmo, where there was another broad valley. There was a river on one side and a meadow with tall mountains on the other side. This meadow was a wider space than we had seen in a while, so we stayed there for about five days. A lot of people had come there from many different places in Tibet. One could camp there and cook and wash, since there was water. This was very close to India. A few miles farther down was a bridge. One side of this bridge was Tibetan territory, and the other side was India. We were still on the Tibetan side so we had to worry a little bit about the Chinese. If they sent planes over they could have dropped soldiers there and caught us, but otherwise they would have had to go through all the mountains like we had. We were more relaxed by now, but we were still not totally at ease.

Many new people continued to arrive at this place all the time. Then a message came that everyone had to go to a place in the Indian Mön territory called Tawang, which was a couple of days away. Before we left Chu Drangmo, everyone's name was put on a list, and they put us into groups of one hundred. This was being organized by some of the Tibetans. We went on to Tawang in these groups, first one group of one hundred, then another, and so on. Many of the people there were from Lhasa, Sera, and Drepung, so they were educated and realized that we had to be organized. I remember that one of the people who took charge of this was a young Drepung lama who was very competent and able and had good handwriting. It turned out that this young man was Samdhong Rinpoché, who would later be the prime minister of the Tibetan government in exile. He was originally from Kham and had studied at Drepung. He was maybe in his twenties at this time, but he was already very mature and a good leader.

Our group, with the two lamas and us geshés, was considered special, so we were put in the first group of one hundred that was sent to Tawang. Each of the groups chose someone as the leader to take charge of the group. He was responsible for handling the messages and overseeing the group. All this was a matter of the Tibetans organizing themselves. Later, when we got to Tawang, the Indian government was organizing along with the Tibetans, so this was just in preparation for getting to the Indian side. We knew that they would welcome us and help us get settled, so we wanted to be organized to make it easier.

One night before we went to Tawang, there was a rumor going

around that India was going to close the bridge at the border. We heard that we might have to go back to Tibet, so we should immediately try get to the other side of the bridge. I remember how wet and muddy it was, and how everybody was in a panic trying to get to the bridge and cross over. It turned out that there was nothing to the rumor, but it had all of us very worried that night. A lot of rumors got started in the camp, and they always spread quickly. Maybe the Chinese would come. Maybe the Indians would close the bridge. But for the most part nothing came of them.

56. Arriving in India

AFTER THIS SCARE, we finally crossed the bridge and arrived at Tawang in India. It was a nice broad valley, and there was a monastery there. There were also government offices there, so we didn't have to worry about the Chinese anymore. This was Indian territory, but culturally it was more Tibetan. To get down to the plains of India, we still had to cross a pass called Sengé Pass and then another called Bumti Pass. The Mön region was an interesting place; it was between being Tibetan and being Indian. The Mön people wore a short red chuba without trousers and a funny kind of hat, and they didn't wear any shoes. When they were carrying a load, they could go very fast, even over rough ground or stones. They could move almost as gracefully as wild animals. Tibetans couldn't do that. The Buddhism of both Mön and Bhutan were very much like the Tibetan system. In fact, the Mönpas were generally Gelukpas, and the Sixth Dalai Lama's birthplace was in Tawang. In the little Mön towns there were prayer flags and mani stones, and one would see prayer flags between two sides of a bridge, just like in Tibet. In one place, I saw a Nepalese-style stupa with eyes on the top part like the one at Bodhnath in Nepal. That was the first time I had ever seen that kind of stupa.

The Mönpas were very kind to us. These were rural people, and they were all Buddhists, so they treated strangers coming from Tibet with great respect and reverence. Whenever we came to a town, they lined up along the road and offered us incense, delicious puffed rice mixed with black raisins, dried meat, and other kinds of food. In the beginning we collected some of these offerings, but later people said that we shouldn't take any food from the Mönpas because they would put poison in the food. There was a well-known old story about a high official who had gone to Mön, eaten the food that he was offered, and then died from poisoning. In the story, it was claimed that the Mönpas believed that if they killed a wealthy person, they would somehow get that person's fortune. We knew of this old story, and when we heard this rumor that the food from the Mönpas was poisoned, we were worried. But no one even got sick, much less died. This may have been some Chinese disinformation or maybe just another baseless rumor circulated among Tibetans. There were some strange ideas going around then. I think this kind of thing happens when a group of people is thrown into troubling and uncertain circumstances.

When we got to Tawang, things got much better. We didn't have to worry anymore, at least not about the Chinese. There were doctors available, and rations were being distributed by Indian soldiers. We received the rations according to the lists that had been made back at Chu Drangmo. There was good rice, powdered milk, tea, sugar, and other staples. From then on, we didn't need our own food. The rations were being supplied by India, but they were coming indirectly from international sources. We had beautiful rice in nice packages, and people were saying that these things had come from America. These rations were airdropped there at Tawang.

Among the refugees, our group was much better off to begin with because we had brought a lot of food, which we were able to do because we had horses and mules to haul it for us. We still had some things left from Phenpo and Gönsar's home. We were fortunate. Many other people had nothing at all. Sometimes on the journey people had asked our group for some tsampa or other food, and we always shared whatever we had.

We spent four or five days in Tawang. Then we were sent on in our groups of one hundred. Each group had two Indian soldiers assigned to it. One went at the head of the group to lead the way, and one stayed at the rear to make sure no one got left behind. We traveled through a valley and then started to climb, coming eventually to Sengé Dzong and Sengé

Pass. We had to stay in the pass one night, but it wasn't like a normal mountain pass—someone, I think some international refugee organization, had set up some bamboo houses and tents. We slept there, and the Indian soldiers patrolled all night to protect us. From then on we were very well treated by the Indian government, and the people helped us a lot. His Holiness was already in Mussoorie, and he was probably asking the government to help his people, so that probably had something to do with it.

At Tawang, we realized that we were going to have some problems regarding the horses and mules. We couldn't take the animals to India with us, because the hot plains would have been hard on them, and it would have been difficult for us to keep them anyway, being refugees. We were going to have to travel on buses, jeeps, or trucks, so there would be no place for the horses. I knew a Bhutanese lama in Tibet who was one of my students. He had come to Sera and lived in Bati Khangtsen. I knew that he had a nice retreat place near Tawang, so I sent him a message and he came to see me. We made arrangements for him to take the animals with him to Bhutan and take care of them for us. We kept the animals until we got up to the pass, and then this lama sent someone there to take the animals back to Bhutan.

This Bhutanese lama was still young, maybe in his twenties. He hadn't received his geshé degree but had gone back to Bhutan already. One of our original plans had been to go from Tawang west to his place in Bhutan, instead of south into the Indian state of Assam, and stay there until things in Tibet settled down. However, the Bhutanese government suddenly changed their policy and stopped allowing Tibetans to come in. They allowed in a couple of the big Nyingma and Kagyü lamas such as Dudjom Rinpoché and Dilgo Khyentsé Rinpoché, but no one else. The rest of us had to go east through Arunachal Pradesh to Assam. Bhutan also had to worry about China at that time, so they were being cautious. So we decided that the lama would keep the horses and we would contact him in maybe a year or two to get the horses back after we had returned to Tibet. That was as far as we planned it.

Rinpoché's horse, my horse, and the mule that the manager rode made it all the way from Sera to Mön. Some of the animals had made it all the way from Khamlung Labrang. We had set out with more than that, maybe seven or so. The few that were left we sent to Bhutan. When we originally set out we weren't thinking at all about the wealth of the labrang or any material things. We were only concerned to have enough food and clothing. We expected to be going back soon. When we gave the animals away, we had to carry whatever provisions were left. By the time we got to Tawang, a lot of the food was used up. We got some rations and we had to carry them too.

The experiences at Sengé Pass were very interesting. We were refugees but we had bodyguards. Not everyone had it this good. From there we kept going down until we got to the last mountain pass, Bumti Pass. There were a lot of Indian soldiers around, some of whom were Sikhs. They were very large, with turbans and beards. We had never seen people like this before, so they looked kind of frightful to us. We stayed at this pass a couple of days while arrangements were being made for us to go to Assam. Our party must have stood out because we were singled out by an Indian military official and given a jeep and a driver. The five of us—the two young lamas, the two tutors, and the elderly manager—got into the jeep, and that was how we traveled down to Assam. The rest of the attendants and our other friends and relatives came later by foot. The day that we were taken down to Assam from Bumti Pass in the jeep was the first time I had ever ridden in a car. The road was very winding and bumpy, and the ride was very hard. I felt like I was going to vomit. Luckily we went down quickly, all in one day. I think other people who came in trucks or buses may have taken two days. I don't know if other people were brought down in jeeps after us; I suppose elderly people, women, disabled people, young lamas, or other young children may have come that way. From what I saw, though, we were the only ones who got this special treatment.

57. Beginning Life as a Refugee

WE STOPPED at an Indian government office at the foot of the mountain. We arrived sooner than the rest of our group, and the Indians had prepared some tea and sweets to eat. We stayed a little while and then got into a big canvas-topped military truck that held twenty or thirty people. We had to hold on to a cord in the back of the truck to keep from falling over. We were already a little carsick and feeling a little weak, and then we had to ride in the truck for two more hours to get to the refugee camp. We were still accompanied by Indian soldiers in the back of the truck. I remember very clearly the noise and the smell of the exhaust; it was not at all pleasant.

When we finally got down to the plains it was very hot, especially for us Tibetans. I looked out from the truck, and everywhere there was nothing but plains. It was green but completely flat. The mountains we had come down from were behind us, but there were no mountains in front of us. In Tibet I never saw such a thing. That was very disorienting. In Tibet, the sun rose from behind the mountains in the east and set behind the mountains in the west. We had the idea that when the sun went down it kept going farther west. In Assam, in the morning this huge red sun came right up from the ground; there was no mountain. The sun seemed to be rising right out of the ground. The day was incredibly hot, but the sun wasn't even directly overhead; it seemed far off in the west. When the sun set, it looked as if it just went straight back into the ground. I thought to myself, "Where is the sun going? Where is it coming from?" It was a very strange feeling.

At the camp hundreds of bamboo houses had been set up. Next to each one was a smaller building that was the kitchen. There were differently sized houses that accommodated twenty to sixty people. We were divided up according to our groups and assigned to the houses. Inside there was a row of bunk beds spaced against the wall in between the windows on each side. The roof was made of bamboo, over which was some kind of grass. That was very useful, because it helped make the house cool and kept out the direct sunlight. Otherwise it was unbearably sunny and hot. We Tibetans couldn't take that kind of heat. We would mostly just stay in bed and sleep or just lie there. Mentally we were sad and disoriented, physically we were miserable. We wondered, "Where are we going from here?" We had no idea of what would happen next. We just knew that we were a long way from home.

When we arrived at the camp, each of us got a towel, toothbrush, washcloth, shirt, and a pair of short pants. Everything was fresh and new. We were told to put our old clothes in one of the bamboo buildings. Our old things were dirty, and the Indians didn't want to touch them. Whatever one had on or had brought with him from Tibet, even fancy clothes, was put in this building. They took all the knives and small pistols and any other weapons that people were carrying. We had nothing left of our own. Then they sent us to another bamboo house where we could wash. After we bathed we dressed in the clothes that they had given us. They were thin, Indian-style clothes.

Everyone wore the same thing. Monk or layperson, man or woman, there were no differences. When I saw high lamas, officials, monks, and everyone all wearing exactly the same thing, everything the same and equal, I had a very strange feeling. I thought, "What have we come to? Where are we? What are we doing? What have the Chinese done to us? We don't have our homes, we don't even have our own way of dress anymore." In Tibet, other than the Muslim people who wore a white shirt, pants, and cap, you would never see something like this. Now we saw everybody in the same white shirt and pants. You didn't know who was a monk, who was a lama, who was an official. You almost couldn't tell who was a man and who was a woman. We were lost. We felt like crying. Now we had no choice of our own; we were in the hands of others. Our clothes were taken away, our things were taken away. Of course you might think that we would welcome these clean new clothes, but at that time, having just come out of Tibet, that wasn't how we were feeling. It was very upsetting.

Every morning they would give us food. During the day it was always terribly hot, but after the sun set it cooled down a little. In the evening they called us all out to a big open space where there was a huge movie screen and loudspeakers. I think this began the first day that we were there. An Indian official would give a speech, though we couldn't understand it, and then a Tibetan official would give a speech. The speeches were very unpleasant. The officials said that we were exiles now and that we would stay in the camp for a little while and then go to different places in India. Being exiles, we would not live comfortably like we did before. We would have to work to survive. There would be food rations for a few months, but after that we would have to take care of ourselves. They said that we Tibetans didn't know about this kind of life, so they would teach us about the realities of life in India. After the speech, they showed a film.

If they had shown a nice film, people would have enjoyed it, but this film showed Indian people doing hard work. We saw a vast flat plain, a couple of cows pulling a plow, and people who were dark and thin working very hard. This, the film said, was how we would have to live. The film showed poor farmers' houses, which looked like little more than run-down huts. In cities in India there were big buildings, but that is not what they showed in the film. Instead they showed people making pottery, weaving, and road workers breaking stones. It was all work. We monks had never had to do this kind of thing. At first they showed us these films every night. Later it was maybe twice a week. They told us that we had to become self-supporting, and the films concentrated on this. For a few months we didn't have to worry; there would be rations and housing, and they would teach us some job skills. But eventually we would have to support ourselves, and these films showed examples of the work that we would have to do. I remember wondering what our lives would be like now.

Earlier, in Lhasa, and even earlier when I was at Ganden Chönkhor, I had seen some pictures of places outside of Tibet, but not of India. This was around the time when the British ruled India, so what we saw was mostly England and the West. Tibetan merchants did business in India, so some of these British things were available in Tibet. I remember someone who had a small viewer with a disc of pictures who came to Ganden Chönkhor. For a small amount of money we got to look at one of these discs. By clicking the little lever the pictures would change. When the twelve pictures were finished our turn was also finished, unless we wanted to pay to see it again. I remember seeing pictures of a road that was nice, black, and shiny. I saw pictures of houses, with black shiny roofs and other nice things, all very clean. I remember seeing pictures of British people, or maybe they were Americans, at parks and some vacation spots. Since we had seen pictures of what the West was like, we thought that India was probably like that, not like what we were being shown in these films. What we saw in the films was completely different from what we expected.

The food that we were given at the camp was also different from what we were accustomed to. They gave us sweet tea, flat bread, rice, dal, and eggs. We didn't eat many eggs in Tibet, and they didn't give us any meat. It was mostly these same few things but they varied it slightly. Of course, we really weren't very hungry anyway. We felt a little sick all the time.

The heat was a big problem. It was too hot for a blanket at night, so we just put a thin sheet over ourselves. During the day it was miserable. We all had heat rash. We developed little red bumps that were filled with pus all over our bodies, and our faces got swollen as well. They gave us white powder to put on, which was helpful, but we had to put so much on our faces that finally we couldn't even recognize ourselves. It didn't happen while our group was there, but among those who stayed in Assam a long time, many people died. I suppose it was from the combination of the heat and the food.

Some of the bamboo houses were bathrooms. There were holes in the floor with a place on each side of the hole to put your feet. Underneath was a big metal container or pot. When this got full we could see everything that was in it, and not only that but there were worms and insects crawling around in it as well. When these pots were completely full, some Indian laborers would take them away and empty them. They would put a metal cover over the top and carry them away on their heads. However, they didn't empty them until they were full, which took several days. When they were mostly empty it was okay, but when they got more full we could see all the dirty things and the worms. Sometimes they put some kind of powder in the pots that was meant to kill things. At least it helped the smell for a short time.

Next to the bathrooms was a big river. In Tibet the rivers are cool and the water is blue and clear. If the river by the camp had been like that it would have been nice, but this river was all muddy. When we'd go there to try to cool off in the water, the water wasn't cold. Nothing there was cold. In addition to being warm, the drinking water also had a bad metallic taste. There was a military camp nearby, so the water was contaminated. When we washed or brushed our teeth, it made everything darker. Day by day, everybody's teeth took on a bluish color, and their faces got increasingly darker. Eventually, our Tibetan faces looked like those of Indians. We were very, very miserable. We didn't know where we would be sent, and we didn't know what we would be doing when we got there. The future was unknown, and the present was miserable.

In the beginning we didn't hear anything about what was happening back at home. There was a radio in the camp, but they didn't talk much about Tibet. Later we began to hear from refugees who had recently left. These refugees told stories about fighting, but there was no news that things were getting better. We stayed at this camp for about two months, but people kept arriving there for four or six months after that.

When I look back at this now, it seems like it wasn't real. It seems like a dream, like it didn't really happen. Sometimes I wonder, is my life now a dream, or is it real? Maybe I'm in Lhasa dreaming all these things. For a long time my dreams were of being in Lhasa, worrying about how to escape. I think maybe all Tibetans had these dreams. Our dreams were full of fear and worry long after we escaped. Even now I sometimes have these dreams.

58. From Assam to Dalhousie

W E STAYED in the refugee camp in Assam for about two months. Some people had to stay longer, maybe six months, before they went elsewhere. The refugees were divided into different categories depending on where we were going next or what we were going to do. For instance, some people were sent to be road workers. Monks were sent to Buxaduar, as I'll discuss later. Every day Tibetan officials came with a list and asked people where they wanted to go, but first they asked a question that was difficult to answer: "Do you want to be self-supporting or do you want the government to send you somewhere?" If you chose the former, you decided yourself where you would go, maybe Kalimpong or Darjeeling or somewhere else. If you had some money and knew someone somewhere in India, then you could choose to go there. For example, Gönsar's mother was a Tibetan official and was fairly wealthy. She had a lot of friends in Kalimpong. This was when our group got split up, because Gönsar Rinpoché's group chose self-support, and they went to Kalimpong. Then our group consisted again of the Dzamling Rinpoché's group, who we had met just before we got to Tsona, and the members of the Khamlung Labrang: the lama, the labrang manager, some attendants, and myself. We could not choose to be self-supporting because we didn't know anyone in India, and we were not wealthy enough to support ourselves. If one chose to be government-supported, then the Tibetan government in exile would assign him a place. Our manager had to make the decision, and under the circumstances, he couldn't choose to be self-supporting and support our whole group. This was really our only choice. We had to do whatever the government said.

Among the places that the government was sending people, the best was Dalhousie. It was in the far north, high up in the mountains and cool, almost like Tibet. That was most people's first choice. High lamas, old geshés, officials from Drepung, Ganden, Sera, or the government, and other privileged people were sent there. If that were what they wanted, they would be sent there, but they could also refuse it. At that time the Tibetan official who was sent to our camp by the Dalai Lama was the manager of Tsidrung Kündeling Labrang. Fortunately, our manager knew this man. The Kündeling Labrang manager told our manager that it would be best to take government support and that Dalhousie was the best place to go. At first Dalhousie sounded wonderful, but then after we had chosen this placement, a rumor started circulating that no one should accept being sent to Dalhousie. One reason given was that Dalhousie was close to Kashmir, where India was at war with Pakistan. It was also close to China, and it would be easy for the Chinese to come across the border.

Many people started to refuse to go to Dalhousie. While at first they had happily accepted this assignment, after this rumor they didn't want to go. We also started to wonder and said to our manager that maybe we shouldn't go. But the Kündeling manager's office reassured us, "No, no, don't worry about it. The Dalai Lama is near there. It is very far from China. There is no danger from China. It is close to the war zone in Kashmir, but the war is now over. The area is peaceful and very pleasant. Back in the British period, the British officers who lived in Delhi and other places on the plains spent their summers in Dalhousie. It is a vacation place. You can't refuse this. Go." Though we were reassured by the Kündeling manager, some people were still reluctant to go to Dalhousie and went to the south or someplace else that was not so close to Tibet. They also remained worried about being close to the war zone in Kashmir. They didn't want to have to flee from another war.

In the end, we decided to go to Dalhousie. The preparations took several days. We had to get Indian visas, have our photographs taken, and complete a great deal of paperwork. We Tibetan refugees couldn't just travel around freely. Finally, after two months of living in the refugee camp in Assam, we left for Dalhousie.

We were among the first groups to leave the camp in Assam. Again we went in a group of one hundred and were escorted by two Indian soldiers. It took a long time to get to Dalhousie, but of course we were going from the far eastern part of India to the far western part. This trip took five days and nights by train. The train ride to Dalhousie was very interesting for me. Traveling brought many novel experiences. Just as I had never ridden in a car or truck until we traveled to Assam, I had also never seen a train up to this point. It looked to me like long houses all lined up. I thought, "How can houses go someplace?" We had no knowledge of these things. Hundreds of people could fit on the train, and it was actually nice and comfortable inside.

The problem came when the train started to move. In one way we were enjoying how these "houses" were going somewhere, but riding on the train was also very hard. When the train was moving, all the trees, fields, plants, and everything else outside looked like they were rushing in the opposite direction. It was just an optical illusion, but it made us dizzy and gave us a headache. Most of the Tibetans sat in the train with their eyes closed or faces covered, unable to look out the window. Later though, when we had been traveling two or three days, and we got to Siliguri, where the Himalayas could be seen in the distance, someone shouted, "Mountains!" and then everyone uncovered their eyes and crowded at the windows to look.

There were several cars on the train that held only Tibetans. There were no Indians with us except the two soldiers that were in charge. They stayed by the door of the car with a stick. They had to watch us, and if they lost anyone it would be their responsibility. They had to keep counting us to make sure we were all there. In the beginning we were a little bit afraid that they were keeping us prisoner, but then we saw that they only had the stick in order to help and protect us. Without them we wouldn't have known what to do. The soldiers worried about us very much; it was like they were taking care of little children. We Tibetans were so hot that when the train stopped, we all ran for the water pump and drank. When the whistle blew for the train to leave again, some Tibetans were still drinking, so the soldiers had to go get them and bring them back onto the train.

Even though we were taking the train across India, we didn't see any big cities, because the train usually went around them. The first time that I saw a city was when we got off the train at Pathankot. We stayed there one night. There was good food and accommodations for the Tibetans getting off the train, which was nice. It seemed like the Indians there were excited to see us Tibetans. The next day we went by bus to Dalhousie, and along the way the villagers we passed welcomed us too. They called all the Tibetans—men, women, and children—"Lama." When the bus stopped along the way, villagers brought big baskets of mangoes, which they offered to us. The baskets would be passed along in the bus, and everyone took a mango. The villagers were happy and seemed to enjoy offering us these fruits. They called out, "Lama! Lama! Lama!"

It was late in the day when we arrived in Dalhousie. There was a central square with a market and other commercial buildings, and many different types of houses went off in different directions from there. There was a big hill that one could walk around, and on top of it was the place where we received our rations. On that first night the Indian officials didn't know much about us. They had a list of people that they had assigned to rooms, but our group was split up. It was very worrisome, because we didn't know where the others were or how we would contact one another. But the next day we found each other, and like most other Tibetans, we traded and rearranged so that we got back together with the people that we knew. We had already been separated from the Geshé Rabten and Gönsar Rinpoché group, so we didn't want to be split up any further. What was left of our group had been together for the whole journey out of Tibet, and of course the people from our own labrang were like our family.

After Gönsar Rinpoché's group went to Kalimpong, we didn't see them anymore. Later, when scholar monks began to go to Buxaduar, we saw some of these people again. Our labrang people and the Ganden lama's group had stayed together in the same bamboo house in Assam, and we ended up in the same house in Dalhousie, along with some other people: the members of two Ganden labrangs, some elderly monk officials from Ganden Shartsé and Jangtsé, and a man who had been about to be appointed one of the Drepung sergeants-at-arms when the Chinese attacked. This house had two stories, with several rooms upstairs and some downstairs. We all lived, cooked, and ate together like a big family. Our younger students went to get the rations when they were distributed. Everything was rationed—rice, milk, sugar, flour, and even firewood. The students who went to the market did the cooking. On the top floor of the house, there was a small room with windows where Khamlung Rinpoché, the manager, and I stayed. Next to that was a bigger room where the two Ganden rinpochés and their people stayed. The kitchen area where our younger students did the cooking was next to this. The monk officials from Ganden and the one from Drepung lived downstairs.

59. Learning to Live in Exile

FOR THREE YEARS we lived in Dalhousie, supported by rations. After that time, the Indian and Tibetan governments made people learn a trade to support themselves. They set up a rug factory, and younger people with some talent were trained to work there. The younger people were also sent to learn the Indian language, and they had to go to school every day. At first, for a little while, the older people had to take language lessons too. They sent a young Indian man to our house to teach the older people some Indian language and customs. This man would come every morning to our house, and we all went down to the open area to listen. At first I couldn't understand him at all, but then I began to understand little by little. He was teaching basic words like "stand up," "sit down," "come," "go," and other simple language that we needed to survive in India.

In the beginning one funny thing happened with this teacher. We Tibetans, especially older lamas, liked to have long fingernails. Back in Tibet, these would be beautifully kept. Zong Rinpoché, for example, had this even later in America. But of course in exile we didn't have any instruments for cutting or cleaning them, so they became rather dirty. The first day our language teacher came, he told everyone to hold out their hands. Many of us had long nails, which he apparently thought was very bad. He said that everyone had to cut their fingernails by the next day. However, we didn't have anything to use to cut them. The next day he told us to show our hands again, but nobody had cut their nails. He got a little bit angry and frustrated, but the next day he brought us nail clippers. This was our first cultural lesson.

At the time I thought, "Why do we have to cut our nails? This is not very important." But later I realized why it was important in our situation in India. Sometimes one was served food on a plate that had different sections, and one had to eat the food with his hands. Knives and spoons were not generally used. There would be rice in one spot, dal in another, and maybe potatoes or something in yet another. I realized that if we were eating like this, it wasn't good to have long dirty nails. In India, they have bathroom customs that are different from those in the West. They don't have toilet paper, and when they go outside somewhere to defecate, they clean themselves with the left hand and water. We had noticed that people had small pots or jars hanging from their belts, but we didn't know what these were for. It turned out that they held the water for cleaning. One was never supposed to use the right hand for this. In this context, it made sense not to have long fingernails. That was their culture, but we were unaware of such things before this time. So nail cutting was our first lesson, but eventually we learned all kinds of practical things that we needed to know in everyday life. Even the old respected lamas had to sit there on the ground and listen to this Indian man. He was actually a very good teacher.

I didn't have to learn a trade like most people, because I was an older man who was the tutor and caretaker of a young lama. In the beginning I thought that I would have to take some kind of job, but fortunately that didn't happen. The Tibetan government people talked to the Indian officials at the camp who were in charge of the rations and training. We had some translators because we didn't know enough Hindi to really communicate. One of our translators was an old man from Ladakh. Oh, his Tibetan was terrible! He also had a very short temper, so when we couldn't understand him he got angry. The Tibetan word for an old Ladakhi man is Ladakhpo. Whenever we saw this man coming we'd say, "Ladakhpo is coming!" and we were a little afraid. He was the person who was supposed to translate things into Tibetan, but we Tibetans couldn't understand him. He spoke Hindi and English too, but I think all of his languages sounded strange. We needed a translator all the time in the beginning, but some of our younger students learned Hindi quickly, at least enough for shopping and everyday needs. We older people never learned much.

Khamlung Rinpoché didn't have to learn a trade either. There was some talk of having the young lamas go off to school, but there was resistance to this idea. People were concerned about what they would be learning. However, in Delhi there was a wealthy older British lady who established the Young Lama's Home School. Trungpa Rinpoché and some other Kagyü lamas went there, and later some of them were sent to Oxford University in England to study. Sharpa Tulku, who I would later be taking care of, also went to the Young Lama's Home School to study English and other modern subjects.

At that time we wondered why we needed to know these things. We just weren't very interested in such things and didn't see the point. Khamlung Rinpoché could have gone to this school, but the manager didn't think it was necessary. He wanted to keep Rinpoché with us. I wasn't interested in him going either. Remember, we were thinking that the exile would only be temporary. We still thought that we would be going back to Tibet soon. The lamas that went to the school learned English well in a few years. Sharpa Tulku learned a lot of English while he was there. Later, when we came to America, Sharpa could understand English when we were in airports and other places, but he was very young and shy; even though he could understand, he wouldn't speak.

So for three years we just stayed in Dalhousie. Khamlung Rinpoché and some of the other younger people did learn some Hindi, and I continued to teach Rinpoché, though he wasn't very interested at that point. In the morning we did a lot of prayer and recitation. Khamlung Rinpoché was memorizing some short texts. In the evening after dinner, we all sat together in the big upstairs room where the Ganden lamas stayed and talked endlessly about Tibet. Sometimes the monk official from Drepung who lived downstairs came up to talk too. At Drepung, there were four men who were high disciplinary officers. Two of them were the sergeants-at-arms, who were higher and more powerful. The other two were of a lower rank called Chaptama. This man had been Chaptama for several years, so we called him Chaptama. He'd say, "Oh those Chinese. If they had not come, I would have been sergeant-at-arms by now!" He had many interesting stories about what had happened to him at Drepung, and one could listen to him for hours, laughing.

60. Trying to Keep Tibetan Culture Alive

WE TIBETANS tried to reestablish some aspects of our culture in Dalhousie. Above the marketplace where they distributed the rations, we gathered together for prayer, pūja, and some debating. Though we took steps to establish some things it was really very meager, and people had little interest. Sometimes talented people like dancers and singers originally from Kham, Amdo, or central Tibet came. There were rehearsals going on for *lhamo*, the traditional Tibetan opera, and other types of dancing and singing, and these people also gave performances. Chaptama was very well versed in singing religious biographies and in lhamo. Later he became the head of that lhamo company. Often foreign visitors came from England, Germany, or America and were very supportive of the Tibetan refugees. High Indian officials also visited from time to time. They would give a talk, and the Tibetans would give a performance for them. Slowly these events became more frequent. The Tibetans were attempting to express and preserve their culture in exile. This was quite nice. I had not seen or heard any artistic performances before, much less ones by Amdowa and Khampa performers. It was fascinating for me.

I was able to study and read a little bit, and occasionally I would have the opportunity to debate. Near the house where we stayed, a little farther down the hill there were a number of empty houses that were left over from the time of British rule when British officials spent their summers in Dalhousie. Later, the houses were used by some wealthy Indian families, who would come and stay for a few weeks in the summer. Other than at those times, the houses had only a caretaker staying there, and some of them were available to rent. Before I did my geshé examination, I sometimes rented one of these places in order to do my studying and text retreat, because I needed a quiet place.

Back in Tibet there had been a very famous lama named Trehor Kyorpön Rinpoché. He had been a top-ranked lharampa but had chosen to be a yogi rather than follow the lharampa path. He was from Drepung, and after he did his geshé examination, he went to Gyümé Tantric College. Then, while he was in his first year, he just left one day. He went east of Lhasa and went into retreat in a cave way up a mountain named Mindrup Tsering. Slowly people learned of this, and he began to attract followers from Drepung and also from Sera. People who wanted to dedicate their lives to yogic practice wanted to follow him. One of my students had gone there on the advice of Geshé Thapkhé Rinpoché. When the Chinese invaded, my student and Trehor Kyorpön Rinpoché escaped through Bhutan and ended up in Dalhousie. They stayed in a house near Dalhousie with some followers. When I stayed in one of the rented houses, this student would come to visit. It was a nice situation.

By this time, His Holiness had established a special monastic camp at Buxaduar, which was before the Sera monks moved to Bylakuppe in the south. There were scholars from Sera, Ganden, and Drepung at Buxaduar. It was close to Bhutan, way up in the hills. It was all trees, hills, and mountains, and one couldn't see the Indian plains at all from there. In the middle of this place was a lone hill with a little bit of flat space around it, on top of which were a bunch of buildings. For a long time, this had been a British prison, and it was where Nehru and Gandhi had been imprisoned. There were many buildings with thick walls and big barred windows. A high metal fence with a big gate surrounded the buildings. Nehru gave this facility to His Holiness as a place to carry on Tibetan religious and educational culture, ensuring that it would not be lost. The reason that Nehru had given this particular place to the Tibetans was symbolic and personal. He said that since the Indian people had won their independence by passing through there, it was auspicious for the

Tibetans to use it as well—they too would regain their independence. This was his express motivation in giving Buxaduar to the Tibetans.

The Tibetans started to reestablish the study of philosophy at Buxaduar, and they began doing geshé examinations there. This happened fairly quickly. His Holiness was very concerned about the fate of the monks, lamas, and scholars. Where were they to go? At first the Indians were going to send them to the border area to do roadwork like many other Tibetan people had to do. They were to work all day digging and breaking rocks to build roads, for which they would be given a small amount of rupees. A lot of laypeople did this roadwork in the beginning, but scholar monks were sent to Buxaduar.

Buxaduar, however, was not such a great place. It was depressing, isolated, and claustrophobic. There was a lot of sickness among the people who went there, and some monks even went insane. In fact, a lot of monks died there. It seemed that the water there wasn't good, and the rations that people got were not as good as what we got in Dalhousie. Having formerly been a prison, the complex was bleak and oppressive. The geography of the place made it so that one couldn't see very far in the distance, and fences closed in the facility itself. There were bars on the windows, and people were very isolated. They felt trapped, and combined with the feelings of being in exile and having lost their homes, it was psychologically unhealthy. The motivation behind Nehru's giving this place to the Tibetans was noble and kind, but the reality of living there was still very unpleasant. Fortunately I never had to live in Buxaduar. I only went there for my geshé examination.

61. An Attempted Trip to Bhutan

THERE WAS a time when I had to go back up to Bumti Pass. As I said, we had left our horses and mules there to be taken care of by the Bhutanese lama that I knew. The labrang manager hadn't known this person, so he sent the horses based on my word alone. For this reason I felt personally responsible in the matter. It wasn't that we expected to get the horses back, but they belonged to the labrang, and we thought that the lama would perhaps buy the animals or provide some compensation. Two or three years had passed and we hadn't heard from him, so our manager wanted to send me and one of my students to see about this matter. Our plan was to try to meet with the lama. If we weren't able to meet with him, we would try to find some information about the animals. We needed to get to Bhutan, but at that time Bhutan's borders were still closed to Tibetans, so we couldn't go.

Trijang Rinpoché had a relative who was a Tibetan official and a close friend of a Bhutanese official. This relative was living in Kalimpong at the time, so we thought it would be good for me to go see him and try to find out something about the animals. It was hoped that through this official I could get a letter or something that would get me into Bhutan. However, there were also problems in my going to Kalimpong. There had been an assassination involving a Khampa lama who was a Chinese spy. I never really knew the details, but they were preventing Tibetans from coming into Kalimpong. This meant that before I could set off for Kalimpong, I had to go to Darjeeling, where Trijang Rinpoché was living. I hadn't seen him since we had left Tibet. There was a little monastery in Darjeeling that belonged to Dromo Geshé Rinpoché. A couple of my former students were running this monastery, so I went there and stayed for four or five days along with my attendant. It was actually quite enjoyable. Of course my students took care of my food and everything else that I needed.

One day Trijang Rinpoché was giving the bhikṣu vows to some monks. The full monk ordination required at least five fully ordained monks. It required ten in the best situations, but at the very least there had to be five. It wasn't so easy to get this together in our situation, so I was asked to come on that day and be one of the five monks of the ordaining quorum. Fortuitously, among the group of people seeking ordination was one man, perhaps forty years old, who was from Kalimpong. He was the prayer leader at a monastery there. Since I was in his ordination ceremony, I got to know him very well, and when he went home to Kalimpong I went with him. Without him, I wouldn't have gotten in.

From Darjeeling, we had to descend from the mountains, cross a bridge on the river, then climb back up again to get to Kalimpong, which was on top of another hill. There were Indian police at both ends of the bridge, and they controlled who could cross. Fortunately, the police chief was the brother of this monk, so we had no problem. The monk told his brother that I was part of his ordination party and that I should be allowed to cross. I didn't have the right papers or anything, but I was still allowed to pass because of this connection. Dromo Geshé Rinpoché also had a monastery in Kalimpong where I was able to stay. But after all this effort to get there, the official that I had come to see was not there, and I left empty-handed.

From there, my attendant and I went to Assam and climbed all the way up to Bumti Pass. There were a lot of Tibetans living there, especially wealthy Khampa merchants. Among them was one person who was very devoted to Trijang Rinpoché. He was a very wealthy man. He gave both my attendant and me a room at his place at Bumti Pass and provided us with food and everything else we needed. We were very comfortable there. In addition to all the Tibetans at Bumti Pass, there were also many

Mönpas and Bhutanese people. When these people found out that I was there, they treated me like a great lama. They came and asked me to do divinations or pūjas, and they brought many offerings. I never did any divinations, but a couple of times I did agree to do pūjas for them.

One day a Bhutanese lady came with a beautiful covered basket. Usually people came with puffed rice and raisins, which as I said was very nice food. The woman had brought the basket with a khatak and a small amount of money as an offering. Though the basket was covered at first, even when it was sitting on the table I thought it smelled a little funny. I didn't open it until after she had left, and when I did I found that it was filled with very small, fresh dead fish. My attendant held his nose when I opened it. I'm sure the woman thought it was a very wonderful gift. I suppose she and her family would have eaten them that night, fried or something, though I didn't really know how they were prepared. I had never had that kind of thing and wondered, "Now what am I supposed to do with these?" In the end, I gave them to the merchant, who said, "Oh, I can use that! Very good!" He gave me some other meat and some good food in return. If the merchant had not wanted it we would probably have taken it someplace and thrown it away. But the woman offered it with pure motivation and the merchant enjoyed it, so in the end it worked out well.

While I was staying at Bumti Pass I was still trying to figure out how I would contact this Bhutanese lama. One day I met a Bhutanese man there who happened to be going back to Bhutan the next day. He knew the place where the lama lived, so I sent a message with him and asked him to give it to the lama. It took about two days to get there, so we had to wait. Finally, the lama sent two people to Bumti Pass to see if it were really me. They saw that it was really me and told me that the horses had already died. There was still a mule or two, but that was all. For some reason, our manager had also sent a small container of half silver coins to this Bhutanese lama when he took the animals. In Tibet people would sometimes cut coins in half, so there were full ones and half ones. Anyway, our manager had left these half coins with the horses, and of course he wanted to know what had happened to them. I asked the messengers to go back and ask the lama to come to Bumti Pass and see me. Then I waited another four or five days. I spent a lot of time just waiting around there. Finally, I got a message back that the lama couldn't come. It was winter then, and apparently the road from Bhutan was bad. The messengers said that the lama had set out but had to turn back because he couldn't get through on horseback. They had come on foot with the message, and they brought a small amount of money with them. Anyway, I never got to see the lama, and I always felt responsible for the loss of the animals and the coins.

62. A Letter from His Holiness

DURING THAT SAME period, around 1961 or 1962, a letter came to Dalhousie from Dharamsala. It said that I was supposed to go to a special school in Nalanda, where there had been a great Buddhist monastery in ancient times. A lama from Drepung and I had both been chosen. When the letter came, I was away on the trip to Kalimpong and Bumti Pass, so they selected someone else. Another letter also came while I was away, and that letter was still waiting for me when I returned. It said that I was to accompany three young lamas who were going to America— Sharpa Tulku, Lama Kunga, and Khamlung Rinpoché. Because I was Khamlung Rinpoché's tutor, I would have to go with him. The lamas were mainly going to learn English, but they would also need a tutor so that their Buddhist training would not suffer. When I got back from my trip and read the letter, my first reaction was, "America? What? No way! Rinpoché can go, but I'm not going." I told the manager that I was getting old—I was almost forty—and I would not go to America. But in order to get permission to stay, I had to go to Dharamsala to talk to His Holiness, from whom the letter had come. So I went to Dharamsala to ask permission not to go.

Before I went to see His Holiness I went to see Trijang Rinpoché, who by this point had moved to Dharamsala. From the time that I had become Khamlung Rinpoché's tutor, I knew Trijang Rinpoché well and he knew me. Before that, I knew him, of course—everybody did—but he wouldn't have known me. Thousands of people, both monks and laypeople, knew him and had been to his teachings and empowerments.

I was one of these people. In that sense I was his student or disciple, but he didn't know me personally before I became the tutor to Khamlung Rinpoché.

Since my family was just a poor farm family from Shang, I came to be who I was seemingly by accident. I believe that my karma is responsible. If we believe that our lives have any meaning or purpose, we have to either believe in karma or in God. It's one or the other. As a Buddhist, I prefer believing in karma rather than God. Whether we have misery, problems, suffering, or good fortune, it is always due to our previous actions. If something bad happens to me, I blame myself rather than God or somebody else. I came to the position that I had through hard work; it didn't have anything to do with my family or social status. But of course, the ultimate cause of my fortune was determined by karma.

The same is true when a tulku is selected. There may be some unusual signs that accompany the births of several boys, but that doesn't necessarily mean that a particular child is this or that lama. Of course these boys don't just say, "I am the reincarnation of such and such." There has to be a divination and examination, and finally it will be determined that one of them is the reincarnation of the lama that is being sought. In any given reincarnation lineage, some of the lamas are renowned and others are less remarkable. This is true even of the lineage of the Dalai Lamas. Some of them were very famous, while others weren't very well known. All of this is determined by their karma.

Anyway, I told Trijang Rinpoché that I was not going to go to America. I hoped that he would support me in getting permission to stay. But instead he gave me a big lecture. He said that it would be better for me to go. All the monks of Sera, Ganden, and Drepung were still getting rations, but after two or three more years, those rations would stop, and everyone would have to find a way of supporting themselves. "Then what will you do?" he said. "Right now you have a great opportunity. America is the most famous place in the world; it is a special place. You can go there to Geshé Wangyal's monastery (which was in New Jersey). Most people desire to go, and you are refusing? You should go." Another reason he gave was that I had been requested by His Holiness to do this. "He has asked you to do this. This is the first time he has asked such a thing. This is a bad situation that we are in. If you were to refuse, it would be very bad. Don't refuse."

Then he showed me a big map that he had on the table. He showed me on the map where North America was and said, "You are going here." He said, "America is far away, but you are not going to go there on foot or train. You are going on an airplane. It will take two days to get there. Going down from Dharamsala to Delhi takes almost the same amount of time. Airplanes are very fast and can go over the ocean and mountains. Go to America and stay a couple of years, and then if you still want to return, then you can ask to come back. Until then, I don't think you should refuse." Then he showed me exactly where in America I was going. I respectfully said, "Yes, yes." After that I was happy about it, and I was determined to go. I didn't even go to see the Dalai Lama. I just quietly went back to Dalhousie, accepting the request.

One of the most important Tibetan officials in Dharamsala at that time was Phalha Drönyer Chenmo. Phalha was a very close friend of our manager and also of Geshé Wangyal. Back in Tibet Geshé Wangyal, who was from Drepung, would stay with Phalha during the Mönlam Festival. Geshé Wangyal knew English, so people respected him. Some Tibetan officials were secretly suspicious that maybe Geshé Wangyal was a spy for the Russians or the British. He was also friends with Hugh Richardson and another British person who was in Lhasa. But despite this suspicion, most people thought that it was better to be friends with Geshé Wangyal than not. While I was in Dharamsala, Phalha gave me a dinner. He said, "Geshé-la, it is wonderful that you are going. I know Geshé Wangyal very well, and he really wants someone to come." After all of that, there was no way I could refuse.

I went back to Dalhousie and started to prepare to go to America. I was still thinking, "Where am I going? What will happen?" But these three lamas had to go, and I had to go with them. It was all very strange. Everything about it was very, very strange. I was just an ordinary person from Tsang who was now going to America at the request of His Holiness the Dalai Lama. That's why I keep saying, as I'm talking about my life, that it seems like a dream. Many times I have had the thought, "Am I really in America?" Some time after I left Tibet, I dreamed that I flew in an airplane back across the ocean and mountains and got to Tibet. When I got there I was worried that the Chinese would come and catch me. I thought, "I shouldn't have come. Now how am I going to fly back?" I was very afraid. Interesting, isn't it? I was still afraid of the Chinese even at that time.

As I said, I never had to live in Buxaduar, but I did go there for my geshé examination. My examination was close to the end of my time in India, just before I went to America. Geshé Tsultim Gyeltsen, who would later start a center in Long Beach, California, was from Ganden and was in the same group as me for the awarding of the geshé degree. In our group we had two people from Sera, and there were some from Drepung as well. Because we all were in this same group, I got to know some geshés from Ganden and Drepung. I also had some students who were living at Buxaduar, and it was nice to see them. Serkong Rinpoché, who was then a tsenshap, came from Dharamsala and made the awards to the candidates. I got my geshé degree in Buxaduar during the Mönlam Festival, and my lharampa ranking was number one. I remember a theater troupe came on the fifteenth day, after the examinations were finished, and that night they gave a performance.

I left India just after my geshé examination. This was in 1962. I went to Buxaduar around January, and on May 2nd I arrived in America. Geshé Tsultim Gyeltsen was chosen by His Holiness to go to Sussex, England, and I was sent to New Jersey in America. This was the first time that His Holiness had sent geshés to other countries. I'm not sure what connection Geshé Gyeltsen may have had that he was chosen for this, but in my case, it was primarily because Khamlung Tulku was one of the three young lamas to be asked to go. Geshé Wangyal had requested three young lamas who could stay at his monastery and learn English. He did not request a geshé, but His Holiness decided to send a geshé with them anyway.

63. The Situation for Those Who Did Not Escape Tibet

AFTER WE LEFT in 1959, things got very bad in Tibet. Many people were rounded up and punished or put in jail for no other reason than who they were. Nobles and especially religious leaders were particularly targeted. Any official, even just a secretary, was in big trouble. The Chinese gathered the names of these people and then found out where they were from. They arrested them and asked them what they did and where. Then they took the prisoners to those places and asked the ordinary people of that area to accuse them. Of course at that time, most people were too afraid of the Chinese to just say nothing about these prisoners. They had to make some kind of accusations. Maybe they were true, maybe false; it didn't really matter. No one would dare to just keep quiet because the Chinese interpreted this as a kind of sympathy with the prisoner, and then the person who did not speak up would be implicated. The Chinese would say, "So you don't want to accuse this person. You must have something to hide!" The Chinese also went around dressing up poor people in new clothes and praising them. They would parade them around to show how much better off they were under the new Communist system. This is what I've heard. It was a very difficult situation. In India, I heard these kinds of things from many people who had escaped. For a while we didn't hear anything at all. No news was coming out. Later when we finally began to hear things, they were always bad.

Someone told me a story about my teacher Gen Thapkhé and Ngödrup Tselné, who had been one of the tsenshaps from Sera Jé. After His Holiness had escaped from the Norbu Lingkha in March of 1959, the

Chinese completely took over Lhasa. One night after this had happened, Gen Thapkhé and the tsenshap were performing the Vajrayoginī prayer ritual in Gen Thapkhé's house in Lhasa. Someone found out about this and reported it to the Chinese officials. Chinese soldiers came and forced my teacher and the tsenshap to walk around the Barkhor, Lhasa's busiest square, holding up the tormas used in the Vajrayoginī ritual. This was intended to be a form of humiliation and punishment, though it doesn't make much sense.

Gen Thapkhé told me later when I returned to Tibet to visit him that the Chinese had forced laborers to build a big dam east of the city on the Kyichu River. These laborers worked from early morning to evening, without much food. Gen Thapkhé was one of these laborers, and he and all the other workers were former officials, high lamas, monks, or dignitaries. The Chinese dressed them in filthy clothes and made them work on this dam at gunpoint. They weren't even allowed to speak to each other. My teacher told me that when he saw birds flying around above him, he was envious of them. He thought, "How fortunate to be one of those birds. I wish I were one of them, flying free." That's the way it was in Tibet. Soldiers were everywhere, and people were forced to work long and hard. There was no freedom.

I believe it can only be because of karma that somehow I was not touched by any of the direct effects of all this. Somehow, I always escaped. It's almost like I was a feather, blown here and there and then, finally, far away. That's all it is. I had no plan. I did not think, "I should do this and then this and then this." There was no plan, no preparation, nothing.

64. Going to America

BEFORE WE LEFT for America we first had to spend some time in Delhi. There were many preparations to complete before we could go. We had to get shots and have x-rays taken, go to the American Embassy several times for visas and passports, and many other things. The x-rays were to prove we didn't have tuberculosis. All these strange experiences we had to go through before leaving were new to us. In Delhi there were modern Western stores, wide paved roads, and other things one only sees in a big city. This was more like the images that I had come across when I was back in Tibet, but this was the first time that I had seen such things in person. There hadn't been anything like that in Assam or Dalhousie or anywhere else I had been.

In Delhi the one making all the arrangements for our departure was Shakabpa, who would later become well known for his history of Tibet. Shakabpa had been a *tsipön* in Tibet before the Chinese takeover, which was a very high position in the government. In the Tibetan governmental system the Dalai Lama was the supreme leader of the country. Beneath him was the Kashak; below them was the Yiktsang; and below them was the Tsikhang, which was made up of four lay officials called *tsipön*. Shakabpa had played an important role in the negotiations with China, India, and the U.S. before 1959. He had been sent as a representative of the Tibetan government to India back in 1950, so he had a great deal of experience with India and its bureaucracy. He certainly knew a lot more than we did.

While we were in Delhi, the days were so hot that we didn't go out at all. Shakabpa had given us some pajamas, which were much cooler than our robes, so we wore them both day and night, not knowing that they were supposed to be just for sleeping. One evening after it had cooled down, one of the young lamas asked, "Shall we go outside for a little while? Wearing all these robes is so hot. Let's go out in these pajamas. When we go in our robes everybody stares and laughs at us. Maybe this will make us look more like Indians." I thought that was a fine idea. We didn't know that pajamas were different from what the Indian people wore outside throughout the day. We thought that they were the same, so we went out in our pajamas. Of course, everybody stared at us again. We were all wearing exactly the same thing. We thought, "These Indians are funny. When we wore our robes they looked at us and laughed. Now tonight they are doing the same thing when we wear their style of clothes. What is wrong?" Much later we discovered that this was not an acceptable thing to wear outside. It had seemed reasonable to us. To us, these clothes looked like the same thing that everyone else was wearing.

When we left India, it was evening, almost sunset. We flew all night. The flight was on Air France, and it was a very nice plane. Of course it was the first time any of us had ever been on an airplane, so it was really frightening for us. The three young lamas sat on one side of the aisle, and I sat on the other side. Beside me there was an elderly French woman with blue eyes, a white dress, and a lot of jewelry. She looked strange to me. Back then airplanes were different than they are now. Now there is a large overhead compartment with a door, but back then there was just a little shelf up above. One had to put any heavy things underneath the seat, and just the light things would go up above. There were pillows, blankets, and that kind of thing on the shelf. Not long after we took off, I think somewhere over Pakistan, we came into some turbulence. The pilot came on the speaker and was saying something, but of course we couldn't understand it. The flight attendants seemed very busy, but soon they sat down too. Then suddenly we hit a very big air pocket and the plane dropped. Some of the pillowcases that were on the shelf fell down on us. That really scared us. The elderly French lady next to me seemed to be doing something inside the bag that she was holding on her lap. When the plane dropped, she cried out and then started mumbling something that I couldn't understand. I saw then that she had a rosary in her hands and I thought, "Well, we are finished." I figured if she were saying mantras or something, we must be in big trouble. I thought something very bad was happening. Of course, it was nothing.

When the food came, it looked very strange to us. Everything was on a little plate and packaged up. The milk was covered, the sugar was covered, and the butter was covered. Everything was covered. There was also a little folded piece of paper. We had never seen anything like that so we didn't know what to do with it. Before we could eat we had to watch the other people around us to see what to do. Sharpa Tulku watched the British man next to him. He knew a little English, so he was able to find out from this man how we were supposed to eat. "What is this little cup? What is this little packet of sugar? What am I supposed to do with this?" Then he told me what to do with these things. After we ate the food, a little desert came on a tiny plate. The food was actually quite delicious, but everything was so small. It looked like baby food. It was all very interesting to us.

As I said, we left Delhi just about the time when the sun was setting. We were flying west, and I noticed that we flew a long time but the sun never seemed to get any closer to the horizon. It just stayed in the same place. I remember thinking, "What is going on here? How strange! When we left Delhi it was almost dark. What is happening?" We had no idea about such things.

Shakabpa had given us a piece of paper with something written on it in English. I presume it said that we had never been out of Tibet before and we didn't know English or any of the things that we needed to do. The note asked that the authorities take care of us, like babies. When we got to the airport in Paris it was early in the morning. The sun hadn't risen, but it was getting light and it was raining. We had been getting special treatment throughout the trip from the flight attendants. They either kept us on the plane until last, or maybe they let us off first; I can't remember now. Anyway, as we were getting off the plane, they gave us each a blanket to cover our heads because it was raining. We thought that it was very nice that they were giving away blankets.

When we went into the airport, we first entered the area downstairs. This is where there were some officials, ticket counters, and that kind of thing. Upstairs there was a much better place, though we didn't know that at the time. We thought that the downstairs area where we were was the only place to go. Somebody showed us a spot where we could sit or even lie down there on the lower level. We stayed there a long time; I think it was maybe six hours. Our next flight was on Pan American Airways, so we had to wait until they called us for that flight. We thought we had to stay downstairs until they called us.

It was my job to watch these young boys and make sure they didn't get lost or get into any trouble. At one point, Sharpa Tulku went to look around the airport. He found an escalator and he was very interested in it. He went up and came back down, over and over. He also found a luggage cart and brought one to us, imitating the people that he saw with carts. I had a difficult time keeping him sitting down with us; he wanted to go explore. Eventually we figured out, probably from Sharpa Tulku's explorations, that we could go upstairs. It was much nicer up there. From there we could see the sun coming through the windows. Before we went upstairs the flight attendant told us that we had to give back the blankets. Up to that point, we thought that we got to keep them. Downstairs we had been sitting or lying down wrapped up in those blankets, which was nice. Now we had to give them up.

Upstairs there were huge windows and many stores. We could see the city in the distance. It probably seems like a silly thing to remember, but I remember this was the first time that I saw a vacuum cleaner. It made a loud whirring noise and sucked up small pieces of things from the floor. I thought this was amazing. Then we met a young Indian man who was studying in Europe someplace. Sharpa and Khamlung knew Hindi very well, so they were very happy to have someone that they could talk to.

After feeling so alien in this place, they felt that this man was almost like a brother. I think the Indian man enjoyed talking to us as well.

Eventually, we needed to go to the bathroom, but we didn't know where to find one or how it would work. The young Indian man said that we might have to pay some money to use the bathroom. He asked us if we had any French money, which we didn't, so we were worried. But finally Sharpa and the Indian man found a bathroom where we didn't have to pay. After that, we were able to relax; it was much more enjoyable. We waited upstairs until someone came to get us when our flight was ready. We didn't have anything to eat or drink because we didn't have any money, and we wouldn't have known how to ask for anything even if we did, so we sat there hungry until it was time to leave. Shakabpa had given us some American money for when we arrived, but we didn't have anything for Paris. Perhaps he hadn't thought of that.

It was afternoon before the Pan American people came and got us and we boarded another plane. It was a very big plane, and the young lamas were excited, saying, "This is an American plane!" We had already been given some blue plastic bags that said "Pan American" and had a globe on them. At that point I thought that Pan American was the only American airline. We had another long flight, this time over the ocean. There is no ocean near Tibet, so we had never seen so much water. We flew and flew over nothing but water. I was a little bit worried. If that plane fell, I didn't know how to swim.

65. Our New Life in New Jersey

O N MAY 2, 1962, we arrived at the airport in New York that was later called Kennedy Airport. There was a group of Mongols there waiting on the runway with khataks in their hands to offer us. Taktser Rinpoché,[63] whom the Americans called Mr. Norbu, and his wife were there, and so was Elvin Jones, who would later become my student and good friend. There were also newspaper reporters there. They must have known ahead of time that we were coming; I guess our arrival was regarded as an important event. We were taken off the plane before everyone else, and I remember all the flashes from the cameras going off as we came down the stairs from the plane. Elvin was dressed in a very elegant suit, wearing a hat. Sharpa Tulku noticed him right away and whispered to me that this man must be an American official or maybe a spy.

We went from New York City to Freewood Acres, New Jersey. It was a small town, but many of the people there were from other countries. There was a group of Mongolians who had escaped from Mongolia during the war there, and a monastery that had been established by Dilowa Hutukhtu, who was a very famous Mongolian lama. He was a great scholar from the older generation, and he had taught at Johns Hopkins. By this point Dilowa Rinpoché was mostly staying in New York City, but he still came to New Jersey from time to time. Geshé Wangyal had initially lived with him at his monastery. Just before we came, Geshé Wangyal bought some land a couple of blocks from this original monastery and established the Lamaist Buddhist Monastery of America in

1958. Next to the land where Geshé Wangyal's little temple was built, two old Russian men had bought some land and built a Russian Orthodox church there. They built it slowly over several years, taking five or ten years altogether. When it was finished it was a very nice building and very beautiful. Having a lot of foreigners around there was good for us. There were Turks, Russians, Mongolians, and now Tibetans.

Prior to this, I had only known Geshé Wangyal by reputation. I had never met him. He had been in New Jersey since 1955. At some point he went to India to see the Dalai Lama in Dharamsala and requested that some young lamas be sent to his center in America. He got a grant from the Tolstoy Foundation with the help of Professor Kenneth Morgan of Colgate University. Originally the plan was that the young lamas and I would be there for a two-year program. We would stay in New Jersey, study English, and then go back. But then Geshé Wangyal and Dr. Morgan got another grant, so we stayed for another two years. After the four years passed we were all supposed to go back, but Geshé Wangyal made a request to His Holiness that the two older monks, Kunga Lama and me, stay on in New Jersey. He agreed; otherwise I would have returned to India with the two young rinpochés. Lama Kunga later went to the San Francisco Bay area and in 1972 founded a center there in Kensington, California.

After the two young lamas went back to India, I was able to become more involved in teaching others, and there was more and more interest on the part of the American students. My English had gotten better, so during this period I also began to teach publicly.

I gave my first public teaching at a seminar in Bucks County, Pennsylvania, in 1968. Jeffrey Hopkins, whom I had known from Geshé Wangyal's center, was the translator. This was before he became a Buddhist scholar. Jeffrey had lived at the center for a while beginning in 1963, as had Robert Thurman and Christopher George.[64] Many others also came to visit. By this time the center was getting to be well known in and around New York. A lot of visitors began to come, and from time to time Geshé Wangyal read Buddhist texts with them. Later, Geshé

Wangyal's book, *The Door of Liberation*, came from a translation of some of these teachings.[65]

Elvin Jones had already been coming to New Jersey for some time when I arrived. He had lived in New York and had studied with Geshé Wangyal, who had taught some classes at Columbia University. Elvin was very excited when we arrived from India, and as I said, he was at the airport to welcome us the moment we arrived. Eventually he bought a house near the Lamaist Buddhist Monastery and the Khamlung Rinpoche and Sharpa Tulku would sometimes go there. That was the beginning of my friendship with Elvin. He was a very good friend. During that time Elvin said that he wanted to study with me. He was studying with Geshé Wangyal along with Robert, Jeffrey, and Christopher, but he said he wanted to study with me separately as well. We studied two of Kamalaśīla's *Stages of Meditation* texts.[66] Elvin knew some Tibetan language by this time, and he was very helpful for my learning philosophical terms in English. That helped in my teaching later.

I first met Professor Richard Robinson when he came to New Jersey one summer. At that point Geshé Wangyal didn't want to always be known as the boss of the monastery, so he decided to name me president, though it was in name only—he was still running things. It was during this time that Robinson came. He was a serious student of Buddhism and had started the Buddhist Studies Program at the University of Wisconsin–Madison in 1960. He had decided that the Tibetan language was important for this study, and that they couldn't only rely on Sanskrit. There were many texts preserved in Tibetan for which the Sanskrit text had been lost, so Robinson decided to find a traditional Tibetan scholar to teach the classical Tibetan language. He could have found many in India, but in America there weren't many to choose from. He heard that there were some geshés in New Jersey, and both Geshé Wangyal's and my name came up. He came and talked to us, and then he invited me to come to Madison to teach the Tibetan language as his teaching assistant. I refused at first, saying, "How can I teach? I don't know English." But he said that I shouldn't worry about that because we would teach together. He knew a little bit of Tibetan. That's how it started. That's the way that we did it. Robinson was very sharp, and it seemed that he was a powerful man in the department, so he was able to arrange for me to come. At that time it was a strange thing for a university to have someone like me teaching there.

66. Beginning to Teach in America

IN 1967, when it was decided that I would go to Madison to teach, Elvin said that he would come along. He was with me from that time until his death in 1997. He was very, very helpful to me, especially at the university, preparing lessons, showing me how to grade, and all that kind of thing. When we got to Madison, Elvin arranged for an apartment and all the daily necessities. I didn't know how to do any of that. He cooked and took care of things, so it wasn't too difficult for me.

We had eight students that first year, including two faculty. One was the Sanskrit teacher, Francis Wilson. The other was Professor Upadhyaya, who was from India. He was both studying and teaching there. Robinson would lecture and run the class, and when questions about pronunciation and grammar came up, I would answer those. That's the way we taught for the first couple of years.

There were a lot of students around who were interested in learning about Buddhism. I was a monk, wearing robes, so that got people's attention. Those first students helped a lot with my learning English. I was very enthusiastic then about learning English. I always had a little dictionary with me, and when students would come, I asked them about English words. Somehow I was able to communicate pretty well that way.

During my time in New Jersey I had lived in a monastic environment, as I had in Tibet. When I came to Wisconsin, I was no longer in a monastery, and I was completely lost. The university was a whole new experience for me. There were thousands of students, and when the class periods ended, they went every direction, like ants. During this time I was teaching in the Van Hise building in the middle of campus, and when I would walk from place to place, people would stare, talk to each other, and sometimes laugh. Sometimes people would go out of their way to walk far away from me. Sometimes students walked by me and then after they passed they'd turn around, looking at this strange person. Of course they had never seen someone in these robes. I was like a white crow among black crows. Among all those students and teachers walking around there was this one red-robed person, standing out. But most people were just interested and helpful. Students and other university people helped me a lot, and so did secretaries in the department. This was my first experience meeting young Westerners. I had some experience in New Jersey because people had come to visit there, but they were mostly there to see Geshé Wangyal. We were in the background. We cooked and sometimes served guests, but that's about all.

Even after I became a teaching assistant at the University of Wisconsin, New Jersey was still my home, so I would go there in the summer and for the winter break. During one of my winter breaks when ordinarily I would have returned to New Jersey, I went to Canada instead. A woman who had attended the Bucks County teaching in 1968 had asked me to come to Canada. She was a teacher if I remember correctly, and she had a group of people coming to her house for lessons on Buddhism. She wanted to start a center there, and she asked me to get two Tibetan teachers, saying she wanted people "just like you." I wasn't sure what that meant, but I tried to select two of my best students and decided on Khensur Losang Tenzin and Geshé Kelsang Gyatso. The plan eventually fell through, however, and the center was not established there after all. But I did travel to Canada to look into the situation before committing to the endeavor.

Since I only had the time between semesters, we had to hurry. Elvin and I drove. At that time, both Elvin and I were new drivers, so we were not very experienced. Elvin had lived for a long time in New York City, but he didn't drive there. We left Wisconsin in the afternoon and drove until late, all the way to Detroit, where we spent the night. The weather was bad; it snowed all night. We left Detroit and went to Toronto on the way to Montreal. My driving teacher had told me not to turn on the heat in the car when driving in the cold and snow and that it was better to wrap up in a blanket and drive like that. If the heat were used, then it would cause a lot of ice to build up on the windshield because it was cold outside and warm inside. If it were kept cold inside, the wipers would be able to keep the windshield completely clean. So that's what we did. We didn't have any heat, and we just stayed bundled up. That was a good lesson in the sense that it kept the windshield clear, but it made for a very long, cold drive.

Along the way, when I was driving, we had an accident. It was dark, and we were on a two-lane road. It was snowing, the road was icy, and the lights from the oncoming cars were shining in my eyes. There was a truck in front of us going very slowly, so I decided that I had to pass it or we would never get there. I think we were close to Montreal by this point. Elvin kept saying, "Now you can pass," but I wasn't able to. He repeated several times, "Now it's okay to pass," but I was still hesitant. Finally, there was a time when no cars at all were coming, so I started to pass. The back corner of the car hit the guardrail, and bang! the car went into a spin, going around several times. The truck was gone, and fortunately there was a pause in the traffic and no other cars were coming. The car ended up sliding into the ditch on the side of the road. The back end was in the ditch, and the front was kind of sticking up in the air. I didn't know anything about cars and accidents, so I thought that the back wheels were broken, like the back leg of a dog. In fact there really wasn't any damage. Elvin was very good, saying, "It's okay, don't worry. Now just don't do anything." I saw some cars coming in the distance. They probably saw our car spin and then go off the road. A couple of cars stopped and the people got out. They had shovels and sand; they were prepared for an emergency. They asked if anything were damaged or if anyone were hurt, and we said that we were okay but we needed help getting out. They helped us get out easily by shoveling and putting down sand. Then we immediately started driving again. There was a big dent in the back of the car, but otherwise it had no problems.

It was strange. I had never had that kind of experience before; no one in Tibet had a car. In one way I was anxious about driving, but in another way I was rather enjoying it. Eventually we reached our destination. I didn't actually teach on this trip. I was just visiting to see how it looked, to see if it would be good for a center. Elvin was always very careful about these things because he was concerned that I not get involved in something without investigating it carefully first. We didn't stay very long because we only had a short time before the start of the next semester.

After I had been teaching Tibetan language at the university for about a year, Jeffrey Hopkins came to Wisconsin. He was officially studying with Robinson, but he was also studying with me. Jeffrey and Robinson rented an old farmhouse in Cambridge, Wisconsin, which is just outside of Madison. Michael Sweet, Leonard Zwilling, Jeffrey, and some other students lived there. The house became something of a Buddhist center. They invited Khensur Ngawang Lekden Rinpoché, who was then living in New Jersey, to live there while he was teaching a seminar at the university. He also did some teaching there at the house. I was living in Madison with Elvin, but I spent a lot of time at the house in Cambridge.

Robinson and I had gotten a grant from the government to write the book that later became *Lectures on Tibetan Religious Culture*. The following fall he was going to go to the University of Hawaii for one year. One day close to the fall semester it was very cold, so he went down to the basement to do something to the furnace. It was very dark down there, and there was a gas leak, but he didn't know it. He lit a match and there was an explosion. He was burned over most of his body, maybe seventy percent. He lived a couple of days in the hospital, but then he died. We went to visit him in the hospital, but he was in a plastic tent so we couldn't get close to him. He looked frightful. He was so badly burned that I couldn't even recognize him. At first he was able to talk, and he talked to me quite a bit. He said that we would work on the book when he recovered. Someone said later that he was probably in shock at that point. Still, he was trying to tell me some things, trying to encourage me. After Robinson's death I continued to teach at the university and was asked to continue to write the book, so Elvin helped me to write it. I remained in Madison and didn't really go back to New Jersey much anymore. Anyway, working on the book kept me there. After that I was stuck in Wisconsin—stuck like glue!

My teaching at the university attracted many students who were interested in Tibetan Buddhism and religion. The Department of South Asian Studies at the university hired me to teach Tibetan language, literature, culture, and Buddhism, even though I didn't hold any Western academic degree. The fact that I was attracting so many students interested the university, but there were some who were not happy about it. Some people weren't sure about having a Tibetan monk as a professor. This was during the Vietnam War and the hippie movement, and a lot of hippies left the U.S. to escape the draft. Many went to India. They had long hair, wore beads, and all that. On campus there were many of these people too. First I was a university teacher and then I became like a guru to the hippies.

In Nepal, Lama Yeshe was attracting many students. Lama Yeshe had been one of my students back in Tibet, and at this point he was getting rather famous among Westerners. He was like a hippie lama. There were some people in Indiana who knew Lama Yeshe, and they invited Lama Yeshe and Lama Zopa to come there. When they did, they also came to Wisconsin to see me and stayed a few days.

67. Starting a Dharma Center

WITH ALL THESE things happening, I was attracting a lot of students. Some people who had gone to India and Nepal learned about me there. Tibetans knew who I was, and they told the Americans that there was a teacher in their own country. John Newman was the first one who came from India to find me. He came right to my house. He stayed with Elvin and me there for some time, and I enjoyed hearing news from India. After that, many other people came, such as Roger Jackson and Beth Solomon, and these people stayed in houses near me. There were some affordable places to live in that part of Madison, and slowly a steady group of people had gathered around me. Eventually these people didn't want just occasional teachings; they wanted to have an actual Buddhist center. The first center was called the Ganden Mahayana Center, and it was right in the house where I lived.

Once the center was established, I taught more regularly, nearly every Sunday. I was living in this rented house when we began the first summer teachings in 1968 or 1969. The house that we were renting had a room big enough for maybe fifteen people. I gave some teachings there, but the first actual special summer teachings held by the center took place at Edgewood College and lasted about one month. Zong Rinpoché taught there, as did a very famous female Tibetan medical doctor from Dharamsala. Geshé Rabten, Lama Yeshe, and I also taught. Four or five monks came with Geshé Rabten from his center in Switzerland. Gönsar Rinpoché may have come too, though I'm not sure now. That first year was very eventful.

That same year I had another automobile accident. It was during the time of the teachings at Edgewood College. Zong Rinpoché was going to give the Vajrayoginī empowerment, and I was bringing the Vajrayoginī statue to the teaching. I had put the statue in a box and put the box on the seat next to me. As I was driving I noticed that the statue was clanging around as if it had fallen over or something. I thought that I should stop and secure the statue correctly in the box. I pulled over behind some cars that were parked on the road so I could take care of the statue. As I went to park the car, right when I should have put on the brake, I pressed down on the gas instead, and I crashed into the car in front of me. My face hit the steering wheel and pushed in my two bottom front teeth, cutting my lip open. There was a lot of blood, but it didn't hurt much. I was just thinking, "What happened?" The car in front of me had been pushed forward and hit the car in front of that, so there were three cars damaged. The front of my car was also leaking water because the radiator was smashed.

I just sat there for a while, wondering what I should do. There was a woman across the street in one of the houses who had heard the crash. She looked out the window and came over right away. She asked if I were all right. When she saw the blood all over me, she hurried back to her house and brought me some paper towels. I told her that I should probably call someone, so I gave her Elvin's phone number, and she said she would call him for me. She said that we should probably call the police, but I told her that she should just first call Elvin and he would know what to do. She did call Elvin, but she also called the police, who were there almost immediately. I heard the sirens, and there they came. They asked what happened, and I told them. They were very sympathetic toward me. The officers said that I should be taken to the hospital to see what needed to be done and that I shouldn't worry about the car and the accident; they would take care of it.

The ambulance came, and I was thinking that I would just walk over and get in it, but the attendants said that I shouldn't walk. Instead, they put me on a stretcher, which made it look very serious. They said that if

I were to just walk into the hospital then the people there wouldn't work on me very quickly. They said I should just lie down on the stretcher so it would seem more serious. I said that I was okay, but they said, "No, no, don't say you're okay." So I just lay down like they said.

When we got to the hospital, the ambulance people wanted to take me to the emergency room so that I would be taken care of right away. I was lying on the stretcher when they took me in. I suppose it looked bad with all the blood. They had to stitch up my lip first, so they didn't do anything about my teeth for the time being. There was another team of doctors that would work on those. The first team just sewed up my lip properly, and then they called the doctor who was to work on my teeth. That took a little while, so I just waited there lying on the stretcher. Then the other doctor came and gave me an injection. Of course I had already had one for the stitches, so this wasn't painful. This second doctor looked everything over, and he moved the teeth back into place. Luckily, they weren't knocked out completely. He said that it was better not to pull the teeth if that could be avoided. If they did not recover then they might have to remove them and replace them with false ones. So he left them in place and said that they might get better, which they did. That's how the doctor left it, and eventually they let me go home.

The people at the event at Edgewood College had heard news that I had been in an accident. When I finally arrived, people came to see how I was. Geshé Rabten said that they didn't know if I were dying or dead or what. He said he had been very afraid. All they had been told was that I was taken to the emergency room, so they thought that it must be very bad. The next day I went to the teaching and participated, no problem. It looked rather frightening, but I didn't feel too much pain. So that was my second accident.

Eventually we were able to buy another house in our area in Madison for the Ganden Mahayana Center. The house was located on the upper part of a hill. The woman who owned it wanted to move to California, so I was able to buy it cheaply. It was not a very nice place when we first moved in. The house was very dark because all the windows were covered with heavy blue curtains, and the walls were covered with dark wooden paneling. It had dirty blue carpeting, which had been ruined by the dogs and cats that belonged to the previous owner. At first it was pretty dark and miserable in there, but my students completely remodeled the house. Downstairs there was a big garage that we turned into the temple and teaching room; we could seat nearly fifty people.

Having the center in a residential neighborhood caused some problems. There were often a lot of cars on the road by the house, and some of the neighbors apparently didn't like that. They were worried about something, though I'm not sure what. Elvin was the first to notice it, then some of the other students noticed it too. We decided that it was probably best to move the center somewhere else. Until then, I asked people to park farther away when they came to teachings on Sundays. This was close to the end of the center being there.

68. His Holiness the Dalai Lama's First Visit to Madison

H is Holiness first came to Madison in 1979. This was the first time he came to America. The trip was arranged by the University of Wisconsin at my request. His Holiness was to give Dharma teachings as well as a general public talk. This was the first time that the Ganden Mahayana Center sponsored a program with His Holiness. We had to have the Dharma event at the St. Benedict Center, a retreat center outside of Madison, because we didn't yet have any space of our own that was large enough. We were able to arrange for His Holiness to stay at the chancellor's house, which was a big mansion that belonged to the university. While he was in Madison, His Holiness visited my house, and I offered him a dinner there.

His Holiness was supposed to give a lecture at the university, but the day chosen for his talk was the same day as the toga party, which was a big yearly student event in Madison. The chancellor said that this was very bad and that we wouldn't be able to have His Holiness speak on campus because of the event. I had never heard of such a thing, so I had to ask, "What is a toga party?" The chancellor said that the students would be wild and disorderly, so it would just not work to have His Holiness on campus the same day that all this was happening. He said that it would be better to arrange for a place away from campus and downtown. So through the university it was arranged that His Holiness would give the public talk in a big auditorium at West High School in Madison. It turned out that this too had to change because they didn't have enough room in the hall for all the people that came. People came all morning, and more and more people arrived throughout the day. Eventually they realized that the hall was not going to be large enough for all these people. We had to wait about an hour while they arranged to move the talk to the gymnasium, which they said was large enough to hold all the people. Finally, after about an hour, the talk began.

During this visit, His Holiness also went to a Catholic college near Milwaukee that had invited him to give a one-day teaching and receive an honorary degree. I went along on the drive to Milwaukee and sat in the back of the car with His Holiness. We talked back and forth for that whole ride. It was on this ride that I asked him to come back and give the Kālacakra empowerment. It was an unprecedented request. It would be the first Kālacakra empowerment in the West. He had already given four in India and a couple in Tibet when he was young. I thought that it would be a good idea for him to give this empowerment in the United States. At first he seemed hesitant, but then he said that such a thing could be done. We decided that we would begin to prepare and that we would do it within three years. That's how it started. We planned for the empowerment over a couple of years. Originally we thought about having it at a big public venue, but then we bought our own place that would become the new Deer Park Buddhist Center.

69. The First Kālacakra
Empowerment in America

A s mentioned, we already had some problems keeping the center in our neighborhood, but the overriding reason we needed to find a new place was because we had finally arranged for His Holiness to come and give the Kālacakra empowerment in 1981. We needed a place that was large enough and where we would be allowed to gather people regularly, so it couldn't be zoned as a residential place. As a result we looked more at the outlying areas of Madison rather than right in the city. There was one place that we liked very much, and we almost bought it, but in the end we didn't. This turned out to be a good thing because we later found out that we wouldn't have been allowed to have a lot of people there.

The county authorities were helpful, but the people in some areas that we were considering were closed-minded and suspicious about us. Some of the places that we considered would have been very nice, but the communities did not want us. In one place they held a meeting to determine whether we should be allowed to have a center there, and the people were worried that we would eat the local box turtles. I never did understand that. They thought some crazy things about Tibetans and Tibetan Buddhists. The realtor who was helping us in our search suggested that we look at Oregon, Wisconsin, a rural community south of Madison, because it was more liberal.

In Oregon again we had to go to a meeting to get approval to establish the center. Here some people were supportive, while others opposed the center. I think they were worried that we might be like the Hari Krishnas or something. During this time the Hari Krishna movement was very popular, and many people were concerned about it. This was also around the time that Bhagawan Shree Rajneesh, later known as Osho, was getting into trouble in Oregon state, so people were worried that we might be like him. Of course we Tibetans didn't know much about this at the time, but these issues were important in those days. People were suspicious of many foreign religious groups, thinking we might be starting cults. I could understand these people's concerns; when I heard about groups like this, I didn't like it either.

Just to be safe, we had checked around and had found some places where we could have the empowerment ceremonies if we didn't find a place of our own. We could have had them at the Sheraton near Madison or at the Dane County Coliseum. His Holiness's younger brother, Ngari Rinpoché, was our main contact about the Kālacakra empowerment. He suggested that it would be much better if we could find a place of our own, because the Kālacakra empowerment would make the site where it took place into a sacred place.

Fortunately we finally found a house in the town of Oregon. Due to financial difficulties, the owners were anxious to sell, and it looked like we would be able to purchase it at a good price. This is now the Deer Park Buddhist Center. When we bought it there were some problems with our property. Just behind the house, where the Kālacakra temple is now, it was as dense as a jungle. The area in front of the temple where the stupa is now was not flat. It was covered with trees and had a hill that sloped down to farmland. Because it was winter when we looked at it, the area was snow-covered, and we couldn't see that this was the case. The front part of the land was then an open field with tall grass. The trees that are there now were planted later. It seemed as though the flat front area was the only possibility for the place to hold the Kālacakra ceremonies. We would be able to put up a big tent, but it would have to be close to the road and wouldn't be very quiet.

I had my doubts about whether this were a suitable place, but we were running out of time and options, and of the pieces of land that we had looked at, this was among the least expensive. It also looked as though getting permission from the community to have the Kālacakra empowerment would be fairly easy. Though there were other places that I liked better, it seemed that this was our best choice, and Elvin thought we should buy it. It turned out well in the end. Now it's very good.

In the spring we started to work on the area behind the house and cleared the trees. John Davenport was the main person supporting this project. He was the engineer. We built a temporary platform there for the empowerment that was later enclosed to make a permanent temple. Many of the students worked on this and also on the house. The students were so kind and helpful, doing all that work. We bought the land in the winter, and it was the following summer that His Holiness came.

In Tibet it is said that the Kālacakra tantra is uniquely effective in this age, in which it is harder than ever for people to adhere to, and make progress in, the Buddhist religion. The Kālacakra empowerment ceremony contains unique and powerful methods that bring blessings and peace to the place where it is held. It also has a special connection with the land of Shambhala, which, according to tradition, is a hidden kingdom where the Kālacakra tradition is upheld and people live in complete peace and harmony. Interestingly, in Tibet they say that America, like Shambhala, is far off to the north, so there was some connection between Shambhala and America in the minds of Tibetans.

I thought that it would be beneficial to have this empowerment here in the U.S. I thought maybe it would have some benefit, like bringing peace and bestowing blessings on this place. Elvin had expressed an interest in this for some time even though he didn't request it specifically. There had been tantric empowerments given outside of Tibet before, both in India and in the West, including in Madison. Several lamas had come and given these, as in the case of Zong Rinpoché giving the Vajrayoginī initiation at Edgewood College. Among my students, there was a lot of pressure for me to give empowerments, but I never did. I never gave tantric teachings either—only sūtra teachings like stages of the path and so on. There were many students who had heard of the tantric practices of Vajrayoginī or Vajrabhairava, or at least had heard these names. Even though they liked my ordinary teachings on stages of the path texts and so on, they were also looking for some high, special teachings. There were also some who had already taken such empowerments and teachings elsewhere, and they wanted this from me. Finally, I invited Zong Rinpoché who gave the Vajrabhairava and Vajrayoginī empowerments. This was back in 1969.

There are three levels of vows in Tibetan Buddhism. The first is the *pratimokṣa* vow, or the vow to strive for individual liberation. This vow stresses ethical conduct for the sake of freeing oneself from the cycle of birth and death. The bodhisattva vow is much higher and more demanding. A person who takes this vow puts the well-being of others before his own. He vows to stay in the cycle as long as others are suffering and vows to lead all beings to liberation. This is a commitment for all one's future lives. The tantric vows are based on this same concern for others but are specific to the unique qualities of tantric methods. These vows are very demanding and are also binding in all one's future lives. For example, one must commit to performing the sādhana of the practice every day, several times a day, forever.

Some of the people who carelessly took these higher vows later realized that it was nearly impossible to live up to them. One such person told me, "I took such and such vow and committed to this and that practice, but I can't do all these things. Every day I have to do these recitations. Can I please give these vows back to you?" I said, "How can I take these back?" I scolded such students a little bit. I had warned them before that this would happen. They just wanted some big empowerment, ignoring the fact that this entailed taking these very demanding vows. They had just been curious. In order to take a tantric empowerment one has to take bodhisattva vows and tantric vows. These are much higher and much more demanding than just the pratimokṣa vow, which is demanding in and of itself. But even students who weren't that serious took all these vows anyway. For this reason, I never put too much emphasis on empowerments and tantric teachings.

The Kālacakra empowerment, however, is different. It is unique among tantric empowerments in the way that it is given by His Holiness to a large group of people. This was so even in Tibet. One could take this empowerment without the same degree of commitment to practice. This was well known in Tibet, and of course there were many students here who were interested. I had taken all this under consideration before I requested that His Holiness give the Kālacakra. In later years, the Dalai Lama also gave this empowerment in California and New York, but the empowerment in Madison was how it all began.

The way the Kālacakra empowerment was performed in Tibet wasn't much different from how it is done in the West now. I received the Kālacakra empowerment when I was young from Ngakchen Rinpoché. I also attended the Kālacakra given by His Holiness later at the Norbu Lingkha. Many people came. The monks and nuns sat inside close to His Holiness, but there were many more laypeople from Lhasa who also attended. They sat outside, brought tea and cookies, talked, and sometimes listened to what was going on. If they were tired, they would go walk around or go off to the bathroom anytime they wanted. It was almost like a big picnic. They didn't know much about Kālacakra, but it was very famous in Tibet so they came. Mostly they were there out of devotion to His Holiness.

The more serious people sat up front, but the laypeople were there for the blessed water and *kusha* grass that were passed around. When these things were distributed, people crowded in to get them. They didn't want to miss even one thing. People are the same everywhere. Actually the people that came to that first Kālacakra at Deer Park were very serious. I was surprised at how serious they were. They listened carefully and even took notes. At the point in the ritual when everyone had to put on the red blindfold before seeing the mandala, even the police officers who were standing around had put them on. That was rather funny to see.

Everything went well for the ceremony, though a few times the weather seemed like it was going to disrupt things. As I said, we built a temporary roofed platform where His Holiness sat with the Namgyal monks, lamas, and other dignitaries. Everyone else sat under a huge circus tent that we rented. On the day that the ceremony was to begin, we had to set up the statues, the throne, and all the other necessary things. We lined up starting from the house and passed things out to the temple. It was raining a little bit, and we were worried that it would get worse. Suddenly there was a rainbow right on top of the temple, and everyone agreed that this was a good omen. Actually, that happened a couple of times over the course of the empowerment ceremonies. It's rather interesting, I think.

People came from all over for this empowerment. Many Tibetans came from Switzerland and other parts of Europe. There were people from India, Japan, and other places in Asia. I think there were about thirteen hundred people that attended the empowerment. Before the actual empowerment His Holiness gave a teaching on the *Thirty-Seven Practices of the Bodhisattva* at the Field House at the university. More than four thousand people came to this teaching, which lasted four days. This teaching was the preliminary teaching for the Kālacakra. We rented several buildings in Madison where people stayed. For instance, most of the Tibetans from Switzerland stayed together in one of these buildings. They came to Deer Park in school buses, and the buses took them home in the evening.

We did have a little difficulty with the Office of Tibet in New York at the very beginning. I had requested His Holiness to come here and give the Kālacakra, but then they got the idea that it should be at a bigger place in California. They wanted to move it there, but they wanted to keep me as the sponsor, to deal with all the expenses and everything. We refused this idea. Later, they did have a bigger one in California, but I think it was better to have a smaller one at Deer Park first.

70. My Return to Tibet

THE FIRST TIME I went back to Tibet was after His Holiness gave the Kālacakra empowerment in Bodh Gaya, India, in 1974. This was toward the end of the Chinese Cultural Revolution, and things were still very bad at that time. In the Lhasa area, many of the familiar things were gone, and many of the large homes of the wealthy had been turned into housing for the poorest classes. This was all part of the Chinese way of making the upper and middle classes pay for their supposed oppression of the lower classes, whether or not this was actually the case. The Chinese said that the higher classes had to pay for their subjugation of the poor—they said that now it was the higher classes' turn to be the oppressed.

In the Potala, the Chinese had made His Holiness's rooms into a museum. A relative of one of my teachers was a caretaker at the Potala, and he had keys, so I got to see these rooms. They had His Holiness's things, like his cup and so on, in glass cases. At Sera Monastery some statues had been removed and taken to China, and many others had been destroyed. The Chinese had deposited many broken statues in the temple in Samlo Khangtsen. Piles of broken heads and arms, all in pieces, were just dumped there. This was a very sad sight.

During the Cultural Revolution, aristocrats and highly educated monks suffered greatly. Religion was regarded as poison. The Chinese said that we Tibetans had enslaved our lower classes, and if one were an educated person, he was punished just the like the old nobility, regardless of whether he had actually ever held any power or privilege. As I mentioned, my teacher Gen Thapkhé Rinpoché was forced to do man-·ual labor on a dam at that time. He told me about these things when I saw him in 1974. By then the worst was over, and he had been given a position of some kind and was not treated too badly. He was still in good health too. Still, I could see that things were very difficult for most people who had remained in Tibet.

On that trip I visited Gen Thapkhé at Sera Jé. We met in a room on top of the Sera Jé temple, which hadn't been destroyed by the Chinese. Upstairs is the Dalai Lama's room and the abbot's room. My teacher stayed in another room up there at that time. This was before he got sick. I offered him a long-life pūja while I was there. That is a good memory. After I saw my teacher and how bad things were around Lhasa, I went back to Tsang. I went to see Ganden Chönkhor, but it had been destroyed. That was hard for me to see. It was rebuilt later, in the 1980s, but at this point, not much of anything was left there, so I had to stay in Shikatsé with some relatives. One of these relatives had gone to China to school, so he knew Chinese as well as Tibetan. Because of this, he had been given a job as the director of a Tibetan drama group that was located near Tashi Lhünpo. I stayed with him and his family on my visit.

In 1987 I went to Tibet again. I went to Lhasa on a university grant, hoping to arrange some kind of exchange program for students to come and learn the Tibetan language. I tried to arrange this through my teacher. I didn't expect it to be a great success, but I hoped that it might begin the discussion of this idea. Some of the Tibetan officials liked the idea, but nothing concrete came of it.

By this time my teacher's health had deteriorated. Now Thapkhé Rinpoché was staying in a room in Ngapö's house in Lhasa. Ngapö Ngawang Jikmé had been a member of the Kashak before 1959. He was one of two members of the Kashak who did not go into exile. This was a period of relative calm and freedom for Tibetans. Deng Xiao Ping was in charge, and he relaxed things quite a bit. He traveled to the U.S. and made other efforts to modernize and grant more freedom to people in both China and Tibet. This was before the events at Tiananmen Square; after that, things got worse again for a while. In 1987, however, things were not bad. Tibetans had more freedom than they had had for years. I stayed in the same house where my teacher was staying in Lhasa, and I was able to visit with him for several days. One night there was a wedding celebration going on just outside in the park where the house was. I could hear the music and celebration from the house. The music was not traditional Tibetan music; it was modern Western music. At that time Western ideas and customs were coming into Tibet more and more, and people were free to do such things. Of course this was both good and bad.

71. Meeting the Panchen Lama and the Passing of Gen Thapkhé Rinpoché

URING THIS SECOND trip to Tibet, my teacher suggested that I visit the Panchen Rinpoché. Generally this wasn't an easy thing to do. The Chinese were very cautious with the Tenth Panchen Lama. He had a bodyguard and other security people who always accompanied him. The Chinese built a new palace for him in Lhasa near the Potala. That is where I visited him. Panchen Rinpoché's Tibetan bodyguard was a lama that I knew, so that made it easier for me to get in to see him. It also helped that Panchen Rinpoché was interested in talking to me because I had come from America and because I was a student of Khensur Lhündrup Thapkhé.

At that time, Thapkhé Rinpoché was rather sick and mostly stayed in his house. Panchen Rinpoché had great respect for Thapkhé Rinpoché, in part because of his connection with the Panchen's own teacher, Ngülchu Rinpoché, and also because both my teacher and Ngülchu Rinpoché were students of Tri Rinpoché. I too had a connection with Ngülchu Rinpoché. Five other monks and I once received a teaching from him, requested by Tri Rinpoché, on the drawing of the lines of a mandala. Ngülchu Rinpoché was a very famous lama and a tantric master. He gave many teachings in a big room at the Panchen Lama's labrang on ritual, and he was a specialist on the fire pūja, which is a ritual done in connection with tantric practice. One other young person and I went there for teachings along with some older monks. The older monks were more interested, so I think they learned more. At that time I was more concerned with philosophy, but Tri Rinpoché said we should go, so we did.

During our visit I discussed many subjects with Panchen Rinpoché. He spoke out against the uncritical acceptance by Tibetans of all things Western. His concern was that our Tibetan culture would be lost if everyone simply adopted whatever was popular in America. I remember one amusing thing about this. Many women were wearing pants and high heels in Lhasa. This was so popular that some enterprising Tibetan businessmen took advantage of it. For a small sum of money, these men would attach heels to whatever shoes one had so that they became high-heeled shoes and the person could be fashionable. That's awfully funny, isn't it? In the end this liberalization was short lived, and the Western idea of protesting and students' rights was part of what caused the government to crack down on the protests in Tiananmen Square. After this, things got worse again both in China and Tibet.

Panchen Rinpoché told me that the Chinese government had recently given him some religious authority again. At that time he was working on the rebuilding of Samyé, and next he was going to turn to Ganden, Drepung, and Sera. Since Ganden was the Gelukpa's mother monastery, he said he was thinking that he would focus on that one. In the old days there were thousands and thousands of monks, from great scholar monks all the way down to dopdops, at Sera, Drepung, and Ganden. Panchen Rinpoché said that he didn't think it was necessary to return the monasteries to that kind of scale, but that those who were serious about study should have places to do it. It was his intention to make this possible. He was concerned with the way that young Tibetans were taking up the modern ways brought by the Chinese. He wanted to use his limited power to revitalize the Tibetan way of life, though he realized it wasn't possible to fully return to the ancient ways. He was also worried that because so many of the lamas and geshés had fled, there wouldn't be many good people left to teach Tibetan monks. He suggested that I should think about coming back to teach. I think he meant for me to come and teach for some short period rather than stay permanently.

During our visit we also discussed my life in America and how my teacher was doing. I told him that Thapkhé Rinpoché had been very sick of late. Suddenly Panchen Rinpoché said that he would go to visit my teacher. He told me to tell my teacher that he would come to see him. When I returned and told my teacher this, he couldn't believe it. He said, "How can he come here, to this house?" He assumed that it was just a polite thing to say or something. Then, a couple of days later, around 8:00 in the morning, a message arrived saying that Panchen Rinpoché was coming at 8:30! My teacher was completely surprised. He quickly began to make arrangements. He had a nice, wooden-frame seat that he usually used himself, so he prepared it for Panchen Rinpoché, moving himself to another. He had someone bring in a nice carpet, some silk wall hangings, and other decorations. He quickly borrowed an ornate silver cup with a lid and base that was used only for special occasions, and many other nice things. He had to make his small, ordinary room into a proper place for Panchen Rinpoché to visit. The Chinese government had provided the place where my teacher was living. It was in a new building on the edge of Lhasa, toward the direction of the road to Sera. It was a fairly large house with a gated garden and several rooms, but they were not big rooms. In fact my teacher's room was rather small.

Panchen Rinpoché did indeed come that day. He was wearing a big chuba like a Khampa. He had two or three Khampa bodyguards with him and one Chinese official who had a camera. The Panchen Lama was not allowed to go anywhere without this Chinese official. I was in the outer room when he arrived, and we talked again briefly. Then he went inside to my teacher's room where he was offered tea, and they talked. After a little while, they were ready to take pictures. Panchen Rinpoché asked me to come in for the pictures and I did. Though Panchen Rinpoché was about the same age as His Holiness, he died in 1989, not long after that visit.

My teacher Thapkhé Rinpoché also died shortly after I saw him in 1987. He had been in poor health for some time. Though many people wanted to look for his reincarnation after his death, Thapkhé Rinpoché had specifically said earlier that he did not want them to do this. He made this choice while he was still alive. This was just what his own teacher, Tri Rinpoché, had done before him. Before his death, Tri Rinpoché had told Thapkhé Rinpoché that looking for the reincarnation for the sake of carrying on the labrang and all its wealth and belongings was not worthwhile and not very sensible. He said that if a lama were really as spiritually realized as people thought, then he would have the power to be born into a wealthy family if he wanted to. Thus there was no point in finding some boy, bringing him into the labrang, and then giving him all his own wealth back. A real lama could take care of that himself. So Tri Rinpoché said that finding his reincarnation for such purposes was unnecessary, and he did not want it done.

Of course, in one sense, the search for the reincarnation of a lama arises out of his former students' desire to see him again. In general, if there are definite signs that a new tulku lineage has begun after a lama's death, then such a search should be done, but the purpose of such a quest should always be examined closely. In Tri Rinpoché's case, he made his feelings about this very clear, so his wishes had to be respected by his students. Gen Thapkhé was Tri Rinpoché's closest and favorite student, and Gen Thapkhé was a very devoted disciple, so when the time approached for him to die, he followed the example of his teacher.

By the time of his death, Thapkhé Rinpoché had regained some of his renown and was respected not only by Tibetans but even by some Chinese officials as well. Earlier, during the Cultural Revolution, Gen Thapkhé had been reduced to forced labor. At that time being well known and respected had counted against one. However, by the time Thapkhé Rinpoché was old, things had turned around again. He was again renowned, though he didn't have any actual political power. He was a member of the Tibetan Autonomous Region Religious Association, along with the Panchen Rinpoché; Phakpa Lha, who was a famous lama from Chamdo who had been a high Tibetan government official before the Chinese invasion; Tsemönling, who was a Sera Mé lama whose previous incarnation was one of the regents of Tibet; and some other famous religious figures. This association was important for Tibetan religion, but it didn't really have any political power.

Thapkhé Rinpoché was not only a great scholar, he was also a greatly realized master. I heard that after his death, he remained in a deep meditative state even after he had breathed his last. This is a well-known phenomenon in Tibetan Buddhism. He remained in this state for several days, during which time many people came to see him, including many Chinese people, both officials and ordinary people.

72. The Recent Past

MANY OF MY Tibetan students and other great geshés and lamas have come to Deer Park over the years, including those who have already been mentioned, and the Ganden Throne Holder Geshé Wangdu, Serkong Rinpoché, Lati Rinpoché, Jangtsé Chöjé Khensur Losang Tenzin, and others. Geshé Dönyö also stayed for a long time, but he eventually had to return to India to be Sera Jé abbot. There are a lot of geshés there these days, but most of them are younger. Older ones who have experience of the monastic system and who lived in Tibet are becoming rare. That's how Deer Park lost Geshé Dönyö.

Before they took Geshé Dönyö, Sera Jé tried to get me to come back too. They wanted me to be abbot and sent a letter requesting me to come. They had to submit a list of candidates to His Holiness for his approval. They told him that I was number one on the list, but he told them that they had to check with me first to see if I would want to do this. I responded that I could not do it. One reason was my age. Another was that I had become kind of Americanized. I had been away from a Tibetan monastery for so long that I no longer knew all the rules and regulations. I knew that now in India some things were different, but I didn't know what had changed and what remained the same. Thirdly, I had knee problems and was using a cane. I wouldn't even be able to ascend to the throne, much less sit on it, because I always have to sit with my leg stretched out. Fortunately, I had all these very nice excuses, so I was able to turn down the offer.

If His Holiness had put his seal on the list with my name on it, it would have been nearly impossible for me to refuse. I was lucky that he told them that they had to check with me first before he approved the list. After I turned them down, they appointed Geshé Dönyö. There had been another time that they wanted me, but that time His Holiness told them not to put me on the list at all. At that point I was still teaching at the university, and he thought that it was important that I continue to work there.

Being abbot is kind of like being governor. The abbot is the head of the monastery, but there isn't much teaching involved; it's more of an administrative position. There are many monks to oversee, and there are always problems. Being abbot means being the top authority of the monastery. If there are major decisions to be made, or if there is punishment to be dealt out, the abbot is responsible. Being abbot is not all that appealing.

I could have taken the position and retired quickly or had my senior students do the work, but I was not interested in that. I could have done it for the prestige, but I wasn't interested in that either. If this were something that I could do for the benefit of the monastery, I would have done it. But I did not have any experience with any administrative position, and I didn't feel qualified to be in charge of a big, complicated, political institution. It didn't seem that there would be any benefit in my doing it.

If I hadn't been sent to America, then I surely would have ended up in this position in India. Four of my students have been abbot now— three abbots of Sera Jé: Khensur Dönyö, Khensur Losang Tsering, and Khensur Jampa Tekchok; and Khensur Losang Tenzin has been abbot of Gyümé Tantric College and is now the Jangtsé Chöjé. Since I came to America, my connections with this system have been cut. If things had been different, and we did not have to flee Tibet, I probably would have gone on to Gyümé Tantric College, and maybe ended up Gyümé abbot, which would have been better, or at least a little quieter. Maybe I would have been the Jangtsé Chöjé, and then, by the age I am now, Ganden Throne Holder. Anyway, those are possibilities, but who knows?

It may seem strange that my story dedicates so little time to the last twenty-five years. It isn't that these years have not been eventful and important; it is simply because for most of these years, my time has been spent maintaining and improving Deer Park and being a university professor, each a lifetime's work on its own. It would be difficult to remember and list everything that I have done or been a part of in these years, but I will highlight a few important things.

We officially established the Deer Park Buddhist Center and Evam Monastery by the end of the 1970s, though teachings had been going on for some time before that. I have taught nearly every Sunday since the beginning of having a center. Some of the people who were there at the beginning are still coming, and many others have come over the years. Throughout the years I have taught many great Buddhists texts, including Śāntideva's *Guide to the Bodhisattva's Way of Life* and Nāgārjuna's *Letter to a Friend*. In the summers we have had numerous visits by great geshés and lamas who come and give empowerments and teachings. I have also offered intensive month-long courses in the summers on several fundamental texts by Tsongkhapa, including his *Essence of Eloquence*[67] and *Illumination of the Intent*,[68] as well as his *Great Exposition on the Stages of the Path*.[69]

In 1992, we sponsored one hundred Tibetan refugees to come to Madison. Because Tibetans are not legally recognized by the United States as refugees, we had to guarantee means of support for the Tibetans before they were allowed to come. Deer Park took responsibility for these people, and many members of the community joined in to help the newly arrived Tibetans. In 1996, Deer Park sponsored a tour of fifteen monks from the relocated Sera Jé monastery in India to come to the U.S. These monks toured the country debating and performing religious dances and other things to raise money for the building of a new assembly hall at their monastery in India.

We have sponsored several visits by His Holiness the Dalai Lama: first in 1979, then the Kālacakra initiation in 1981, and then again shortly after His Holiness was nominated for the Nobel Peace Prize in 1989, at which time he dedicated the Kālacakra stupa at Deer Park. In 1998 His Holiness came again to Madison and taught the middle-length *Stages of Meditation*, gave a public talk to thousands of people, and received an honorary degree from the university. His Holiness visited again in 2007 and 2008. My activities in connection with Deer Park have been very extensive and, I hope, worthwhile. We have many ambitious future plans for Deer Park, as I will discuss later.

I have already talked about how I came to teach at the University of Wisconsin. It seems like it was almost an accident, but here I am, almost forty years later, still living in Wisconsin. After Professor Robinson died, I continued teaching and slowly moved up from lecturer to assistant professor, associate professor, and finally to full professor in 1985. I was appointed Distinguished Visiting Professor for a semester at the University of New Mexico in 1975. In addition to teaching, my work has included writing scholarly articles and books, delivering lectures in the U.S. and elsewhere in the world, participating in numerous professional and humanitarian organizations, and receiving several grants and fellowships, including two Fulbright Fellowships.

During this time I have had many students, both undergraduate and graduate. I supervised more than twenty doctoral dissertations over a wide range of topics in Buddhist Studies. Many of my graduate students have gone on to teach Buddhist Studies at universities all over the U.S.

I have published numerous articles and several books, including two Tibetan language books, and two books on Tibetan Buddhist doctrine and philosophy, one of which has been translated into German, Italian, and Spanish. More recently I have published a volume on Kadam mind-training texts with two of my former students, and am now working on publishing a multi-volume commentary on Tsongkhapa's *Great Exposition on the Stages of the Path* in collaboration with several of my former students, three volumes of which have already been published. Additionally, I have recently published a translation of Thuken Chökyi Nyima's 1803 survey of religion, *Crystal Mirror of Philosophical Systems*, again in collaboration with several of my former students.

Throughout my time as a professor, I had many opportunities to travel and lecture all over the world and throughout the United States. I have given lectures and Dharma teachings in Canada, Mexico, Italy, Switzerland, England, France, Australia, New Zealand, Malaysia, Hong Kong, Singapore, Taiwan, Indonesia, Japan, Tibet, India, Nepal, Thailand, Puerto Rico, Costa Rica, Venezuela, and Brazil. I have been very fortunate to have seen so much of the world and met so many people interested in the Dharma and Tibet.

In 1996, I became a member of the Trustees of the International Peace Council, an interfaith organization that meets regularly to promote peaceful resolution of differences. Since that time I have attended meetings organized by this group in England, Mexico, and Israel. In 1997, I retired from the University of Wisconsin and was given emeritus status. Since retirement, I have continued to travel to Buddhist centers all over the world teaching the Dharma.

When not traveling and teaching, I have been trying to devote more time to practice. While I was teaching at the university and Deer Park at the same time, there was little time for me to practice. Since retirement I have completed retreats on the practices of all three of the major tantric practice lineages revered by the Geluk sect: Guhyasamāja, Cakrasaṃvara, and Vajrabhairava. This has been a precious opportunity for which I am very grateful.

Though I ended up in very different circumstances from what I thought I would when I was a scholar monk at Sera Jé, it's curious how, in one sense, I'm not much worse off in terms of having time to dedicate to practice. If the Chinese had not come, and I had progressed up through the ranks of the tantric college and maybe even up to Ganden Throne Holder, I would not have had much more time to devote to intensive practice. As I discussed, my teacher Gen Riksal, and before him Geshé Chönden, turned away from following the path of the scholar monk to its completion for this reason. Tri Rinpoché himself told me that though the pursuit of the scholar monk was important, it was just as important to be cultivating practice. Fortunately, I have lived long enough to get to the point in my life when I can spend more time on practice. If it had been otherwise, how much would I have really accomplished?

Not long after I came to America, I saw that people were very interested in Tibetan Buddhism. They seemed to want more spiritual things in their lives. People here have plenty of material things, possessions, money, and all that, but they still aren't happy. There is something else that they seek, and many people think that this is to be found in the Tibetan Buddhist Dharma. Generally, we Tibetans were less interested in material things alone, at least before the exile. Whereas we were more concerned with religious development and the purification of our karma through pūja and prayers, in the U.S. it seems that most people are more concerned with this life and the eight worldly goals that I discussed earlier. But if one sees the world from the perspective of the Dharma, when one does not have worldly success or when bad things happen, one sees it as the result of one's previous karma. This isn't supposed to make one feel better; it should have the effect of changing one's behavior. If these bad things are the result of previous negative actions, one should strive to avoid negative actions, and then such misfortune will not come again in the future. This attitude is much more helpful for oneself and for society in general.

Not very long ago, people in the West knew little or nothing about Tibet and Tibetan Buddhism. People thought that there were these strange, backward people high up in the mountains who were poor and stupid. They had some supernatural king called the Dalai Lama who sat on a high throne where everyone worshiped him, while the poor common people had no material well-being or any education at all. Of course, this was a superficial understanding based on a lack of real information and on the assumption that any advanced culture would be just like the Western ones, or, for that matter, like that of the Chinese Communists. In a curious way, the Chinese Communists were responsible for bringing Tibetan religious culture to the rest of the world. It's like they broke the ice dam that was holding all these things up in Tibet so that they could flow to every part of the globe. Now people know a lot more about Tibetan culture and Buddhism, and it seems that the interest is still growing. Even in China these days young people are taking an interest in Buddhism again. Though the intention of the Chinese Communists was to destroy this culture, their actions have turned out to make it available to the whole world. It's interesting, isn't it?

Now it seems that people are beginning to better understand the Dharma here in the West, and of course it is my wish that Deer Park will be a resource for this to continue to happen. But it's still very early in the transmission of the Dharma to the West, so the results are rather mixed. While there seems to be a better understanding of the principles of the Buddha's teachings, there are some pretty strange ideas out there as well. Over the years, I have had a lot of people come to me with odd conceptions about Tibetan Buddhism and what I have to offer. Not very long ago, a person came to me and said that he had had a bad experience with someone and now couldn't get it out of his head. The person said that he couldn't shake his obsession with this event, and he asked me if there was some Buddhist healing technique that I knew that would make this affliction go away. Apparently this person thought that I must have some supernatural power that would heal him. I had to tell him that I didn't. I don't have that kind of power.

I am neither a great meditator nor a great practitioner, but I enjoy teaching the Dharma, which I learned from my own revered teachers and the renowned monastic universities of Tibet. It seems that over the years, when people have come to me looking for solutions to their problems and I don't have what they're looking for, they aren't interested in what I do have to offer. If someone shows up looking for magical cures and I try to tell her about the teachings of the Buddha, she doesn't stay around very long. I am happy to share my meager knowledge with people who are interested in learning the Buddhadharma. That is what I have to offer.

There are certainly some very difficult things about understanding the teachings of the Buddha, but there are also some very practical, simple things that everyone can understand. Understanding emptiness is not easy for anyone, but that is not the only thing the Buddha taught. In Nāgārjuna's *Precious Garland*,[70] he says, "Until one is able to completely clear away the self-cherishing view, one should practice giving, morality, and patience." The actual eradication of the false view of self comes only through a direct realization of emptiness, but in the meantime, one should cultivate these three qualities. That's a good start.

In Candrakīrti's *Guide to the Middle Way*[71] it says, "There are six perfections: giving, morality, patience, diligence, meditation, and wisdom. Among these, the Buddha primarily taught the first three to laypeople." This is true, but many people might not like this fact. It seems most people want higher teachings and think that these simple ethical prescriptions are not very interesting.

This isn't just a Western idea; Tibetans can be like this too, though they tend to have a different perspective. Most Tibetans believe in karma and have a basically Buddhist outlook, so even if they're uneducated and want the highest teachings, at least the desire arises from a Buddhist motivation. Tibetan people understand suffering, sickness, and misfortune to be the result of karma. There are some things, some sicknesses for example, that one simply has to work through by suffering them. While other people assume that there must always be a cure, a solution, Tibetans will say that some sufferings have to be endured; there is no cure or treatment that will fix the situation. That probably seems like a strange perspective, but that is how we see it. In the West it seems that people assume that everything can be fixed, and that there must always be a solution. We don't see it that way. It seems too that in the U.S. people only believe what they can see with their own eyes. If one can't see it, it must not exist. We Tibetans don't think this way either. There is no reason to assume that we can always see everything there is in the world. There are many things in this world that we cannot see.

73. The Future

THE FIRST TEMPLE at Deer Park was a temporary pavilion that was built for the Kālacakra empowerment in 1981. Later we closed that structure in to make the temple that we now call the Kālacakra temple. That temple eventually became too small, what with all the Tibetans in Madison and the continued growth in interest among Americans. Over the years, the old temple had become less stable. When I sat in the temple during the Nyungné retreat when all the people in the temple were doing prostrations, I noticed the building started to shake, and I was a little worried that it wouldn't hold up. So I decided that we should build a larger and better temple so that we could accommodate more people and activities. That temple was completed several years ago and consecrated by His Holiness in the summer of 2008. This was all thanks to the great generosity and tireless efforts of many people, both locally and internationally. Even after I die, I want this place to be valuable for others.

There are many Tibetan Buddhist centers in this country, but there are very few places that are what we Tibetans would consider monasteries. Buddhist centers and monasteries are not the same thing. Buddhist centers are often run by lay people, but monasteries are run exclusively by monks. In the centers, there are facilities for people who want to study Tibetan Buddhism, and some provide temporary residence for these people, both men and women. It is much harder, however, to find a place to go if one wants to take up the monastic life. I think this is very important, and I want Deer Park to continue to offer this possibility, while also expanding the facilities so that other monks—even if they aren't geshés—nuns, and laypeople will be able to come here.

Monks have the responsibility of teaching others, and the monastic nature of our center means that laypeople can always come here to learn but not stay like they could at a Dharma center. A monastery is a place bound by all the rules of the Vinaya, which means that it is run according to the strict discipline laid down by the Buddha himself. It is a place that only monks can stay, and this specifically means that women are not permitted to stay the night within its walls. This is important for the monastic life. Monks, geshés, and lamas need a place where they can live according to the monastic lifestyle and it is very important to me that Deer Park be able to provide this for them. For centuries in Tibet there was a resistance to modernization and secularism. There were more monasteries and nunneries there than almost anywhere else in the world. These monastic centers were the heart of our religious culture. They were centers where people could come and dedicate their whole lives to religion. But laypeople also benefited from this situation because they were taught by these monastic scholars and teachers. Even the government in Tibet had both of these components. We characterized our government as the union of the Dharma and the secular. It was a very beneficial situation for everyone. I've long thought that this system had much to offer other cultures.

Still, sometimes I suspect that much of the attention that Tibetan Buddhism receives in the West arises largely out of a desire for entertainment and exoticism. It's almost like being interested in a television show. I want to make sure that there is more to it than that. I want to make sure that this interest isn't just something that looks serious for a while but then is gone. There is a saying in Tibetan that some things disappear "like the fog on a mirror on which one has breathed." First it looks like something real, but then it disappears as if it were never there. I don't want this to be the case with Tibetan Buddhism in America. If we can create a solid, traditional basis here, even if it is small, then there will at least be some foundation for others who want to come to know about Tibetan Buddhism in the future.

I always quote a passage from the last chapter of Śāntideva's *Guide to the Bodhisattva's Way of Life* that says, "The pure Dharma teachings are the only medicine able to permanently clear away the sufferings of sentient beings." Of course, for temporary relief there are medicines and other kinds of treatment, but only the Dharma is capable of providing complete mental freedom for all beings. It is also the source of true happiness. Temporary happiness can be had from material things, but permanent peace and happiness can only be found through the Dharma. These two things, relief from suffering and real happiness, come only from the pure teachings of the Buddha. Śāntideva continues, "May these teachings long endure in the world with material support and honor." People's respect and interest and the material support for the Dharma must continue in order for the teachings to remain and thrive. There must be a place for these teachings to be available to people. The teachings can't just live in the sky; there must be support from the people for the teachings of the Buddha to continue. Though these things were said by an Indian master, many great Tibetan lamas like Tsongkhapa have said this same thing for hundreds of years. The Dharma is medicine for all beings, so we must make the teachings available all over the world for the sake of all these beings. This is only possible through the kind of dedication and commitment that Śāntideva talks about. I wish Deer Park to be valuable to others—that's my intention. I want this place to be valuable not just for people now but on into the future.

There's a saying that goes, "A pool from which a stream flows but which has no spring to feed it will soon dry up and disappear." Likewise, a center where the teachings of the Buddha are upheld and taught will not last long if there is no source producing new teachers. In our case, we have the resources of Sera from which to draw. His Holiness has established the three great monasteries of Sera, Drepung, and Ganden in India, where the traditional training is just like it was in Tibet, with meditation and philosophical and scholarly components as well. Because these great monasteries are there, and specifically Sera Jé, we will have a continuing source from which to draw in the form of traditionally trained, highly educated monks who can come to Deer Park to teach. Deer Park exists to provide a place where these monks can come and benefit many people. The primary purpose and value of this place is as a monastery that will serve as a resource for the teachings of the Dharma. As a monastery, there are rules that must govern how it is run, assuring that monks have a place that supports their desire to live in accord with the ideals set forth by the Buddha. At the same time, Deer Park will also serve the public, so that many people can benefit. The new temple is making it possible for even more people to participate.

It is difficult to believe that I am in a position to have to consider such matters today. When I left my home in Tsang I could never have dreamed where my life would take me. I left Tibet with practically nothing. All I had was a cup. Then, because of the way things worked out, I ended up with so much: this land, this house, the temple, and hundreds of dedicated students. Before I die I want to make sure that all of this will continue to be of use for the benefit of others. That is my intention. One can't know how he came to be where he is, or what will happen next. One can, however, take charge of one's future by cultivating good thoughts and actions now. By being mindful of one's intentions, it becomes possible to sow the seeds for good results, both for oneself and for others. Whatever little merit I have I dedicate to the continued presence of the Dharma here, and all over the world, and to the alleviation of the suffering of all beings everywhere.

Table of Tibetan Spellings

THE FOLLOWING is a list of the Wylie equivalents for the phonetic spellings given in the text. This work follows the conventions used by Wisdom Publications; however, some phonetic renderings follow more popular usages and conventional spellings.

amban . . . . am ban
Amdo . . . . a mdo
Ashang-la . . . . a zhang lags
Barkhor . . . . bar skor
Bati Khangtsen . . . . sba ti khang tshan
Bön . . . . bon
Bongbu Sotsik . . . . bong bu so tshig
Bumti . . . . 'bum ti
Buti . . . . bu khrid
Chaksam Chuwori . . . . lcags zam chu bo ri
cham (dance) . . . . 'cham
Chamdo . . . . chab mdo
Chamsing . . . . lcam sring
chang . . . . chang
chanzö . . . . phyag mdzod
Chaptama . . . . chab rta ma
charkepa . . . . 'char skad pa

chö (Dharma) . . . . chos
chö (severance) . . . . gcod
chogawa . . . . cho ga ba
chöjökyi gegen . . . . chos brjod kyi dge rgan
chöra . . . . chos rwa
chöra nup . . . . chos rwa nub
chöra shar . . . . chos rwa shar
chörai gegen . . . . chos rwa'i dge rgan
chöthok . . . . chos thog
Chu Drangmo . . . . chu grang mo
chuba . . . . phyu pa
Chusang . . . . chu bzang
Dakpo Ngari . . . . dwags po mnga' ris
Dechen Rapgyé . . . . bde chen rab rgyas
Dema Gönsar Rinpoché . . . . bde ma mgon gsar rin po che
densasum . . . . gdan sa gsum
Deyang . . . . bde dbyangs
Dompelpa-la . . . . sdom dpal pa lags
Dönyö, Geshé . . . . don yod, dge bshes
dopdop . . . . ldob ldob
Dorjé Drakden . . . . rdo rje brag ldan
Dorjé Shukden . . . . rdo rje shugs ldan
Dorjé Tsering . . . . rdo rje tshe ring
Drakri . . . . brag ri
dratsang . . . . grwa tshang
Drepung . . . . 'bras spungs
Drokmi Lotsāwa Shākya Yeshé . . . . 'brog mi lo tsā ba shā kya ye shes
drölma . . . . sgrol ma
Dromo . . . . gro mo
Dromtön Gyalwai Jungné . . . . 'brom ston rgyal ba'i 'byung gnas
Drupkhang Rinpoché . . . . sgrub khang

düra .... bsdud grwa

Dzamling Rinpoché .... 'dzam gling rin po che

dzokrimpa .... rdzogs rim pa

Dzong .... rdzong

Galuk .... dga' lugs

Gampopa Sönam Rinchen .... sgam po pa bsod nams rin chen

Ganden .... dga' ldan

Ganden Chönkhor .... dga' ldan chos 'khor

Ganden Tripa .... dga' ldan khri pa

Ganden Trisur .... dga' ldan khri zur

Gangchen .... gangs chen

gekö .... dge bskos

gelong .... dge slong

Geluk .... dge lugs

Gen .... rgan

Gen Mönlam-la .... rgan smon lam lags

Gen Tharchin .... rgan mthar phyin

Gesar .... ge sar

geshé .... dge bshes

geshé damja .... dge bshes dam bca'

getsül .... dge tshul

Gomang .... sgo mang

Gongpa Rapsal .... dgongs pa rab gsal

Gönsar Rinpoché .... dgon gsar

Gyaltsap Jé Darma Rinchen .... rgyal tshab rje dar ma rin chen

Gyalwa Ensapa .... rgyal ba dben sa pa

Gyantsé .... rgyal rtse

Gyümé .... rgyud smad

Gyütö .... rgyud stod

Hardong .... har gdong

Hralsum .... hral gsum

Jamchen Chöjé Shākya Yeshé	'jam chen chos rje shā kya ye shes
Jampa Trinlé	byams pa 'phrin las
Jamyang Chöjé	'jam dbyangs chos rje
Jamyang Karpo	'jam dbyangs dkar po
jang günchö	'jang dgun chos
Jangtsé	byang rtse
Jangtsé Chöjé	byang rtse chos rje
Jé (Sera college)	byes
jenang	rjes snang
jepa	byes pa
Jokhang	jo khang
jorlam	sbyor lam
kachen	bka' chen
Kadam	bka' gdams
Kagyü	bka' brgyud
Kalön Tripa	bka' blon khri pa
kamtsok	skam tshogs
kang	rkang
kangsowa	skang gso ba
Kangyur	bka' 'gyur
karam	bka' ram
Karma Kagyü	kar ma bka' brgyud
Karmapa	kar ma pa
Kashak	bka' shag
Katsé	bka' rtse
Kelsang Gyatso, Geshé	skal bzang rgya mtsho, dge bshes
Keutsang	ke'u tshang
Kham	khams
Khamlung	kham lung
khangtsen	khang tshan

khapsé	kha zas
khatak	kha btags
Khedrup Jé Gelek Palsang	mkhas grub rje dge legs dpal bzang
Khenchen Rinpoché	mkhan chen rin po che
khenpo	mkhan po
Khensur	mkhan zur
Khön Könchok Gyalpo	'khon dkon mchog rgyal po
Khyamra	'khyam ra
Khyungpo Naljor	khyung po rnal 'byor
Künkhyen Lodrö Rinchen Sengé	kun khyen blo gros rin chen seng ge
Künphel-la	kun 'phel lags
kunyer	sku gnyer
Kunyer Tsöndrü	sku gnyer brtson 'grus
kyérimpa	bskyed rim pa
Kyichu	skyid chu
labrang	bla brang
Lajang Khan	lha bzang han
lama	bla ma
lama umzé	bla ma dbu mdzad
Langdarma	glang dar ma
Laru Dratsang	lwa rul grwa tshang
Lati Rinpoché	bla ti rin po che
lhakhang chenmo	lha khang chen mo
Lhalu	lha klu
Lhalung Palgyi Dorjé	lha lung dpal gyi rdo rje
lharam	lha rams
Lhasa	lha sa
Lhatsé	lha rtse
Lhündrup Gönpo	lhun grub mgon po
Lhündrup Tengyé	lhun grub bstan rgyas

Lhündrup Thapkhé . . . . lhun grub thabs mkhas

Lhündrup Tsöndrü . . . . lhun grub brtson 'grus
(Tri Rinpoché) . . . . (khri rin po che)

Lhundub Sopa . . . . lhun grub bzod pa

Lhüntsé Dzong . . . . lhun rtse rdzong

Ling Rinpoché . . . . gling rin po ché

lingsé . . . . gling bsre

löntsok . . . . rlon tshogs

Losang Chökyi Gyaltsen . . . . blo bzang chos kyi rgyal mtshan

Losang Chönden . . . . blo bzang chos ldan

Losang Mönlam . . . . blo bzang smon lam

Losang Sangyé . . . . blo bzang sangs rgyas

Losang Tashi . . . . blo bzang bkra shis

Losang Tenzin, Khensur . . . . blo bzang bstan 'dzin

Loseling . . . . blo gsal ling

Lukhangwa . . . . klu khang ba

lung . . . . lung

Marpa Chökyi Lodrö . . . . mar pa chos kyi blo gros

Mé . . . . smad

Meru . . . . sme ru

Milarepa . . . . mi la ras pa

Mindrup Tsering . . . . smin 'grub tshe ring

mingtak . . . . ming brtags

mitsen . . . . mi mtshan

Mön . . . . mon

Mönlam Chenmo . . . . smon lam chen mo

Namgyal . . . . rnam rgyal

Namling . . . . rnam gling

namthar . . . . rnam thar

Nechung . . . . gnas chung

Nenang . . . . gnas nang

Ngak(pa) . . . . sngags (pa)

Ngakchen Rinpoché . . . . sngags chen rin po che

Ngapö Ngawang Jikmé. . . . . nga bod ngag dbang 'jigs med

Ngari. . . . . mnga' ri

Ngawang Gendün . . . . ngag dbang dge 'dun

Ngawang Gyatso, Geshé . . . . ngag dbang rgya mtsho, dge bshes

Ngawang Lekden. . . . . ngag dbang

Ngawang Losang Gyatso
(5th Dalai Lama) . . . . ngag dbang blo bzang rgya mtsho

Ngawang Riksal . . . . ngag dbang rigs gsal

Ngödrup Tselné. dngos grub

Ngülchu Rinpoché. . . . . dngul chu rin po che

Norbu Lingkha . . . . nor bu gling kha

Nyethang. . . . . snye thang

Nyingma . . . . rnying ma

Nyuk. . . . . nyug

Palden Lhamo . . . . dpal ldan lha mo

Palden-la. . . . . dpal ldan lags

Panchen Losang   paṇ chen blo bzang chos kyi
Chökyi Gyaltsen . . . . rgyal mtshan

parma. . . . . 'phar ma

pechai gegen . . . . dpe cha'i dge rgan

petri. . . . . dpe khrid

petsam. . . . . dpe tsam / dpe mtshams

Phabongkha Rinpoché . . . . pha bong kha rin po che

Phakpa Lha. . . . . 'phags pa lha

Phakpa Lodrö Gyaltsen . . . . 'phags pa blo gros rgyal mtshan

Phalha Drönyer Chenmo. . . . . pha lha mgron gnyer chen mo

Phenpo . . . . 'phan po

phodrang. . . . . pho brang

Pholhané . . . . pho lha nas

Phordok . . . . phor dog

Phuntsokling . . . . phun tshogs gling

phurba . . . . phur ba

Phurbuchok Jampa Rinpoché . . . . spur bu lcogs 'byams pa rin po che

Potala . . . . po ta la

Rabten, Geshé . . . . rab brtan, dge bshes

Ralpachen . . . . ral pa chen

Ramoché . . . . rwa mo che

rang ja . . . . rang ja

rapjampa . . . . rab 'byams pa

rapjung . . . . rab byung

rapjung parma . . . . rab byung phar ma

Ratö . . . . ra stod

Reting Rinpoché . . . . rwa sgreng rin po che

Richen Gong . . . . ri chen gong

rikchen . . . . rigs chen

rikchung . . . . rigs chung

rikram . . . . rigs rams

Rinchen Sangpo . . . . rin chen bzang po

Rinchen Sengé . . . . rin chen seng ge

ritrö . . . . ri khrod

sadak . . . . sa bdag

Sakya . . . . sa skya

Sakya Pandita Künga Gyaltsen . . . . . . sa skya paṇḍita kun dga' rgyal
mtshan

Samdhong Rinpoché . . . . zam gdong

Samlo . . . . bsam lo

Samyé . . . . bsam yas

sendregasum . . . . se 'bras dga' gsum

Sengé Dzong . . . . seng ge rdzong

senril . . . . zan ril

Sera . . . . se ra

Sera Jetsünpa . . . . se ra rje btsun pa

Serkhang . . . . gser khang

Serkong Rinoché . . . . gser kong rin po che

Shakabpa . . . . zhwa sgab pa

shaktsang . . . . shag tshang

Shākya . . . . shākya

shalngo . . . . zhal ngo

Shang . . . . shangs

shapten . . . . zhabs rtan

Sharkyu . . . . shar kyu

Sharpa Tulku . . . . shar pa sprul sku

Shartsé . . . . shar rtse

Shartsé Chöjé . . . . shar rtse chos rje

Shelkar . . . . shel dkar

Sherap Gyatso, Geshé . . . . shes rab rgya mtsho, dge bshes

Shidé . . . . bzhi sde

shika . . . . gzhis ka

Shikatsé . . . . gzhi ka rtse

shinglong . . . . shing longs

Shöl . . . . zhol

shukja . . . . zhugs ja

Shum . . . . bshums

sokté . . . . srog gtad

Sönam Gyatso . . . . bsod nams rgya mtsho

Songtsen Gampo . . . . srong btsan sgam po

Sungchöra . . . . gsung chos rwa

tak . . . . rtags / stag

Takdrak Rinpoché . . . . stag brag rin po che

takrik . . . . rtags rigs

takrikpa . . . . rtags rigs pa

Taktser Rinpoché	stag tsher rin po che
takzik	stag gzig
Tashi Lhünpo	bkra shis lhun po
Tawang	rta dbang
Tendar, Geshé	bstan dar, dge bshes
Tengyur	bstan 'gyur
tenja	thon ja
thangka	thang ka
Thapkhé Rinpoché	thabs mkhas rin po che
theurang	the'u rang
Thuken Chökyi Nyima	thu'u bkwan chos kyi nyi ma
thukpa	thug pa
ṭīkā kyorpön	ṭī kā skyor dpon
Tö	stod
torma	gtor ma
trasasum	grwa sa gsum
Trehor Khangtsen	tre hor khang mtshan
Trehor Kyorpön Rinpoché	tre hor skyor dpon
Tri Rinpoché	khri rin po che
Trijang Rinpoché	khri byang rin po che
Trisong Detsen	khri srong lde'u btsan
Trisur	khri zur
tsampa	rtsam pa
Tsang	gtsang
Tsangpa	gtsang pa
Tsangpo	gtsang po
tsawai gegen	rtsa ba'i dge rgan
Tsemönling	tshe smon gling
tsenshap	mtshan zhabs
Tsethang	rtse thang
Tsidrung Kündeling Labrang	rtse drung kun bde gling bla brang

Tsikhang	rtsis khang
tsipön	rtsis dpon
Tsokchö	tshogs mchod
tsokram	tshogs rams
Tsomo	mtsho mo
Tsona	mtsho sna
Tsongkhapa Losang Drakpa	tsong kha pa blo bzang grags pa
Tsultim Gyeltsen, Geshé	tshul khrims rgyal mtshan, dge bshes
Tsurphu	mtshur phu
tulku	sprul sku
Ü	dbu
umzé	dbu mdzad
Wangdu, Geshé	dbang 'dus, dge bshes
Wangyal, Geshé	dbang rgyal, dge bshes
Yangsi Rinpoché	yang srid rin po che
Yeshé Ö	ye shes 'od
Yeshe, Lama	ye shes, bla ma
yikcha	yig cha
Yiktsang	yig tshang
yongzin	yongs 'dzin
zik	gzig
Zong Rinpoché	zong rin po che
Zopa, Lama	bzod pa, bla ma

Notes

1 In the Tibetan language, the suffix *-pa* often serves to indicate a person who is from, or connected to, the basic noun in question. So, for example, a person who belongs to the Kagyü sect is a Kagyüpa. Similarly, someone who is from the Kham region of Tibet is called a Khampa.

2 Tsang is roughly modern Shigatse Prefecture. The Shang region, now called Namling County, is northeast of Shigatse surrounding the south-flowing Shang River. The valley of Shum (Qiumuxiang) is just south of Namling, west of the river.

3 The animals, in the order of their succession, are: dragon, snake, horse, sheep, monkey, bird, dog, pig, rat, ox, tiger, and hare. The elements, in order, are: iron, water, wood, fire, and earth.

4 The cardinal directions, the intermediate directions—northeast, northwest, etc.—as well as up and down.

5 "I go for refuge to the Buddha, his teachings (Dharma), and the Buddhist community (Sangha)."

6 The Nechung oracle is the principal oracle consulted by the Dalai Lama's government on important religious and secular matters. The medium enters a trance and is possessed by the Dharma protector Dorjé Drakden. Questions are then posed, to which the deity responds, and the answers are written down by a trained attendant. Local oracles such as the one described here are consulted for more everyday matters, and the deities who speak through them are local, worldly spirits.

7 *Ashang* is what Tibetans call an older relative on their mother's side, and *la* is a word that indicates respect.

8 For a history of the early period of Tibet, see Tsepon Shakabpa, *Tibet, A Political History* (New Haven, CT: Yale University Press, 1967).

9 A *stupa* (Tib. *chos rten*) is a reliquary containing the physical remains of the Buddha or another realized master. Stupas are regarded as symbolic of the awakened mind of a buddha. Gesar is the legendary hero and king of Tibet's most ancient period.

10 Protector deities and their propitiation are important features of Tibetan Buddhism. Many of these deities are understood to be the indigenous deities of Tibet that were converted by Padmasambhava. These deities were sworn to protect Buddhism from that time forward. Some protectors are believed to be emanations of buddhas or high bodhisattvas.

11 This text belongs to the perfection of wisdom class of Mahāyāna sūtras. It can be read

in translation in Edward Conze, *Buddhist Wisdom: The Diamond Sūtra and The Heart Sūtra* (New York: Vintage, 2001).

12 The *Bar do thos grol* has been translated several times into English.

13 The Sakya, Kagyü, and Geluk schools divide tantric practices into four categories: *kriyā, caryā, yoga,* and *anuttarayoga*. These categories are understood to be in ascending order of profundity and complexity.

14 The vajra and bell are the chief ritual implements used in Tibetan Buddhism. The vajra, which is held in the right hand, is symbolic of a bodhisattva's skillful methods, as well as compassion. The bell symbolizes the liberating wisdom of all the buddhas.

15 These are the five precepts for all Buddhists—(1) not to kill, (2) not to steal, (3) not to engage in sexual misconduct, (4) not to lie or engage in harmful speech, and (5) not to partake of intoxicants—with the addition of (6) not to eat after noon, (7) not to engage in entertainment, (8) not to wear jewelry or other adornment, (9) not to sleep on high or luxurious beds, and (10) not to handle money. Furthermore, the precept against sexual misconduct means celibacy for the novice.

16 Geshé Sopa's name is written as Lhundub in this work because this is how he writes his name, and it is the name under which he has published. Otherwise the transcription convention used in this book spells this name as Lhündrup.

17 The Vinaya is the collection of scriptures containing the rules for monastic discipline.

18 Contrary to popular notions, this term is not an oxymoron. Monks from wealthy families lived better than monks from poor families. They had better food, better accommodations, better furnishings, and so forth. Based on the renunciant ideals of Buddhist monasticism, these worldly benefits were sometimes seen as hindrances to spiritual progress.

19 This very brief sūtra is very popular all over the Buddhist world of Central and East Asia. It belongs to the perfection of wisdom class of Mahāyāna sūtras. For a translation with commentary, see the Dalai Lama, *Essence of the Heart Sutra: The Dalai Lama's Heart of Wisdom Teachings*, Thupten Jinpa, trans. (Boston: Wisdom Publications, 2005).

20 Nāgārjuna was a second-century Indian Buddhist master who is regarded as the founder of the Madhayamaka, or Middle Way, school of Mahāyāna philosophy.

21 For a study of these monks, see Melvyn C. Goldstein, "A Study of the *ldab ldob*," *Central Asian Journal* 9 (1964): 123–41.

22 For a translation of this text, see Tsangnyon Heruka, *The Life of Milarepa*, Andrew Quintman, trans. (New York: Penguin Books, 2010).

23 *Chik (gcig)* is the Tibetan word for the number one, *nyi (gnyis)* is two, *sum (gsum)* is three, and so on.

24 Khensur *(mkhan zur)* is a title meaning former abbot.

25 A lama's manager *(phyag mdzod)* was a much more important figure than the English word *manager* conveys. The manager was in charge of all the economic and other secular matters of the labrang. He also tended to be the lama's closest and most influential advisor.

26 Sera Jetsün Chökyi Gyaltsen (1469–1544) was a famous early Geluk scholar and defender of the teachings of Tsongkhapa and his student Khedrup Jé. His textbooks displaced those of Sera Monastery's first abbot.

27 Phurbuchok Ngawang Jampa Rinpoché (1682–1762) was a famous and influential lama at Sera Jé monastery during the era of the Seventh Dalai Lama.

28 Abhidharma is the collection of texts on Buddhist ontology and systematic philosophy. Both Abhidharma and Vinaya are major collections of texts in the Buddhist canon, but they are also topics studied toward the end of a monk's education.

29 *Stages of the path* (*lam rim*) is a genre of Tibetan Buddhist literature that has its origins in a text by the great master Atiśa composed in the eleventh century. Texts in this genre offer practical, comprehensive, step-by-step guidance to practicing the Buddhist path. Tsongkhapa composed several such texts that continue to be revered in the Geluk sect. Teachings by Geshé Sopa on the largest of these, the *Great Exposition of the Stages of the Path*, are being published in five volumes.

30 This dichotomy of sūtra and tantra refers to the two different classes of texts found in the Tibetan Buddhist canon. Doctrinally, *sūtra* refers to the exoteric teachings of the Buddha. These are considered to be the foundation of Mahāyāna doctrine and practice. *Tantra* refers to the esoteric teachings of the Buddha that employ advanced yogic methods, such as mudra, mantra, and visualization, to expedite one's progress toward full awakening. Tantric doctrine and practice are only for those who are already accomplished practitioners. This is especially true for the Geluk sect. For an accessible description of tantric Buddhism, see Lama Thubten Yeshé, *Introduction to Tantra: The Transformation of Desire* (Boston: Wisdom Publications, 2001). For a more scholarly, but also quite accessible, discussion, see Anthony Tribe's chapter on the Vajrayāna in Paul Williams, *Buddhist Thought: A Complete Introduction* (London: Routledge, 2000).

31 Ngakchen Rinpoché was the Ninth Panchen Lama's representative to the central government in Lhasa. The Panchen Lama fled to Mongolia and then China in 1923 due in part to conflicts between the Panchen's government and the central government in Lhasa. The Ninth Panchen Lama died in Jyekundo, Eastern Tibet, in 1937.

32 Though the title *geshé* had been used by some of the major figures of the Kadam sect as far back as the eleventh century, at that time it did not refer to the kind of scholastic degree that modern Geluk scholars now attain. The Seventh Dalai Lama (1708–57) established *geshé lharampa* as the highest scholarly title. This system was further refined and codified by the Thirteenth Dalai Lama in the early twentieth century.

33 A *chuba* (*phyu ba*) is the traditional garb of Tibetan laypeople, both men and women. Wearing a red chuba and shaving the head implies a semi-renunciant status between lay life and that of ordained monks and nuns.

34 The Kangyur (*bka' gyur*) and Tengyur (*bstan gyur*) constitute the Tibetan Buddhist canon. The Kangyur contains the Tibetan translations of the scriptures of the Buddha. The Tengyur contains the Tibetan translations of the writings of the great Indian Buddhist masters.

35 A *maṇi wheel* is a large cylinder with the mantra of Avalokiteśvara written on the outside of it. There are also mantras written on long rolls of paper inside, so every time the wheel is turned, hundreds or thousands of mantra repetitions are accomplished.

36 Gyaltsap Darma Rinchen was Tsongkhapa's successor and thus was the second Throne Holder of Ganden. Khedrup Jé, another disciple of Tsongkhapa, was the third Throne Holder of Ganden.

37 *Mé* (*smad*) literally means "lower" and refers to the physical location of the monastery—Mé College was lower than the other part of the monastery. *Tö* (*stod*) means "higher." This is the same as in the names of the two tantric colleges: Gyümé and Gyütö.

38 Geshé Lhündrup Thapkhé is also often referred to in this book as Thapkhé Rinpoché. The use of the honorific title Rinpoché often refers to someone who is a reincarnate lama, but that is not the case here. He is also referred to as Gen Thapkhé.

39 Strictly speaking, the title Tri Rinpoché is only accurate when referring to the time during which Lhündrup Tsöndrü actually held the throne of Ganden. When he completed his tenure in this position, he became emeritus Throne Holder, or Trisur (*khri zur*). For the sake of simplicity and to avoid confusion, in this text he is referred to as Tri Rinpoché regardless of what time period is being discussed.

40 The Mönlam Chenmo, or Great Prayer Festival, was instituted by Tsongkhapa. It is celebrated during the first month of the Tibetan calendar. The Tsokchö Festival, which commemorates the Fifth Dalai Lama's death, is celebrated in the second month.

41 This is the *Bodhicaryāvatāra* of the great eighth-century Indian master Śāntideva. This is one of the most influential and beloved texts of Tibetan Buddhists. An excellent translation from the original Sanskrit is by Kate Crosby and Andrew Skilton in Śāntideva, *The Bodhicaryāvatāra* (New York: Oxford University Press, 1998).

42 This is Tsongkhapa's *Lamrim Chenmo*. Geshé Sopa is publishing a commentary on the entire work in five volumes. The first three have already been published by Wisdom Publications under the title, *Steps on the Path to Enlightenment*.

43 Lama Yeshe was a student of Geshé Sopa's at Sera Jé until 1959 when the Chinese began the crackdown on Tibet. In exile, Lama Yeshe founded Kopan Monastery in the Kathmandu Valley, attracting many Western disciples. He traveled extensively in the West and founded the Foundation for the Preservation of the Mahayana Tradition (FPMT). Yangsi Rinpoché earned his geshé lharampa degree in 1995. He was a resident teacher at Geshé Sopa's center in Wisconsin for five years and is now president of Maitripa College in Portland, Oregon.

44 This particular education system was in place at each of the Three Seats, but it was unique to the Geluk sect. Other Tibetan Buddhist sects had different methods of education and placed different degrees of emphasis on scholastic education. For an excellent study of the differences between the Geluk system and that of the other sects, both in Tibet and in exile, see Georges Dreyfus, *The Sound of Two Hands Clapping: The Education of a Tibetan Buddhist Monk* (Berkeley: University of California Press, 2003). Though the discussion below is in the past tense, the system of education and categories of study at the relocated Sera Monastery in India remain largely the same today.

45 These seven are: *Pramāṇavārttika, Pramāṇaviniścaya, Nyāyabindu, Sambandhaparīkṣā, Hetubindu, Samānāntarasiddhi,* and the *Vādanyāya.*

46 The three turnings of the wheel of Dharma, laid out in the *Saṃdhinirmocana Sūtra,* is a classic elucidation of the apparent contradiction between the realist philosophy of the so-called Hīnayāna teachings and the radical negation of all self-existent entities that is found in the perfection of wisdom texts. The buddha nature (*tathāgatagarbha*) teachings, found in a number of Mahāyāna sūtras, are those that employ the rhetoric

of an immanent awakened state, though Geluk scholars have typically interpreted this rhetoric to refer to the potential for enlightenment rather than immanence.

47 In ancient times, King Songtsen Gampo had two wives, one from China and one from Nepal. Each one brought a statue of Buddha Śākyamuni with her from her home. The statue that was brought from China is in the Jokhang Temple, and the statue that came from Nepal is housed in the Ramoché Temple.

48 The Yiktsang (*yig tshang*) was a body of four monk officials that ruled over religious/ monastic affairs. The Kashak (*bka' shag*), a body of three lay officials and one monk official, was its secular counterpart. Above these two bodies were the prime minister(s) (*blon chen* or *sri tshab*) and, finally, the Dalai Lama—or his regent if the former were still a minor or not yet found. A prime minister would only rule in the event of a Dalai Lama's temporary inability, such as in the period of the Fourteenth Dalai Lama's temporary exile in 1950. In that period there were two prime ministers, a monk and a layman.

49 The *kriyā* class of tantras are the so-called "lower tantras." Practices in these texts tend to be more limited and pragmatic than the better-known highest yoga tantras in that they are not regarded as sufficient means to attain awakening. The more familiar tantras and their practices, such as the Kālacakra and Guhyasamāja, belong to the highest yoga class.

50 A *sādhana* is the basic practice text in Tibetan Vajrayāna Buddhism. The text generally consists of verses that are recited or chanted and that describe the visualizations to be done.

51 The *Legs bshad snying po* is Tsongkhapa's text on distinguishing between definitive Buddhist teachings and those that require interpretation.

52 For a contemporary scholarly discussion of this protector and the controversies surrounding him, see Georges Dreyfus's "The Shukden Affair: History and Nature of a Quarrel." *Journal of the International Association of Buddhist Studies* 21.2 (1998): 227–70.

53 These tantras and their practices are the principal ones emphasized and utilized by the Geluk sect. They are all of the highest yoga class. Vajrabhairava is also commonly referred to as Yamantaka.

54 The name Drakri is often rendered phonetically as Pari based on a common pronunciation.

55 This very popular practice consists of a visionary dismemberment and offering of one's own body to all hungry beings, including animals, demons, and other unfortunate beings. *Gcod* (pronounced *chö*) practitioners often undertake this practice in marginal, frightening locations such as cemeteries.

56 The *tsok* worship (*tshogs mchod*) is a ritual obligation for all who have taken the higher tantric empowerments. It is observed on the tenth and the twenty-fifth of the lunar month.

57 In Vajrayāna Buddhist offering rituals, a portion of the offerings is taken outside for the benefit of the hungry ghosts, pathetic beings who perpetually suffer from hunger and thirst and who are thought to congregate outside of temples and other sites of religious practice.

58 There is some disagreement about where the weapons came from. Tsering Shakya says that the weapons at Shang Ganden Chönkhor were actually those of the Changtang

regiment of the Tibetan army. He says that they were placed there shortly after that regiment was withdrawn and disbanded after the signing of the Seventeen-Point Agreement in 1951. Tsering Shakya, *The Dragon in the Land of Snows: A History of Modern Tibet since 1947* (New York: Columbia University Press, 1999), p. 183.

59   A recent translation of this text can be found in *Buddha Nature: The Mahayana Uttaratantra Shasta with Commentary*, by Arya Maitreya, commentaries by Jamgön Kongtrül Lodrö Thayé and Khenpo Tsultrim Gyamtso, translated by Rosemary Fuchs (Ithaca, NY: Snow Lion Publications, 2005).

60   For an account by one of the Sera monks who participated in this incident, see Tashi Khedrup's *Adventures of a Tibetan Fighting Monk* (Bangkok: Orchid Press, 1998).

61   Geshé Rabten's story can be read in Geshé Rabten and B. Alan Wallace, *The Life and Teaching of Geshé Rabten: A Tibetan Lama's Search for Truth* (London: George Allen & Unwin, 1980). A selection from the work can also be found on the website of the Tibetan and Himalayan Digital Library: http://www.thlib.org/places/monasteries/sera/

62   This monastery, mentioned above in chapter 3, is distinct from Shang Ganden Chönkhor.

63   Taktser Rinpoché is the Dalai Lama's elder brother. He fled Amdo in 1950, and his firsthand account of the Chinese occupation was one of the contributing factors in the Dalai Lama's flight from Lhasa in that year.

64   Murray Illson, "Ex–Ivy Leaguers Aim to Be Monks," *New York Times*, December 14, 1963.

65   Geshe Wangyal, *The Door of Liberation: Essential Teachings of the Tibetan Buddhist Tradition* (Boston, Wisdom Publications, 1995). This re-issue of the book first published in 1973 contains an eighteen-page biography of Geshe Wangyal by Joshua Cutler.

66   There are three *Bhāvanākramas* of Kamalaśīla. For a translation and commentary on the middle one, see His Holiness the Dalai Lama, *Stages of Meditation* (Ithaca, NY: Snow Lion Publications, 2001).

67   The *Drang nges legs bshad snying po*. This has been translated by Robert Thurman as *The Central Philosophy of Tibet: A Translation and Study of Jéy Tsong Khapa's Essence of True Eloquence* (Princeton, NJ: Princeton University Press, 1991).

68   The *Dbu ma dgongs pa rab gsal*. Anne Klein has published a translation of part of the sixth chapter of this text, along with the oral commentary of Khensur Yeshe Tupden, as *Path to the Middle: The Spoken Scholarship of Khensur Yeshey Tupden* (Albany: State University of New York Press, 1994).

69   The *Lam rim chen mo*. See the bibliography for the in-print and forthcoming volumes of these teachings by Geshé Sopa.

70   This is Nāgārjuna's *Ratnāvalī*. One can find a translation with commentary in Jeffrey Hopkins' *Buddhist Advice for Living and Liberation: Nāgārjuna's Precious Garland* (Ithaca, NY: Snow Lion Publications, 1998).

71   This is Candrakīrti's *Madhyamakāvatāra*. A recent translation by the Padmakara Translation Group is found in *Introduction to the Middle Way: Chandrakirti's Madhyamakavatara with Commentary by Ju Mipham* (Boston: Shambhala Publications, 2002).

Glossary

Abhidharma (*chos mngon pa*). One of the three sections of the Buddhist canon, this collection deals with the categorization of existent entities according to Buddhist teachings. Abhidharma is also one of the five topics studied by scholar monks working toward the geshé degree.

Amdo (*a mdo*). The northwestern region of Tibet, now included in the Chinese provinces of Qinghai, Gansu, and Sichuan.

Collected Topics (*'dus grwa*). Elementary logic and epistemology (*tshad ma*; Skt. *pramāṇa*) texts used to introduce scholar monks to these subjects and to the practice of debate.

dopdop (*ldob ldob*). A monk who works in the monastery rather than following the scholastic path to the geshé degree. Dopdops include all kinds of workers, such as kitchen workers, bodyguards, and monastery policemen.

Geluk (*dge lugs*). The sect founded by Tsongkhapa Losang Drakpa in the fourteenth century. The Geluk sect places a heavy emphasis on monastic discipline, scholarship, and relatively restricted access to higher tantric practices and doctrines. The Geluk sect came to political predominance in the seventeenth century due to the political skill of the Fifth Dalai Lama and the military support of the Mongol khans.

geshé (*dge bshes*). The degree earned by scholar monks at the three great Geluk monasteries: Ganden, Sera, and Drepung. The degree typically takes over twenty years of study and debate to earn, and the recipients are ranked according to their performance, with the highest rank, the geshé lharampa, qualifying the monk for the highest honors and positions in the monastic hierarchy.

Gyümé (*rgyud smad*). One of the two highest institutions of learning in the Geluk sect. The curriculum here is entirely tantric texts and practices. Gyümé means "lower tantric college," but the term refers to the physical location of the center, which is lower than the other tantric college, not any hierarchical ranking between the two.

Gyütö (*rgyud stod*). One of the two highest institutions of learning in the Geluk sect. The curriculum here is entirely tantric texts and practices. Gyütö means "upper tantric college," but the term refers to the physical location of the center, which is higher than the other tantric college, not to any hierarchical ranking between the two.

Kadam (*bka' gdams*). The sect of Tibetan Buddhism founded in the eleventh century by Dromtön, the Tibetan disciple of the great Indian master Atiśa. The Kadam sect emphasized monastic discipline and had a relatively minor emphasis on tantric ideology and practice. The Kadam sect influenced all of the sects of the second propagation of Buddhism in Tibet, and was effectively absorbed by the Geluk sect after the latter arose in the early fifteenth century.

Kagyü (*bka' brgyud*). The sect that primarily traces its origins back to the Indian siddha Nāropa. The lineage was brought to Tibet by Marpa the translator in the eleventh century and was passed by him to his famous disciple, the beloved yogi Milarepa. After Milarepa, several subsects of the Kagyü arose, including the Karma Kagyü, which was politically powerful in central Tibet prior to the ascendance of the Geluk. In the time of the Fifth Dalai Lama, many Karma Kagyü monasteries were converted to Geluk centers, one of which was Shang Ganden Chönkhor, Geshé Sopa's first monastery.

karam (*bka' rams*). The class entered by geshé candidates after their completion of the final topic of the curriculum, either Vinaya or Abhidharma, depending on the monastery. From the karam class, the most promising candidates are singled out by the abbot and are moved to the lharam class. The rest of the candidates must continue to wait for the opportunity to be awarded the geshé degree, which could take many years, since the number of geshé degrees awarded each year was limited.

Kashak (*bka' shag*). The political body immediately below the Dalai Lama that oversaw secular and political matters. It typically consisted of three lay officials and one monk official and was the secular counterpart to the Yiktsang.

Kham (*khams*). The southwestern region of Tibet, now included in the PRC provinces of the Tibetan Autonomous Region, Qinghai, Sichuan, and Yunnan.

khatak (*kha btags*). A silk scarf widely used by Tibetans as an offering to revered beings and to others out of respect.

labrang (*bla brang*). A lama's estate. Labrangs typically hold property and other forms of wealth, which are passed from one incarnation to the next. A labrang usually consists of a lama, a tutor if the lama is still young and learning, his labrang manager, and several other officials and servants.

lharam (*lha rams*). The highest honor for those earning the geshé degree. The lharam geshés are entitled to admission to the upper division of study at one of the two tantric colleges located in the Lhasa area. The very best of these geshés rise up through the ranks of the tantric college and are eligible to become the abbot of the tantric college and eventually the Ganden Throne Holder, the highest position within the Geluk sect.

Madhyamaka (*dbu ma*). The central philosophy of Mahāyāna Buddhism that avoids the ontological extremes of nihilism and eternalism. The Madhyamaka is said to be the elucidation of the perfection of wisdom texts of the Buddhist canon.

Mahāyāna (*theg pa chen po*). The form of Buddhism characterized by the bodhisattva path, which puts the welfare of others before concern for self. The Mahāyana leads not to individual liberation, removing one from the cycle of birth and death, but rather to engaged buddhahood for the sake of all sentient beings.

Mönlam Festival (*smon lam chen mo*). The great prayer festival established by Tsongkhapa. It coincides with the Tibetan New Year. Lharam geshés are awarded their degrees during this period.

Nyingma (*rnying ma*). The sect that traces its origin to the great siddha Padmasambhava, who is regarded as instrumental in the establishment of Buddhism in Tibet in the eighth century. The Nyingma as a unified sect arose in the centuries following the second diffusion of Buddhism in Tibet in the eleventh century.

Perfection of Wisdom (*phar spyin*). A class of Mahāyāna Buddhist literature dealing with the supreme philosophical expression of Buddhist wisdom. The most well-known texts in this genre are the *Heart Sūtra* and *Diamond-Cutter Sūtra*. When Geluk monks study the Perfection of Wisdom as part of the monastic curriculum, they do so through study of Maitreya's *Ornament of Clear Realization* (*Abhisamayālaṃkāra*) and its commentaries.

pūja (*mchod pa*). Ritual worship of a buddha or deity. Pūja typically takes the form of making offerings that are pleasing to the five senses (sight, sound, smell, taste, touch) accompanied by chanting a liturgy that describes the visualization of more elaborate offerings and frequently includes prayers, confessions, and the dedication of merit. *See also* tsok

rikchen (*rigs chen*). Honor bestowed upon the best students at the time of karam class. The rikchen debate before the entire body of Sera monks in the great assembly hall. Being named rikchen, and the ranking given at that time, are important in determining whether or not one will be moved up to the lharam class.

rikchung (*rigs chung*). Honor bestowed upon the best students at the time of junior Perfection of Wisdom class. The rikchung debate in front of the assembly of Sera Jé.

Rinpoché (*rin po che*). An honorific title meaning "precious one." The title is most frequently associated with tulkus or lamas, but a student or disciple can also use the term to refer to his revered teacher.

sādhana (*sgrub thabs*). Liturgical texts that serve as the foundation for tantric practice. The texts are read or recited from memory and guide the practitioner through worship and visualization of the mandala of a particular tantric deity.

Sakya (*sa skya*). The sect that traces its lineage to the Indian siddha Virūpa, whose lineage was brought to Tibet by Gayadhara and was passed to the great translator Drokmi. Drokmi's most important disciple was Khön Könchok Gyalpo, who was the first patriarch of the Sakya sect. In the twelfth century, the Mongol prince Köden appointed the great scholar Sakya Pandita Künga Gyaltsen as the ruler of Tibet, and his nephew Phakpa was later named imperial preceptor and viceroy of Tibet by Kublai Khan, emperor of China. These events established the precedent for Tibetan reliance on Mongol power and for the monastic rule of the country.

siddha (*grub thob*). As the paradigmatic masters of tantric Buddhism, the siddhas possessed supernatural powers and typically lived on the fringes of society, living neither as householders nor as monks.

stages of the path (*lam rim*). A genre of Buddhist literature that teaches the steps toward awakening. This genre is immensely important in Tibet, and most such works are elaborations on Atiśa's paradigmatic *Lamp for the Path to Enlightenment (Bodhipathapradīpa)*. All the sects of Tibetan Buddhism have texts of this genre, with important and influential ones being the *Great Exposition on the Stages of the Path* by Tsongkhapa and the *Jewel Ornament of Liberation* by Gampopa.

sūtra (*mdo*). One of the three sections of the Buddhist canon, this is the collection of the discourses of the Buddha. The term also refers to particular discourses; for instance, the *Heart Sūtra*.

tantra/Vajrayāna (*rgyud / rdo rje theg pa*). *Tantra* refers to the esoteric teachings of the Buddha that employ advanced yogic methods to expedite one's progress toward full awakening. Tantric doctrine and practice is only for those who are already accomplished practitioners. The term Vajrayāna refers to the same body of practices but distinguishes Buddhist from Hindu tantra. This term fits in an idea of three distinct but complementary vehicles: the Hīnayāna or lesser vehicle, the Mahāyāna or greater vehicle, and the Vajrayāna or adamantine vehicle.

Three Seats (*gdan sag sum*). The three great monasteries of the Geluk sect: Sera, Drepung, and Ganden.

torma (*gtor ma*). Ritual cakes used as offerings in tantra. Tormas are used in expiatory rituals and as propitiatory offerings to Buddhist deities and other kinds of supernatural beings such as Dharma protectors.

tsampa (*rtsam pa*). Roasted barley flour. Tsampa is a Tibetan staple that is usually mixed with butter tea to make a ball of dough that is eaten.

Tsang (*gtsang*). The western portion of central Tibet.

tsenshap (*mtshan zhabs*). The teachers and debate partners of the Dalai Lama as he prepared for his geshé examination. The tsenshaps were chosen from among the very best scholar monks, one coming from each of the colleges of the Three Seats.

tsok (*tshogs*). In the general sense, an assembly of monks or offerings. In the tantric sense, the twice-monthly ritual observance required of initiates into the practices of the highest yoga tantras of the Vajrayāna.

Tsokchö Festival (*tshogs mchod chen mo*). The festival commemorating the death of the Fifth Dalai Lama in the second month of the Tibetan year. Tsokram geshés are awarded their degrees during this period.

tsokram (*tshogs rams*). The second highest level of geshé degree. Tsokram geshés are still considered "big geshés" but do not have the same status or opportunities as the lharam geshés. Tsokram geshés were awarded their degrees during the Tsokchö Festival in Lhasa.

tulku (*sprul sku*). The Tibetan translation of the Sanskrit *nirmāṇakāya*, "magical emanation body," which in Mahāyāna Buddhism denotes a physical manifestation of awakening in the world, such as the Buddha Śākyamuni. In Tibet, this concept is applied to buddhas/bodhisattvas who chose to return to the world after death to continue their work for all sentient beings. This became institutionalized in Tibet in the form of lineages of "reincarnate lamas," such as the Dalai Lamas and the Karmapas, as well as numerous lesser-known lineages. Such tulkus are sometimes also referred to as *rinpochés* and, more informally, as *lamas*, though this latter term is also often used more broadly.

Vajrayāna. *See* tantra

Vinaya (*'dul ba*). One of the three collections constituting the Buddhist canon; this collection deals with monastic discipline.

Yiktsang (*yig tshang*). A body of four monk government officials that ruled over religious/monastic affairs. Its secular counterpart was the Kashak, though the Yiktsang was slightly lower in governmental power.

Select Bibliography

Arjia Rinpoche. *Surviving the Dragon: A Tibetan Lama's Account of Forty Years under Chinese Rule.* New York: Rodale Books, 2010.

Avedon, John. *In Exile from the Land of Snows: The Definitive Account of the Dalai Lama and Tibet since the Chinese Conquest.* New York: Alfred A. Knopf, 1984.

Cabezon, José, and Roger Jackson, eds. *Tibetan Literature: Studies in Genre. Essays in Honor of Geshé Lhundup Sopa.* Ithaca, NY: Snow Lion, 1995.

Dalai Lama, Tenzin Gyatso, the Fourteenth. *Essence of the Heart Sutra: The Dalai Lama's Heart of Wisdom Teachings.* Translated and edited by Thupten Jinpa. Boston: Wisdom Publications, 2005.

———. *Freedom in Exile: The Autobiography of the Dalai Lama.* San Francisco: Harper, 1991.

———. *My Land and My People: The Original Autobiography of His Holiness the Dalai Lama of Tibet.* New York: Warner Books, 1997.

———. *Stages of Meditation.* Ithaca, NY: Snow Lion Publications, 2001.

Davidson, Ronald M. *Tibetan Renaissance: Tantric Buddhism in the Rebirth of Tibetan Culture.* New York: Columbia University Press, 2005.

Dilgo Khyentse. *Brilliant Moon: The Autobiography of Dilgo Khyentse.* Translated by Ani Jinba Palmo. Boston: Shambhala Publications, 2008.

Dreyfus, Georges B. J. "The Shukden Affair: History and Nature of a Quarrel." *Journal of the International Association of Buddhist Studies* 21.2 (1998): 227–70.

————. *The Sound of Two Hands Clapping: The Education of a Tibetan Buddhist Monk*. Berkeley: University of California Press, 2003.

Goldstein, Melvyn C. "A Study of the *ldab ldob*." *Central Asian Journal* 9 (1964): 123–41.

————. *The Snow Lion and the Dragon: China, Tibet, and the Dalai Lama*. Berkeley: University of California Press, 1997.

————. *A History of Modern Tibet, volume 2: The Calm before the Storm: 1951–1955*. Berkeley: University of California Press, 2007.

Goldstein, Melvyn, with the help of Gelek Rimpoche. *A History of Modern Tibet, 1913–1951: The Demise of the Lamaist State*. Berkeley: University of California Press, 1989.

Goldstein, Melvyn and Matthew Kapstein, eds. *Buddhism in Contemporary Tibet: Religious Revival and Cultural Identity*. Berkeley: University of California Press, 1998.

Gruber, Elmer. *From the Heart of Tibet: The Biography of Drikung Chetsang Rinpoche*. Boston: Shambhala Publications, 2010.

Hopkins, Jeffrey. *Buddhist Advice for Living and Liberation: Nāgārjuna's Precious Garland*. Ithaca, NY: Snow Lion Publications, 1998.

Jackson, David P. *A Saint in Seattle: The Life of the Tibetan Mystic Dezhung Rinpoche*. Boston: Wisdom Publications, 2004.

Kapstein, Matthew. *The Tibetans*. Malden, MA and Oxford: Blackwell Publishing, 2006.

Khedrup, Tashi. *Adventures of a Tibetan Fighting Monk*. Compiled by Hugh Richardson, edited by Tadeusz Skorupski. Bangkok: Orchid Press, 1998.

Klein, Anne. *Path to the Middle: The Spoken Scholarship of Khensur Yeshey Tupden*. Albany: State University of New York Press, 1994.

Lobsang Gyatso. *Memoirs of a Tibetan Lama*. Translated and edited by Gareth Sparham. Ithaca, NY: Snow Lion, 1998.

Lopez, Donald. *Prisoners of Shangri-la: Tibetan Buddhism and the West*. Chicago: University of Chicago Press, 1999.

Mills, Martin A. *Identity, Ritual and State in Tibetan Buddhism: The Foundations of Authority in Gelukpa Monasticism.* London and New York: Routledge, 2003.

Norbu, Thubten Jigme. *Tibet Is My Country: Autobiography of Thubten Jigme Norbu, Brother of the Dalai Lama, as Told to Heinrich Harrar.* London: Wisdom Publications, 1986.

Pabongka Rinpoché. *Liberation in the Palm of Your Hand: A Concise Discourse on the Path to Enlightenment*, rev. ed. Edited by Trijang Rinpoché, translated by Michael Richards. Boston: Wisdom Publications, 2006.

Padmakara Translation Group, trans. *Introduction to the Middle Way: Chandrakirti's Madhyamakavatara with Commentary by Ju Mipham.* Boston: Shambhala Publications, 2002.

Palden Gyatso. *The Autobiography of a Tibetan Monk.* Translated by Tsering Shakya. New York: Grove Press, 1998.

Powers, John. *History As Propaganda: Tibetan Exiles versus the People's Republic of China.* New York: Oxford University Press, 2004.

———. *Introduction to Tibetan Buddhism*, rev. ed. Ithaca, NY: Snow Lion Publications, 2007.

Rabten, Geshe, and B. Alan Wallace. *The Life and Teaching of Geshe Rabten: A Tibetan Lama's Search for Truth.* London: George Allen & Unwin, 1980.

Samuel, Geoffrey. *Civilized Shamans: Buddhism in Tibetan Societies.* Washington DC: Smithsonian Institution Press, 1993.

Śāntideva. *The Bodhicaryāvatāra.* Translated by Andrew Skilton and Kate Crosby. New York: Oxford University Press, 1998.

Shakabpa, Tsepon W. D. *Tibet, A Political History.* New Haven, CT: Yale University Press, 1967. (Repr., New Delhi: Paljor, 2010).

Shakya, Tsering. *The Dragon in the Land of Snows: A History of Modern Tibet since 1947.* New York: Columbia University Press, 1999.

Sperling, Elliot. *The Tibet-China Conflict: History and Polemics.* Washington DC: East-West Center, 2004.

Thurman, Robert A. F. *The Central Philosophy of Tibet: A Translation and Study of Jey Tsong Khapa's "Essence of True Eloquence."* Princeton, NJ: Princeton University Press, 1991.

Trungpa, Chögyam. *Born in Tibet.* Boston: Shambhala Publications, 1995.

Tsangnyon Heruka. *The Life of Milarepa.* Translated by Andrew Quintman. New York: Penguin Books, 2010.

Wangmo, Jamyang. *The Lawudo Lama: Stories of Reincarnation from the Mount Everest Region.* Boston: Wisdom Publications, 2005.

Williams, Paul and Anthony Tribe. *Buddhist Thought: A Complete Introduction to the Indian Tradition.* London and New York: Routledge, 2000.

Yeshe, Lama Thubten. *Introduction to Tantra: The Transformation of Desire.* Edited and introduced by Jonathan Landaw. Boston: Wisdom Publications, 2001.

Books by Geshé Sopa

1976. With Jeffrey Hopkins. *The Practice and Theory of Tibetan Buddhism.* New York: Grove Press. Second edition released as *Cutting Through Appearances.* Ithaca, NY: Snow Lion Publications, 1990.

1991. With Roger Jackson and John Newman. *The Wheel of Time: Kalachakra in Context.* Ithaca, NY: Snow Lion. First published in 1985 by Deer Park Books.

2001. *Peacock in the Poison Grove: Two Buddhist Texts on Training the Mind.* Edited and introduced by Michael Sweet and Leonard Zwilling. Boston: Wisdom Publications.

2004. *Lectures on Tibetan Religious Culture.* Dharamsala, India: Library of Tibetan Works and Archives. First published 1972. First LTWA edition, 1983.

2004. *Steps on the Path to Enlightenment: A Commentary on the Lamrim Chenmo, Vol. 1: The Foundation Practices.* Edited by David Patt and Beth Newman. Boston: Wisdom Publications.

2005. *Steps on the Path to Enlightenment: A Commentary on the Lamrim Chenmo, Vol. 2: Karma.* Edited by David Patt. Boston: Wisdom Publications.

2007. *Steps on the Path to Enlightenment: A Commentary on the Lamrim Chenmo, Vol. 3: The Way of the Bodhisattva.* Edited by Beth Newman. Boston: Wisdom Publications.

2009. Translator with Roger Jackson, editor: Thuken Losang Chökyi Nyima. *The Crystal Mirror of Philosophical Systems: A Tibetan Study of Asian Religious Thought.* Vol. 25 in the Library of Tibetan Classics. Boston: Wisdom Publications.

forthcoming. *Steps on the Path to Enlightenment: A Commentary on the Lamrim Chenmo, Vol. 4: Śamatha.* Edited by James Blumenthal. Boston: Wisdom Publications.

forthcoming. *Steps on the Path to Enlightenment: A Commentary on the Lamrim Chenmo, Vol. 5: Special Insight.* Edited by Susan Dechen Rochard. Boston: Wisdom Publications.

Index

A

abbot
  position of, 159, 296
  first meetings with, 93–94
  in debating sessions, 129
Abhidharma, 72, 122–23, 143,
  321n28
Altan Khan, 5
animals of the monastery, 58
Army Protecting the Teachings,
  202
Ashang-la. *See* uncle of Geshé
  Sopa
Assam refugee camp, 232, 233–38,
  239
assemblies, monastic, 46–47,
  53–54, 128
Atiśa, 3, 90, 180, 321n29
auto accidents, 272–73, 276–77
Avalokiteśvara, 18, 53
awakening the lineage, 208

B

belief in God *vs.* karma, 256
Bhutan, attempted travel to, 251–54
birth deities, 21

bodhisattva vow, 284
Bön religion, 2
Bongbu Sotsik, 136
books written by Geshé Sopa, 298,
  321n29, 322n42
breakfast, monastic, 59
Buddha, 118, 150, 302, 323n47
butter tea, Tibetan, 60–61, 114
Buxaduar monastic camp, 249–
  50, 258

C

Cakrasaṃvara empowerment, 184,
  323n53
Candrakīrti, 302, 324n71
cemeteries, Tibetan, 23–24
ceremonies
  geshé damja (geshé thesis cer-
    emony), 152–54
  offerings of rikchung students,
    141
  rikchen debate ceremony, 144
  shukja, upon entering the lharam
    class, 146
  See also rituals

About Wisdom Publications

Wisdom Publications is dedicated to offering works relating to and inspired by Buddhist traditions.

To learn more about us or to explore our other books, please visit our website at www.wisdompubs.org.

You can subscribe to our e-newsletter or request our print catalog online, or by writing to:

Wisdom Publications
199 Elm Street
Somerville, Massachusetts 02144 USA
You can also contact us at 617-776-7416,
or info@wisdompubs.org.

Wisdom is a nonprofit, charitable 501(c)(3) organization and donations in support of our mission are tax deductible.

Wisdom Publications is affiliated with the Foundation for the Preservation of the Mahayana Tradition (FPMT).